07/08

Telephone Renewals: 01902 321333 or 0845 408 1631
Please Return this item on or before the last date shown above.
Fines will be charged if items are returned late.
See tariff of fines displayed at the Counter.

Real Language Series

General Editors:

Jennifer Coates, Roehampton Institute, London
Jenny Cheshire, Queen Mary and Westfield College, University of London,
and
Euan Reid, Institute of Education, University of London

Titles published in the series:

David Lee Competing Discourses: Perspective and Ideology in Language
Norman Fairclough (Editor) Critical Language Awareness
James Milroy and Lesley Milroy (Editors) Real English: The Grammar of
  English Dialects in the British Isles
Mark Sebba London Jamaican: Language Systems in Interaction
Janet Holmes Women, Men and Politeness
Ben Rampton Crossing: Language and Ethnicity Among Adolescents
Brian V. Street Social Literacies: Critical Approaches to Literacy in
  Development, Ethnography and Education
Srikant Sarangi and Stefaan Slembrouck Language, Bureaucracy and Social
  Control
Ruth Wodak Disorders of Discourse
Victoria L. Bergvall, Janet M. Bing and Alice F. Freed (Editors) Rethinking
  Language and Gender Research: Theory and Practice
Anne Pauwels Women Changing Language

Women Changing Language

Anne Pauwels

LONGMAN
London and New York

Addison Wesley Longman Limited
Edinburgh Gate
Harlow, Essex CM20 2JE
England

and Associated Companies throughout the world

*Published in the United States of America
by Addison Wesley Longman Inc., New York*

First published 1998

ISBN 0 582 099625 Paper
ISBN 0 582 099617 Cased

British Library Cataloguing-in-Publication Data
A catalogue record for this book is
available from the British Library

Library of Congress Cataloging-in-Publication Data
Pauwels, Anne.
 Women changing language / Anne Pauwels.
  p. cm. — (Real language series)
 Includes bibliographical references and index.
 ISBN 0–582–09961–7 (Cased). — ISBN 0–582–09962–5 (Paper)
 1. Women—Language. 2. Sexism in language. 3. Nonsexist
language. 4. Language planning. I. Title. II. Series.
P120.W66P38 1998
408.2—dc21   97–41151
                                                  CIP

Set by 35 in 10/12 pt Sabon
Produced by Longman Singapore Publishers (Pte) Ltd.
Printed in Singapore

Contents

Publisher's acknowledgements   viii

Author's acknowledgements   ix

Introduction   x

1   Language planning and the sexes   1

2   Sexism in language: an international phenomenon?   16

3   Should sexist language be changed?   81

4   How should sexist language be changed?   94

5   Implementing non-sexist language change: guidelines   139

6   Evaluating feminist language planning   168

7   Is change occurring?   192

Concluding remarks   222

Appendix: Drafting non-sexist language guidelines   228

Bibliography   236

Author Index   261

Subject Index   265

For JW, thanks for love and constant inspiration

Publisher's acknowledgements

We have unfortunately been unable to trace the copyright holders of a letter which appeared in *The Australian* 2.11.88 and a letter by Robyn Murphy which appeared in *The West Australian* 13.10.88 and would appreciate any information which would enable us to do so.

Author's acknowledgements

My thanks go to many colleagues, friends and feminist organisations mainly in Europe, Australia, and the US who have provided me with data as well as inspiration for this book. In particular I wish to thank Iris Bogaers, Tove Bull, Mirna Cicioni, Viviane Claessens, Kirsten Gomard, Antje Hornscheidt, Uwe K. Nissen, Kerstin Nordenstam, and Ruth Wodak for providing me with interesting data on feminist language use and change. Much appreciation also goes to Joanne Winter for commenting critically on many drafts and for her continuous encouragement. I am also grateful to the editors of the *Real Language Series*, especially Jennifer Coates and Euan Reid who were very helpful in making useful suggestions.

Introduction

Feminism and language reform: international perspectives

There is no doubt that feminism has been, and continues to be, one of the main social movements of this century. Many spheres of life around the world have been, or are being, affected by this movement which strives, among other things, for the elimination of gender discrimination, for the equal treatment of women and men in all spheres of life and for the greater recognition of women's contributions to society.

This book is about one of the many impacts feminism is having on society. It concerns the feminist impact on language – one of our most powerful means of communication and expression. The book documents and discusses *feminist language reform*: the efforts, the initiatives and actions of feminists around the world to change the biased representation of the sexes in language. The bias concerns the portrayal of men as the norm and women as the appendage or as the exception in language. This phenomenon is often called *linguistic sexism* or *androcentrism*.

The book also pays tribute to the activities of many feminists – well known as well as anonymous – who have helped and are helping to debunk some myths about the relationship between women and language. Women are often portrayed as 'consumers' of language, or as passive recipients of knowledge about language. A powerful stereotype is that of the so-called 'schoolmarm' whose role is to enforce and reinforce language rules rather than make these rules. Men, on the other hand, are more often seen as the makers of meaning and the creators of language rules. In this book I highlight the role of women as makers of meaning; I show how women shape language by engaging in critical discussions about the linguistic portrayal of the sexes and by proposing language reform (LR) in many different ways. This book reveals women as language activists challenging linguistic sexist assumptions and practices and as language planners proposing as well as implementing changes.

In this book I approach the description and the discussion of feminist LR from a language planning (LP) perspective,[1] mainly because of my interest in this field of language research and because of my linguistic training. Clearly the topic of this book could have been approached from a variety of other perspectives. For example, Cameron (1995) discusses instances of feminist LR in the context of the debate about political correctness. Furthermore, contributions to this topic have come from feminists working in fields such as philosophy, theology, psychology and psychoanalysis, in cultural and literary studies, semiotics as well as anthropology and sociology.[2] Wherever appropriate I shall acknowledge these and include references for more detailed comments on alternative views and perspectives.

With this book I also hope to broaden the minds of those working in the field of LP by presenting feminist LR as a genuine case worthy of attention. To this day the fast-growing literature on LP has largely ignored the issue of feminist LR. Yet this form of LP has the potential to contribute to a better understanding of the interaction between language, LP and social change.[3]

An important feature of this book is its attempt to provide a multilingual and multicultural focus. The book examines feminist views and actions on LR in different languages and in different societies. To my knowledge[4] this is the first book to bring together extensive information and data on linguistic sexism and feminist LR from a diverse range of languages, especially European languages and some Asian languages. The multilingual database reveals both diversity and similarity among languages and speech communities in their expression and encoding of sexism. The focus on a diverse range of societies and speech communities also implies taking into account the different cultural and linguistic expressions of feminism, the different cultural attitudes towards deliberate language change (language reform) and the extent of interest in feminist language issues. All these will affect the type of language reforms and the extent to which they are successfully implemented and adopted.

Furthermore I draw attention to the fact that cultural and linguistic differences are neither the only nor the main issues to affect different responses to sexism in language. Just as there are many faces of feminism, there are also many feminist reactions to the issue of sexism in language. Those who believe that language is the main force in shaping people's view of reality are greatly affected by the finding that language may be androcentric. They often see a direct, even causal, link between women's subordinate status in society and the androcentrism in language. For them LR is a key to changing women's subordination in society. Other views among feminists do not assign such a central role to language. Consequently their desire for language change is less urgent. Some believe it important to eliminate this form of sexism, whereas others think it unnecessary to expend energy on a relatively trivial matter of sexual inequality. In this book I shall show how these different opinions affect the process of LR.

Finally, I wish to alert readers to the fact that LR or LP is usually a very complex and often very messy activity which seldom follows the programmatic stages identified in the LP literature. In other words, the descriptions and discussions do not always reflect the often chaotic and disorganised nature of the activities. I too am guilty of retreating to a certain level of abstraction which does not always do justice to the complexity of the issue in order to explain the principles, stages and activities of feminist LR.

Sources and data for this book

The data for this book have come from a very diverse range of sources which vary in quality and reliability. This is not unusual for research of an exploratory nature. Because this documentation and examination of feminist LR is in many respects a first comprehensive exploration of the topic, the data often come from less traditional academic sources, such as personal observations and comments, diary entries and similar sources. Of course, I relied heavily on the 'traditional' academic sources of information for documenting feminist LR. These include scholarly articles and books on the subject, theses, unpublished conference and research papers, statistical and survey information as well as transcripts of interviews and results of 'laboratory' tests and experiments. However, important 'alternative' sources upon which I drew for this discussion of feminist LR include the personal and professional opinions and observations of many colleagues, friends and acquaintances around the world. Other important sources have been articles, letters, advertisements, comments and opinions on aspects of gender and LR collected from the print and electronic media in a variety of languages. Written materials such as student essays, internal memos, minutes of meetings, personal and official correspondence, shopping lists, instruction manuals, legal contracts, insurance forms, etc., provided further data for my own investigations of feminist LR for such languages as Dutch, English, French and German. The personal notes which I have kept on this subject have also proved extremely valuable.

The amount and quality of information gathered on each language varies substantially: for some languages my only source of information was an unpublished academic paper on the observations and opinions of individuals, whereas for other languages I had access to a variety of sources ranging from academic articles on feminist LP to the personal views and experiences of friends and colleagues involved in LP exercises. But I hope that these variations in the data used throughout this book will not adversely affect the quality of the documentation and discussion of feminist LR.

Structure of the book

The book is structured around eight chapters. The remainder of this introduction provides some background information on the impact of feminism on the study of language, which should help the reader to place the study of feminist LR in the broader field of gender and language research.

In Chapter 1 I explain the concept of LP in general and discuss the main features of feminist LP. I also outline the planning framework which I adopt in this book.

Chapters 2 to 7 each discuss a major aspect or stage in the feminist LP/LR process. Chapter 2 also describes and discusses the many ways in which sexism is encoded in language.

In Chapter 3 I raise the question 'Should sexist language be changed?' and discuss some of the prominent views for and against any such change.

The question posed in Chapter 4, 'How should sexist language be changed?', assumes a positive answer to the question in Chapter 3, and discusses the strategies and methods of feminist LR.

The issue of implementing feminist LR in societies around the world is addressed in Chapter 5, which especially highlights the use of language guidelines as an implementation strategy.

Chapter 6 raises the question of evaluation of feminist LR and focuses in particular on public reactions to LR as a way of evaluation.

Chapter 7 addresses the question 'Is change occurring?' and comments on some of the outcomes of feminist LR.

Finally, there are some concluding remarks on the issue of feminist LR and ideas for further research and action.

In the appendix I have also included an elaborate section on drafting non-sexist language guidelines. This section provides practical information and advice on the topic of non-sexist (feminist) LR. It specifically targets equal opportunity and affirmative action for staff or any individuals, groups or committees charged with the formulation and implementation of initiatives or policies about non-discriminatory language.

Feminism and the study of language

The feminist movement, also called the women's movement or the women's liberation movement, undoubtedly has been and still is one of the major social movements of this century.

Its aims, actions and ideologies have touched the lives of many women and men in various ways and have made an impact on societal structures, institutions and social practices. Feminism has also had an effect on epistemology, and approaches to research in many disciplines: for example, feminists have challenged long-held views on what constitutes knowledge, they have exposed the male bias in the study of many phenomena and have proposed alternative ways of doing research. In the social sciences, and the humanities in particular, feminist approaches to the study of social and cultural phenomena have emerged and, in the respective disciplines, have commanded a position which can no longer be regarded as marginal. This applies in particular to such disciplines as philosophy, theology, literary and cultural studies, sociology and anthropology. Feminist approaches and perspectives have also made inroads in the study of law, economics, education and some of the 'pure' sciences.

Since the 1970s feminism has also made an impact on the study of language in the discipline of linguistics in a variety of ways. For example, linguists speaking from a feminist position have exposed the masculine bias prevalent in many dialectological, sociodialectological as well as sociolinguistic studies of people's language behaviour and use (e.g. Brouwer *et al.* 1978, Coates 1986, Coates and Cameron 1988, Key 1975). The latter have shown that many language studies which claimed to investigate *people's* use(s) of language in effect mainly examined *men's* linguistic behaviour. Feminist linguists pointed out that this practice of basing speaker behaviour on the linguistic behaviour of male speakers established male linguistic behaviour as the norm and as the topic of linguistic investigation. This relegated the study of women's uses of language and linguistic behaviours to the realm of the exceptional: the study of women's language was considered of interest only in terms of illustrating differences and deviations from the norm of language behaviour (i.e. male linguistic behaviour). Often cited as an example of this approach is Jespersen's (1922) classic work *Language: Its nature, development and origins.* Jespersen includes a chapter on the language behaviour of women, children and foreigners. However, conspicuously absent is a chapter on male language behaviour.

Another effect of feminism was to trigger the interest of some linguists and other language professionals in examining the different ways in which languages represent and treat women and men – a research area that became known as the study of *sexism in language* or *linguistic sexism.*[5] The subject of this book can be said to have grown from this area of language and gender research.

Feminism, furthermore, stimulated research on women's ways of using language and investigations of the extent of differences between the sexes in their use(s) of language. A feminist orientation in linguists and language researchers has also been responsible for the critical re-examining of previous findings and explanations of gender differences in language use (e.g. Cameron and Coates 1985, Cameron 1985, Eckert and McConnell-Ginet 1992, Gal 1994, Henley and Kramarae 1991).

Although feminist approaches to the study of language are most prevalent in those areas of linguistics which study language use in (social) context – especially sociolinguistics, sociology of language, social linguistics, critical linguistics, pragmatics and discourse analysis – they are also increasingly applied to fields such as historical linguistics, lexicology and lexicography as well as linguistic theory (e.g. Cameron 1985, Kochskämper 1991).

The growing number of textbooks and monographs on language and gender issues which adopt a feminist approach are testimony to the fact that 'feminist' linguistics is coming of age. In addition, feminism as a social movement striving for the liberation of women and the equality of the sexes has itself been a rich source of data for linguistic study. Not only has this social movement given rise to new expressions, coinages and phrases (e.g. male chauvinism, sexual harassment, femocrats) which have had an impact on the structure of vocabularies, but it has also engaged in a programme of LP in order to eliminate the gender-bias found in the structures and uses of many languages. Feminist programmes and initiatives for LR present challenging data for the study of LP as well as of language change. As mentioned earlier, the study of feminist LR, LP and change has to date been largely ignored by scholars working in the 'mainstream' (or, in feminist terms, 'malestream') language planning and policy arena. Despite this lack of attention from the mainstream to feminist LP initiatives, feminist linguists (e.g. Frank 1985b, Frank and Treichler 1989, Hellinger 1985a, 1990, Henley 1987, Pauwels 1989a, 1991a, 1991b, Penelope 1990, Schräpel 1985, Stanley 1978) have argued that a feminist programme for LR is an instance of LP whose study could provide not only important insights into the process of planned language change but also contribute to a theory of LP.

Furthermore, evaluating current feminist LR from a planning perspective may help identify factors which facilitate or obstruct the successful adoption of reform. This information in turn will aid future programmes of linguistic reform, especially those concerning the representation of minorities in language. With this book on feminist LP and LR I hope to contribute not only to the study of language and gender but also to that of language planning and policy.

Notes

1. Broadly speaking, language planning concerns making deliberate changes to the status or to an aspect of a language.
2. For example, Vetterling-Braggin (1981) in philosophy, Daly (1978) for theology, and works by Hélène Cixous, Luce Irigaray, Julia Kristeva in the areas of psychoanalysis, semiotics, and cultural and literary studies.
3. The only notable exception in the language planning literature is the work by Cooper (1989) which describes the efforts of the American women's liberation movement in terms of language planning.
4. I acknowledge the existence of Hellinger (1985a) which contains articles on German, English, Italian, Danish, Norwegian, Spanish, Dutch and Modern Greek. Hellinger (1990) is an extensive contrastive analysis of sexism in German and English. Other contrastive approaches exist mainly for northern European languages.
5. For detailed references on the study of linguistic sexism, please consult the annotated bibliography in Thorne *et al.* (1983). Among the first extensive descriptions of linguistic sexism are Guentherodt *et al.* (1980), Lakoff (1975), Nilsen *et al.* (1977) and Spender (1980).

1 Language planning and the sexes

What is language planning?

In the Introduction I mentioned that initiatives directed at exposing and eliminating sexism in language are a form of language planning (LP) which I described as deliberate language change. However, such a brief description is not sufficient for a book focusing on the topic of feminist LP. I shall therefore elaborate on this issue here by explaining what LP is and by attempting to place feminist language reform (LR) in the LP framework.

The workings of language are often a mystery to ordinary people. Indeed, many people believe or wish to believe that language is some sort of organism that lives a life of its own and operates independently from its users. Although they recognise that language can change, they do not understand the processes that contribute to language change. Such people also often refuse to believe that language users or speakers can bring about changes in a deliberate manner.

This belief about the impossibility of planned language change can be the result of implicit or explicit negative attitudes towards language change or 'interference' with the workings of language. Newspaper sections such as *Letters to the Editor* or *Readers' comments* frequently provide many poignant examples of people's negative attitudes to change in language: readers complain about the increased influence of foreign languages on their own language; they bemoan the loss of stricter rules of grammar; they warn of the imminent threat to the freedom of speech when language reforms are advocated; they despise any form of **meddling** with **their** language (see also Cameron 1995).

Yet, despite these popular beliefs and myths about the nature of language and language change, there have been many successful and unsuccessful attempts throughout the centuries at planning languages, at creating new language systems and at reforming or 'interfering' with language.

A fundamental form of LP is the development of a writing system, called *graphisation* by many language planners. Other obvious examples include spelling reforms, the development of style manuals (or handbooks for good writing) as well as the selection of an official or national language in a new nation or society, or in a multilingual community. Many people would have heard of these forms of LP but often do not think of them as *planned* language change.

It is not only the lay person who has difficulty understanding the concept of LP. Linguistic scholars also seem to find it difficult to reach a consensus about what exactly LP is. A survey of the extensive literature on the subject gives the reader the impression that there are possibly as many definitions of LP as there are authors writing about it. Cooper's work on LP and social change, for example, quotes twelve different definitions (Cooper 1989), which range from minimalist and rather vague descriptions such as 'an explicit choice among [language] alternatives' (Fasold 1984: 246) to lengthy and more specific ones such as the definition by Rubin and Jernudd (1971b: xiv):

> Language planning is *deliberate* language change; that is, changes in the systems of language code or speaking or both that are planned by organizations that are established for such purposes or given a mandate to fulfill such purposes. As such, language planning focuses on problem solving and is characterized by the formulation and evaluation of alternatives for solving language problems to find the best (or optimal, most efficient) decision.

or the definition by Gorman (1973: 73):

> The term language planning is most appropriately used in my view to refer to coordinated measures taken to select, codify and, in some cases, to elaborate orthographic, grammatical, lexical, or semantic features of a language and to disseminate the corpus agreed upon.

The lack of consensus among scholars on a definition is reflected in the great variety of terms that exist to describe LP. These include the terms *linguistic reform, language reform, deliberate language change, planned language change and language treatment* as well as terms such as *language engineering* (Miller 1950), *language development* (Noss 1967), *language management* (Jernudd and Neustupny 1986), *language determination* (Jernudd 1973) and *language regulation* (Gorman 1973).

According to Cooper (1989), *language planning* has become the more popular term to denote activities and efforts which focus on making deliberate or planned changes to language and language use or on influencing language behaviour. He notes, however, that the term *language planning* was neither the first nor the undisputed term to be used for denoting deliberate language change, as the list above illustrates.

The multitude of definitions of LP is also a consequence of the many different approaches to the subject. Cooper (1989) therefore suggests that a better understanding of language planning can be gained by reviewing its existing definitions and descriptions in terms of a set of features formulated in the question '*Who* plans *what* for *whom* and *how?*'. I shall discuss these elements (who, what, for whom, and how) here, because they assist in understanding the framework within which feminist language reform (LR) is placed.

Who are the language planners?

Although LP activities are often associated with governments or official agencies, they are certainly not exclusively linked to or undertaken by such agencies. In fact most LP scholars would agree that almost anyone can engage in LP activities. It therefore makes sense to attempt to differentiate between different types of language planners. For example, Jernudd (1973) makes a distinction between five major groups of language planners or LP agencies. These include (a) *governments*, (b) *national, non-government agencies*, (c) *private agencies*, (d) *a newsreader's proofreading function* and (e) *the individual author, letter-writer* or *even after-dinner speaker*. Many LP scholars agree that limiting LP activities to authorised language-regulating bodies is too restrictive because it ignores some of the most interesting cases of LP. These include the LP efforts of individuals and minority groups which have often brought about major changes in language. Cooper (1989: 31) mentions the work of individuals such as Ben Yehuda in Palestine, Samuel Johnson in England, Aasen in Norway, Korais in Greece, Stur in Slovakia, Mistral in Provence, Dobrovsky in Bohemia, Aavik in Estonia and Jablonski in Lithuania. Similarly, the demand for official recognition of a minority language seldom comes from a government or official language agency but mainly from the minority group.

Furthermore, LP does not need to be carried out by linguistic experts. In fact, many LP activities are in the hands of people with a strong interest in language and language issues but without specific training in LP or linguistics.

What is being planned?

Although language is, of course, the focus of the planning activities, there is tremendous variation in the type of focus on language. Examples of LP include the selection of a language (code) for official communications in a society, the development of a regional language variety or unwritten dialect into a standard, national language, the reform of orthography, the development of a new function for a language (e.g. for education or scientific purposes), the regulation of terminology for a particular discipline and the establishment of a language academy (that is, a language-regulating body).

The available literature usually distinguishes between two main categories or types of LP. The first type is concerned with the *regulation* of aspects of an existing language or language variety: this involves, for example, reforms to orthography, the adoption of a new script, the coinage of new words and modifications to existing language forms. The terms *corpus planning* (Kloss 1969), *language cultivation* (Neustupny 1970) and *language development* (Jernudd 1973) have been used to describe this type of LP.

The second major type is referred to as *status planning* (Kloss 1969), or the *policy approach* (Neustupny 1970) or *language determination* (Jernudd 1973). Its primary focus is on selecting a language code for a specific purpose, on allocating functions to specific language(s) and on regulating the use of languages in a community. The choice of Swahili as the official language over many other indigenous languages and language varieties as well as English in Tanzania is an example of this type. Another instance of status planning is the functional and status allocation of language varieties in a multilingual nation: this involves identifying which language varieties should be used, for example, as the medium of education or instruction, in the media and in government-related administration. The status and function allocated to such languages as Dutch, French and German in Belgium, French and English in Quebec are also the results of language planning and language policy.

Although this distinction between two main types of LP helps to clarify the object of planning activities, several scholars (e.g. Fishman 1983, Cooper 1989) have pointed out that this distinction of LP types is clearer in *theory* than in *practice*. Consequently many cases involve activities associated with both types. Cooper (1989: 33) illustrates this with the example of the establishment of the *Académie Française* (the French Language Academy) by Cardinal Richelieu:

> Richelieu's decision to found an official language academy, while an effort to regulate the forms of the French language – corpus planning – may also be viewed as an effort to promote the use of French for functions which hitherto had been occupied by Latin, an instance of status planning.

Sometimes further subtypes are distinguished within either type of LP. For example, within corpus planning – the type most relevant to the topic of this book – a distinction is usually made between *graphisation, standardisation* (sometimes called *codification*) and *modernisation* (also called *elaboration*). *Graphisation* refers to the development of writing systems for unwritten languages. *Standardisation* or *codification* is a very complex activity involving the development of a grammar, the writing of a dictionary of the chosen language (variety), developing and writing rules for the pronunciation and the orthography of this language. *Modernisation* or *elaboration* are the terms used to refer to a process whereby changes or modifications are made to a language to enable it to fulfil new functions, to become an adequate medium for the discussion of new topics, and to cope with new domains and new modes of discourse. The processes of standardisation and modernisation often go hand in hand. An interesting case of modernisation or elaboration concerns Modern Hebrew in Israel. After selecting Hebrew to become an official language of the state of Israel, language planners had to modernise Classical Hebrew to allow this ancient variety, mainly used in religious contexts, to serve the communication needs of a modern people.

Cooper (1989: 154) adds another subtype of LP which he names *renovation* and defines it as 'an effort to change an already developed code, whether in the efficiency, aesthetics, or national or political ideology'.

There are, of course, many other distinctions made in LP types which are, however, not directly relevant to the type of LP described in this book.[1]

Who is the language planning for?

The target audience for LP activities can range from specific groups such as the students in a language classroom, the members of a congregation, journalists and editors working for a particular newspaper, to more general groups of language users such as all public (civil) servants in a country, all members of a speech community or even all users of a certain language, irrespective of national boundaries.

In some cases, language planners adopt a *top-down* approach: they target their changes at a macro-level agency in the hope that this will enable the spread of changes to smaller units and groups. An example of this would be the formulation of language reforms at the level of the ministry of education to be implemented through the school system.

In the *bottom-up* or *grassroots* approach, LP initiatives often originate in a specific section of the population which is most affected by a particular language issue or problem. They then promote the need for reform or sometimes formulate reform proposals which they hope will spread from their group to the speech community at large. The recognition of a minority language as an official language in a country is an example of planning initiated at the grassroots. In reality, many cases of LP demonstrate a close interaction between these two approaches to a target audience.

How is language planned?

This is perhaps the most crucial question for language planners. Indeed this question addresses the issue of the activities, stages and processes that make up LP. Here it is important to make a distinction between what LP involves in *theory*, and how it evolves in *practice*. The study of actual examples of LP quickly shows that there is sometimes a considerable difference between scholars' views on how language *should* be planned and how language *is* planned in real cases. Some planning scholars (e.g. Neustupny 1983: 2) define LP as a 'systematic, theory-based, rational' activity. Others (e.g. Cooper 1989) consider such definitions to represent a LP ideal which is hardly ever realised in practice. The current lack of a theoretical framework for guiding LP activities is another hindrance to dealing with the issue of how language is or should be planned.

Fasold (1984) comments that the *how* of LP is also influenced by the approach taken to the subject. He distinguishes between language planners who adopt an *instrumental* approach and those who adopt a *sociolinguistic* approach. The instrumental approach is mainly concerned with improving the efficiency of language as a tool for communication: it involves making decisions about modifications, and changes to language, purely from the angle of linguistic efficiency. Other functions of language (e.g. as a marker of identity) are not taken into account. The socio-linguistic approach sees 'language as a resource that can be used in improving social life' (Fasold 1984: 250). Those who adopt a socio-linguistic approach are concerned with determining which linguistic alternative or solution is most appropriate in improving or alleviating the social problem to which it is linked. Thus, the process of LP involves not only making decisions about language from the angle of linguistic efficiency but also from a sociopolitical angle.

The discussion of feminist LR is best done from a socio-linguistic approach because the reforms are aimed at achieving greater linguistic, social and political equality of the sexes. I shall elaborate this point later in the chapter.

Language planning scholars working within this approach (e.g. Rubin 1971, 1973, Jernudd and Das Gupta 1971, Jernudd 1973, Fasold 1984, Cooper 1989) usually identify four stages in the LP process: the *fact-finding* stage, the *planning* stage, the *implementation* stage and the *evaluation and feedback* stage.

In the *fact-finding* stage the language planners gather data about the problematic language issue(s). These data are then analysed and made known to the affected community. The data that are gathered for analysis not only include linguistic details but also social and political facts associated with the language issue.

In the *planning* stage, decisions about appropriate actions to deal with the language issue at stake are made. First of all, the language planner decides whether or not changes can or should be made. Secondly, the language planner needs to establish the goals of the reforms and select the strategies by which to attain the changes. Alternatives to problematic forms, language varieties or other language issues then need to be identified and evaluated, which may involve a type of cost–benefit analysis (e.g. Fasold 1984); finally, the language planner needs to make a prognosis about the outcome of the proposed changes.

In the *implementation* stage decisions are made about the best methods and avenues for implementing and promoting the reforms. The implementation stage should be carefully designed and executed: if a variety of methods or avenues for implementation are available to the language planner, each should be evaluated.

The final stage concerns *evaluation and feedback*. Here the language planner should assess the extent to which the planning and implementation of the proposed reforms have been successful. This is mainly done by means of checking the extent to which the proposed reforms (a) have been adopted and spread throughout the target community and beyond and (b) have alleviated the social problem associated with the language issue.

Here I shall briefly discuss feminist LR as a case of LP using the sociolinguistic framework and focusing on the question 'who plans what for whom and how'.

Feminist language reform, non-sexist language reform, feminist linguistic intervention? The nomenclature surrounding language planning and the sexes

Up to this point I have been talking about 'feminist language reform' or 'non-sexist language reform' to describe the activities and initiatives of feminists to eliminate the discriminatory portrayal and representation of women and men in language. Considering the multitude of terms designating LP, it is not surprising that this particular type of LP is also known by many different names. First of all, there is some variety with regard to the description of the discriminatory portrayal of the sexes in language: for English, the most common terms include *sexist* language, *androcentric* language, *gender-biased* or *male-biased* language as well as *gender-exclusive* language. In other languages, we find similar terms such as *sexistische/androzentrische Sprache* (German), *langue sexiste* (French), *lingua sessista* (Italian) and others such as *frauenfeindliche Sprache* (German, 'women-hating' language). Secondly, variation also exists in the terms which describe the efforts to change the gender bias found in language: for example, *sexist language reform* or *non-sexist language reform*, *feminist language planning*, *feminist language reform* or *feminist language policy*, *reform of gender-biased language* or, more generally, *linguistic intervention*. Again other languages in which such LP has taken place have a range of terms equivalent to those in English. The desired outcome of the planning efforts has similarly been indicated by a variety of terms including *non-sexist language*, *gender-inclusive language*, *gender-neutral language*, *sex-fair language*, *linguistic equality of the sexes*, or by more general terms such as *inclusive language*, *non-discriminatory language*, *positive language*, *bias-free language*. Although the choice of a particular term over another is to some extent motivated by the selector's ideological stance *vis-à-vis* the issue as well as her or his social and linguistic approach to language planning,[2] many terms are nevertheless often used synonymously.

In this book I shall use the terms *feminist language reform*, *non-sexist language reform*, and *feminist language planning* interchangeably to refer to LP efforts and activities concerning the non-discriminatory portrayal of women and men in language. I shall refer to the desired outcome of planning efforts as either *non-sexist language, linguistic equality of the sexes* or *sex/gender-fair language*. Other terms such as *gender-inclusive* and *gender-neutral language* will be used to identify particular strategies to be used in attaining linguistic equality of the sexes.

Feminist language reform: an instance of corpus planning?

The object of feminist LP is the non-sexist representation and treatment of the sexes in language use. Indeed the stimulus for non-sexist language reform is the problematic nature of language use about the sexes: the way in which we speak or write about women and men is marked by inequality and discrimination. Men are treated and represented as the norm in language. Women's linguistic representation, on the other hand, is always done in reference to this norm. Women are subsumed under the linguistic norm which is based on, or identical to, men's representation, leading to their invisibility. Sometimes they are made visible only to display their difference, i.e. their deviation from the male norm. The latter leads to their 'marked' linguistic treatment. In Chapter 2 I shall elaborate on the sexist practices in language use including women's invisibility in language, women's marked status in language and men's status as the linguistic norm.

The ways in which languages are being used in speech communities around the world confirm the linguistic inequality of the sexes. Sometimes this linguistic inequality is mainly found in the vocabularies of languages, or in the making and development of meaning(s), and sometimes it is also located in grammatical structures of a language. In the languages which have been subjected to an analysis of sexism, the linguistic bias has been found to be mainly in favour of the representation of the man, the male and masculine as the norm and against the woman, the female and the feminine. This bias has been called 'sexist' in line with other discriminatory practices based on gender and/or sex.

Broadly speaking, the aims of feminist LR are to expose this bias, to rid languages of sexism by eliminating sexist practices from language use, and by replacing them with non-sexist ones or, by creating new ways of expression which avoid gender bias.

Feminist language planning efforts have a predominantly social (and political) rather than a linguistic motivation: LR is believed to contribute to an improvement in social equality, and to lead to an alleviation of a social problem, that is the discrimination on the basis of one's gender. Many forms of feminist LP involve the processes of *modification, replacement* and, to some extent, *creation*. Sexist practices are modified, sexist forms are replaced by non-sexist ones which can occur through either selection of existing non-sexist alternatives or through the creation of new ways of expression. Feminist LP can thus be considered as an instance of *language development* (Jernudd 1973) or *corpus planning* (e.g. Kloss 1969). It is concerned with the selection and promotion of variants within a language: that is, non-sexist practices, alternatives and forms are selected and promoted as replacements for sexist ones. In fact Cooper (1989) treats the American feminist campaign for non-sexist language usage as a particular instance of corpus planning which he calls *renovation*. According to Cooper (1989: 154)

> . . . the plain language movement, and the feminist campaign [for non-sexist language usage, *my comment*] all represent renovation – an effort to change an already developed code, whether in the name of efficiency, aesthetics, or national or political ideology . . . the renovated language fulfills no new communicative functions. But if the new forms carry out old communicative functions, they also contribute to the nonlinguistic goals which motivated the linguistic renovation, whether the limitation of new elites, the discrediting of old ones, the mobilization of political support, or the raising of consciousness.

Some feminist theorists and feminist language planners would take issue with Cooper's characterisation of the American feminist campaign for non-sexist language use as not leading to new communicative functions for the renovated language. They argue that the use of new forms to carry old meanings and to fulfil old communicative functions is not what feminist LR is about (see Chapters 3 and 4). However, Cooper's label of *renovation* is appropriate for a range of feminist LP efforts. In fact, many guidelines for non-sexist language use which have resulted from LP efforts stress and argue that non-sexist language use does not *in any way alter the communicative functions or restrict the communicative range of a language*.

Before I address the question of 'who plans what for whom and how' in relation to feminist LR, it is relevant to reflect briefly on the limitations of a LP framework for the discussion and description of feminist LR.

Applying a LP framework to the examination of feminist LR facilitates the understanding of the *processes* involved in dealing with the problem of sexist representation in language. Although such a framework takes account of the social, political and ideological conditions which have led to the desire, or sometimes demand, for LR, it does not examine these in detail. Similarly, LP approaches take an interest in the reasons why change is desirable or not, but the reasons themselves will not be scrutinised in terms of their philosophical validity, ideological stance or social relevance. From a LP perspective, the interest in a problematic language issue lies not so much in discovering *what caused the problem* as *how to address or solve the problem.*

Feminist LP focuses on the question of how to deal with this problematic issue of linguistic sexism. The emphasis is on documenting and examining the extent of the problem, on making decisions on how to eliminate the problem and on proposing ways of implementing reforms. Discovering the reasons for the existence of linguistic sexism or pondering the question whether or not language is sexist are only marginally addressed.

Notwithstanding these limitations, a LP perspective nevertheless does contribute to theoretical insights into the nature of sexism, and into language action as social action. It also highlights women's initiatives at meaning-making.

Feminist language reform: who plans what for whom and how?

Who are the language planners?

Women associated with the women's movement (both first[3] and second wave) were among the first to openly express concern about the discriminatory treatment of women in language and to call for the elimination of discriminatory language practices. Early feminist LP was very much a grassroots phenomenon. Women from all walks of life who were active in the women's movement not only discussed the ways in which language was used to demean women but also publicised their concerns in consciousness raising groups, in parent, teacher or school council meetings, in pamphlets, in letters to newspapers and to publishers and so on. Often they also developed strategies and proposals to eliminate gender bias in language.

Pioneers in feminist LP who publicised the need for reform and their reform proposals included for (American) English, such individuals as Casey Miller and Kate Swift, two freelance editors,

Bobbye Sorrels Persing and Alma Graham, a lexicographer, among many others. Pioneers in other countries include Marina Yaguello and Benoîte Groult in France, Ingrid Guentherodt in collaboration with Marlis Hellinger, Senta Trömel-Plötz and Luise Pusch in Germany, Dédé Brouwer and Ingrid Van Alphen in The Netherlands, Alma Sabatini in Italy, Theodossia Pavlidou in Greece and E. Zaikauskas in Lithuania.

Besides individual women, women's groups, feminist collectives, task forces and working parties on women's and equality issues made up an important group of the more 'visible' feminist language planners. These groups encouraged and put pressure on their respective organisations, companies or institutions to address the issue of gender bias in language. Early examples of this category of language planners include some American publishing houses with large educational sections such as Scott, Foresman and Co (1972), McGraw-Hill Book Company (1972), Macmillan (1975) and Random House (1976) and some professional associations like the American Psychological Association (1975), the National Council of the Teachers of English (1976) and the International Association of Business Communication (1977). Included in this group of language planners are also equal opportunity committees, women's task forces and advisory committees of tertiary (educational) institutions, union organisations, media organisations who joined the ranks of the publishing houses and the professional organisations in acting as language planners. In such countries as Germany, France, Belgium, The Netherlands, and in some Scandinavian countries, these types of language planners usually preceded publishing houses and other commercial or private enterprises in reform efforts.

A third group acting as language planners in the area of non-sexist language are government or semi-government agencies that were formed to comply with the linguistic implications of legislation outlawing sex discrimination in employment and other spheres of life. The LP of such groups usually confined itself to eliminating sex discrimination in job and occupational titles. Examples include: for the USA, the US Department of Labor, Manpower [*sic*] Administration (1975); for Germany, the 'Deutscher Städtetag' (1986); for Italy the 'Presidenza del Consiglio dei Ministri, Direzione Generale delle Informazioni della Editoria e della Proprietà Letteraria Artistica e Scientifica' (1986); for France, the 'Commission de féminisation des noms de métiers' (1984–86); for French-speaking Canada, the 'Conseil du status de la femme – Office de la langue française' (1979); and for Spain, the 'Ministerio de Educación y Ciencia' (1988).

Finally, some international or supernational organisations have also engaged in non-sexist LP. For example, UNESCO has issued guidelines for non-sexist language for English and French in 1989 and for German in 1993.

It thus appears that feminist LP or non-sexist LR is undertaken by a great variety of 'planners' ranging from enthusiastic feminist individuals who are privately and professionally committed to changing sexist language, feminist activists and lobby groups, and women's action committees in large organisations to language task forces of government agencies and even language academies. The considerable political, ideological and social differences among these groups of language planners affect the *what* and *how* of their planning activities. Similarly, these different groups have different methods of implementation as they vary in their access to agencies promoting language spread (e.g. legislation, media, education). Language planners also differ greatly in *how* they carry out their reform activities: for example, they may differ in the amount of attention they pay to each of the stages in the planning process. Some focus primarily on the *fact-finding* stage whereas others concentrate much more on the *actual planning* or *implementation stages*. For example, some government agencies do not engage in their own fact finding and pay little attention to the formulation of alternatives, but focus primarily on implementing proposals.

What is planned?

I have already identified feminist LR as a type of corpus planning whose subject is the portrayal of women and men in language – that is, a concern with the way people use language *about* and *to* women and men.

Feminist LR affects almost all aspects of language: the writing system, the lexicon, the morphology and the syntax, the construction of meaning and of discourse.[4] Observations and investigations of language use have shown that the portrayal of the sexes is characterised by 'sexism': i.e. language practices and usage express a bias against women in favour of men. It is the task of the language planners to examine and expose the extent of sexism in language, to formulate non-sexist alternatives which should *replace* the sexist ones. Although in principle all forms of language use are subject to the language planner's attention, in practice it is mainly forms of written discourse and some forms of public speech that are scrutinised most thoroughly.

Who is the language planning directed at?

Although the ultimate aim of most feminist language planners is to influence and change the language behaviour of an *entire speech community*, many do in fact aim their proposals at more specific audiences. They also often identify the types of language uses for which their proposals are primarily intended.

Among the prime target audiences for non-sexist language reform are publishers of all kinds of educational materials such as first readers, textbooks, instruction manuals and learning guides. Journalists, editors, presenters and others working in the mass media (both print and electronic) form another major target group, as do bureaucrats, educators (especially school teachers) and legislative bodies.

Feminist language planners focus on these groups because they believe that these groups are key agencies in influencing and/or 'regulating' the language behaviour of the speech community at large. Later we shall see that the choice of the target audience is partly influenced by the language planners' strategies for promoting the proposals and partly by their understanding of how language spreads.

How is feminist language planning done?

I have drawn attention to the fact that the practice of LP seldom resembles the 'systematic, theory-based, rational activity' some LP scholars believe it to be (e.g. Neustupny 1983: 2). In fact, I agree with Cooper (1989: 41), who comments that 'language planning can be a messy affair – ad hoc, haphazard and emotionally driven'.

There are indeed many factors that have an impact on how the LP process is conducted. They include the grassroots nature of many feminist LP initiatives, the differences between language planners, the diverse range of views on what constitutes feminist LP, and the social, political and ideological motivations for LR. The fact that few of the early language planners saw themselves in that role also influences the way in which reforms are brought about.

It is therefore almost impossible to find examples of feminist LP that rigorously stick to the execution of the crucial LP stages: fact finding, planning, implementation and evaluation. Nevertheless, if we look at feminist LP as a phenomenon in its entirety, it is possible to find evidence that the stages of fact finding, planning, implementation and evaluation have occurred.

Notes

1. Further reading on language planning in general can be found in Eastman (1983), Edwards (1985), Wardhaugh (1987) as well as Cobarrubias and Fishman (1983), Fishman (1974), Fishman *et al.* (1968), Kennedy (1984), Rubin and Jernudd (1971a) and Rubin and Shuy (1973).
2. For instance, Hellinger (1993) distinguishes between feminist language planning/reform/policy and the other terms, e.g. (non-)sexist language reform to mark differences in language planners. For her, *feminist language planning* is restricted to those planning activities which involve feminist language planners, whereas *non-sexist language reform* can refer to the planning efforts of agencies with regard to the issue of linguistic equality. Similarly, some authors (Frank and Treichler 1989: 17–18) comment on the differences in meaning relating to terms such as 'non-sexist language', 'gender-neutral language':

   > The use of gender-neutral language is not sufficient, because gender-neutral language is not synonymous with nonsexist language . . . It is important, then, to distinguish between the terms *gender-neutral* and *nonsexist*. *Gender-neutral* is a linguistic description: a gender-neutral term is formally, linguistically unmarked for gender: *police officer, domestic violence, flight attendant* in place of gender-marked *policeman, wife battering, stewardess*. *Nonsexist* is a social, functional description; a nonsexist term works against sexism in society. While many gender-neutral terms are consistent with nonsexist usage, the two are not the same . . .

3. A brief documentation of early concerns about sexism in language is presented in Chapter 2. More information can also be found in Stannard (1977) and Miller and Swift (1991).
4. To my knowledge there are no investigations of sexism in phonology.

2 Sexism in language: an international phenomenon?

Introduction

Non-sexist language planning, like most other forms of language planning (LP) arises out of a concern with language, an aspect of language *per se*, a language situation or a communication issue which affects its speakers adversely. In the case of non-sexist language reform (LR), it is the linguistic portrayal of women and men, which is considered problematic. This problem has been labelled *sexist language, sex-exclusive language, gender-biased language* or *androcentric language*.

A first major stage in the planning process is to identify, document and describe the problematic language issue. This forms the fact-finding stage. Depending on the type of language issue involved, this stage may not always be linked directly to the following stages of the planning process, these being *planning, implementation* and *evaluation*. In the case of feminist LP, the 'identifiers' of the problem were not always those who proposed changes or who were responsible for their implementation.

In this chapter I survey work that has been done to document sexist language use in a variety of languages. The survey of linguistic sexism presented here is far from exhaustive: the pool of languages for which linguistic sexism has been documented is vast and is constantly expanding. Whereas the Germanic languages, especially English and German, have been subjected to very detailed and expansive analyses since the mid-1970s, the documentation of sexist practices in other languages and language groups is much less extensive and/or of a very recent nature (e.g. Lithuanian, Chinese). The extent and depth of the documentation of linguistic sexism in a language is of course in no way related to the extent of sexist linguistic practices found in a particular speech community. It is more a question of the level of feminist activity in a community and the importance assigned to language in feminist concerns. For example, Violeta Kalėdaitė (1995), in a paper on language and gender issues in Lithuania, quotes Marija Ausrine Pavilioniene, the president of the Lithuanian University Women's Association, who claims that the women's movement was stimulated by the idea of an independent Lithuania. Consequently, Kalėdaitė comments, feminist concerns with language issues are of a very recent nature in Lithuania.

The aims of this chapter are, firstly, to provide an insight into the fact-finding stage of this increasingly international LP activity by documenting linguistic sexism and sexist language practices across texts, domains and languages. Because of the wealth of data available I have had to be very selective in the presentation of material. Although I have tried to select data representative of a variety of languages, texts and approaches I may not always have succeeded, especially in relation to the range of languages represented here.

Secondly, this chapter aims to give a description of the major forms of linguistic sexism and common sexist practices found in a variety of languages. Although the chapter provides substantial evidence that the way sexism is embedded in and expressed through language is often language specific, it nevertheless shows that there are common forms of linguistic sexism and common sexist practices across languages.

It is not my intention to critically examine the extent to which these 'allegations' and observations of linguistic sexism are genuine or 'true'. The focus is purely on documenting a stage in the LP process and on extrapolating common trends in the analyses of linguistic sexism across languages. Issues of criticism will be dealt with in later chapters.

Sexism in language: old and new

Concern with the linguistic treatment and representation of women is said to be a characteristic of the second wave of the women's movement which started in the late 1960s and early 1970s mainly in Western English-speaking nations. Feminist scholarship of and investigations into the issue of sexism in language and, more generally, women's relationship to language started in the mid-1970s, as various bibliographies on the subject testify (e.g. Froitzheim 1980, Thorne and Henley 1975, Thorne *et al.* 1983).

The topic of the discriminatory treatment of the sexes in language, however, is not a new activity or concern exclusive to the women's movement since the 1970s. Various language issues such as women's access to words, women's representation in language and women's naming practices had received attention in earlier times.

A woman's right to maintain her name after marriage was a central feature of the Lucy Stone League in the United States of America (see Stannard 1977). Kramarae and Treichler (1985) report that Charlotte Carmichael Stopes challenged the generic use of 'he' and 'man' as early as 1908 and that Mary Ritter wrote a feminist critique of the *Encyclopaedia Brittanica* in 1941. Miller and Swift (1991) mention that in the United States Dorothy L. Sayers, a writer, Mary Beard, a historian and Sophie Drinker, a musicologist, had commented on androcentrism in language as early as the 1930s and 1940s. In Denmark in 1912 Lis Jacobsen published a study on the Danish language in the Middle Ages, in which she researched human agent nouns: she commented that men were named according to their social status in society whereas women were named according to their relationship with the man or men in their lives.

Of course, in previous centuries and earlier this century matters concerning female language behaviour as well as the portrayal of women in language were at times 'hot' topics of debate among male linguists and language guardians. These language custodians were often preoccupied with defining the role of women in language change: were women the guardians of the old and pure language forms or were they agents of decay? They expressed a similar preoccupation with prescribing the status of women in language and with their linguistic representation.[1] Their concern (with very few exceptions) could hardly be called feminist. On the contrary, in most instances they were worried about *man's* supremacy in language being diminished by the linguistic presence of women. This will become clear in some extracts from their work quoted in the following sections on sexism.

Despite these earlier preoccupations with the topic, the *systematic* study of linguistic sexism is squarely linked to the second wave of the women's movement.

Documenting linguistic sexism across texts, domains and languages

Surveying the entire field of research on linguistic sexism pertaining to a wide range of languages is simply impossible within the confines of a single book. For English alone – which has been subjected most thoroughly and widely to analyses of sexism – this would amount to a volume much larger than the present book. In addition, the number of studies investigating sexism in languages other than English is also rapidly increasing. Nevertheless I shall try to convey the wide scope and diversity of this field by identifying the language domains, and the major (types of) texts for which analyses of linguistic sexism have been conducted, by illustrating the latter with examples drawn from a variety of languages and by briefly commenting on the investigative methods used in analysing sexism in language.

The identification and documentation of linguistic sexism has never been the exclusive domain of language professionals, let alone linguists. On the contrary, language experts and those with linguistic expertise have long been a minority in this field, especially with regard to the English language. Both the grassroots character of the non-sexist LP movement and the fact that linguistic sexism is intricately linked to other forms of sex and gender-based discrimination have meant that authors, journalists, bureaucrats, editors, administrators, educationalists, psychologists, historians, sociologists, media commentators, school teachers, publishers, students and lawyers, among many others, were and are engaged in documenting gender bias in language. Some have commented on gender bias in language because of their own personal experiences in this area; others have become involved in the debate through their professional activities. This personal and professional diversity of people concerned about sexism in language is not only reflected in the types of texts and discourses that have been subjected to analysis but also in the focus of the analysis.

Language commentators other than linguists tend to focus their analysis on features and phenomena such as gender-stereotyping, asymmetry in the use of parallel expressions for women and men, women's invisibility in language or on the construction of sexist discourses.

Linguistic investigations of sexism tend to be influenced by the researcher's linguistic approach and training. For example, Hellinger's (1990) work on German and English sexism adopts the methods of *contrastive linguistics*. Poynton's (1985) work on gender and terms of address in Australian English is firmly couched within a *systemic linguistic* approach based on the work of the linguist, Michael Halliday. Researchers working on the semantic derogation of female terms often employ methods found in *historical linguistics* to trace the changes in meaning (e.g. Kochskämper 1991, Penelope and McGowan 1979). The emergence of *critical discourse analysis* (e.g. Fairclough 1992) has brought about a greater focus on the analysis of sexist discourses from a critical linguistic perspective which moves away from investigations of sexism at or below sentence level.

Almost any major text type, genre or form of discourse found and used in a wide range of domains has been subjected to an analysis of linguistic sexism: texts belonging to the domains of (language) education, the media, law, business, public administration, science and (institutionalised) religion have been widely scrutinised for sexism, not only for English but also for a range of other languages.

In the following sections I shall review some studies of linguistic sexism in these domains of language use.

Sexism in educational materials

Educational texts and resource materials for young learners[2] were among the first to be subjected to analysis. This is not surprising because there is a strong belief that the effects of sexism, including linguistic sexism, were most pernicious in the early stages of socialisation – that is, in the pre-schooling and schooling periods. From children's picture books, first readers and first school books, a textual and visual image emerged which was sex-stereotyped and biased against the portrayal of girls and women. Both female and male characters displayed highly sex-stereotyped behaviour and engaged mainly in activities considered appropriate for their sex. Furthermore, male characters were visually and verbally more prominent. Usually there was also a greater diversity of male characters who engaged in a greater and more diverse range of activities than women and girl characters.

I have chosen an Australian-based study into gender representation in children's early readers to illustrate the type of findings emerging from analyses of linguistic sexism in the domain of language use. The examination by Freebody and Baker (1987) covered 163 reading books in English which were (and some still are) commonly used as first readers in a large educational division in New South Wales, Australia. Their main aim was to examine the construction and operation of gender distinctions in such literature. The authors not only examined the obvious and blatant forms of gender-stereotyping and male-centredness but also focused on exposing the more subtle ways of constructing gender-stereotypes in these readers. Their research revealed a quantitative imbalance in the use of gender terms. For example, for child characters the ratio of the word 'boy(s)' to the word 'girl(s)' is 3 : 2. They found a similar imbalance in relation to proper names used for boys and girls: approximately 2,000 names for boys as opposed to 1,400 for girls were used in the corpus. The authors commented that 'thus proper names reinforce, rather than compensate for, the prevalence of boys over girls shown in the use of general terms' (Freebody and Baker 1987: 83). Freebody and Baker also investigated the elaboration of gender terms: this refers to the kinds of events and activities, mainly expressed through verbs and adjectives with which boys and girls are associated. Their findings also confirmed strong tendencies for gender-stereotyping in this area. In relation to the expression of boys' and girls' activities they found (*ibid.*: 87) that

> there is a wide range of verbs associated with boys but not with girls (as subject: *answer, hurt, shout, think, work*; as object: *come to, jump with, like, play with, talk to, walk with*, and a small subset of verbs of which girls are the object and never boys in these texts (*hold on to, kiss*).

Their analysis of adjectives associated with girls and boys in the readers (*ibid.*) mirrored the above:

> we found that the most frequent adjective in the corpus is *little* and that this adjective is not equivalently associated with *boy/s* and *girl/s*. About 30 per cent of the boys appearing in these books are described as *little*, while slightly more than half of the girls are so described. In addition, there are a number of adjectives applied uniquely to either boys or girls. Boys, but never girls, are described as: *new, sad, kind, brave, tiny, naughty*. Girls, on the other hand are exclusively attached to the following adjectives *young, dancing*, and *pretty*.

The depiction of girl characters in these books is characterised by the 'cuddle factor' according to Freebody and Baker. They define this as a direct association between girls (and other female characters) and more emotional states of mind as well as less physical and gregarious activities.

Gender-stereotyping was not only prevalent in the depiction of characters but also in the description of home and family life.

A very interesting aspect of Freebody and Baker's analysis is their observation of the way in which conversational exchanges between boy and girl characters were represented. Patterns of turn-taking, the amount of speech attributed to girl and boy characters, type of turns all reflected the dominance of the male in conversation: girls were allowed to introduce topics but only boys expanded them. Girls' utterances often functioned as providing support to those of boys, as illustrated in the following extract from one of the readers (*ibid.*: 99):

> 'Let us make a little play house with this,' says Jane.
> 'Yes,' says Peter. 'It will be fun. There will be no danger.'
> Then he says, 'We will not make a little house, we will make a big one to play in. Then you and I, and the dog can get in it.'
> 'Good,' says Jane.

Freebody and Baker concluded their analysis with the observation that many materials still in use in (Australian) schools portrayed gender and gender relations in sexist terms, even if the more blatant forms of gender stereotyping were diminishing (*ibid.*: 103):

> In the books' recasting of gender relations in non-school, usually family, settings, further evidence of the books' work of cultural assimilation can be seen. The child characters perform and view gender practices in relation to parents, grandparents, siblings, and friends. The private world of the family is restructured along the lines of public, institutional expectations.

In addition to first readers, many other types of educational materials have been examined for forms of gender bias, including textbooks, resource materials and test papers (e.g. Tittle *et al.* 1974). The analysis of these texts have yielded similar results to those found in relation to children's early readers. Most texts have an androcentric orientation: they present their material and knowledge from a masculine-generic perspective, while females are largely invisible in the text or are treated as secondary. There is no significant difference between male and female textbook authors in the use of sexist language practices, nor is there one between different subjects and topics of textbook materials. Both male and female writers often assume their readers to be male unless proven otherwise.

In the domain of language education it is worthwhile highlighting the research on linguistic sexism in foreign language learning materials. Exposing and tackling the sexism in foreign language textbooks is considered an important task, especially for the more widely taught and learned languages around the world, because it helps prevent the spread of sexist language practices to new users of a language. With English being the most widely taught second and foreign language[3] in the world, it is not surprising that ESL and EFL textbooks have been thoroughly scrutinised for gender-stereotyping and other sexist language practices.[4] Research on sexism in ESL/EFL materials has sometimes acted as a catalyst for research on linguistic sexism in other languages: for example, graduate students and language teachers undertaking ESL/EFL and other language studies in English-speaking countries have been confronted with the issue of linguistic sexism in English which has inspired some to examine the phenomenon in their own language. In the past few years a number of my graduate students in applied linguistics have become inspired to examine sexist language practices in Vietnamese, Korean, Chinese, Romanian and Japanese as a result of their exposure to issues of linguistic sexism in English.

The language textbooks for foreign languages other than English display a similar bias against women in their portrayal of male and female characters, their actions and roles. There is a high level of stereotyping the sexes. Stern (1976) analysed the contents and visual images in twenty-five foreign language textbooks (French, German, Italian, Latin, Russian and Spanish) published after 1970 and used in the USA. She found that women were either largely invisible in the texts or, when they were present, gender-role stereotyping was accentuated. The female characters were portrayed as wives, mothers and housewives and were described in physical terms. Harres and Truckenbrodt (1992) and Rendes (1988) analysed the linguistic portrayal of the sexes in current and new textbooks for German, finding that the most blatant forms of stereotyping have partly disappeared only to be replaced by more subtle forms (e.g. Harres and Truckenbrodt 1992).

Sexism in language reference materials

The exploration and documentation of linguistic sexism in grammars, dictionaries, language and style manuals[5] is of specific interest to language planners because of their alleged importance as repositories of, and authoritative reference works for, language and linguistic knowledge. Nichols (1988) points out that in countries without official language academies, dictionaries, handbooks of style as well as literary anthologies often have the role of 'semiofficial' language authorities. In countries with an official language academy, it is usually the responsibility of the academy to sanction or determine what can or cannot be recorded in dictionaries and what should or should not be considered acceptable grammatical practices. Feminist language professionals, especially linguists, have shown that such tools of linguistic knowledge reflect, contribute to and perpetuate the sexist use of language and the sexist nature of society.

In particular, dictionaries and the process of dictionary making have attracted considerable criticism. For instance, feminist linguists and lexicographers have shown for a variety of languages that women are more often than not excluded as meaning makers or as sources of meaning and words. This exclusion or omission is generally the result of the criteria selected for inclusion of material. An important criterion is the number of times a word or meaning is used or cited in certain publications. It is rare that feminist or women-oriented publications are well represented among the primary sources for dictionaries. As a matter of fact, the works of the 'best', 'male' authors were the main sources of information for entries in older dictionaries. Such dictionary-making practices are seen to have contributed to the late entry of new words like 'sexism' or even 'women's movement' or to the delayed recording of new meanings of words such as 'feminism'. For example, Pusch (1984b: 130) mentions for German that until recently the main meaning recorded for *Feminismus* (feminism) in several German dictionaries was 'the presence of feminine and female traits in a man' rather than the meaning commonly associated with the word since the 1970s. She also exposes a male bias and anti-feminist stance in the recording of new words and expressions in the German language. Pusch (1984a: 78–9) reveals that linguistic changes and innovations under the impact of the women's movement in Germany were completely ignored in articles, essays and collection of new acquisitions to the German language: in the 1970s, for instance, the essay by Uwe Förster of the *Gesellschaft für Deutsche Sprache* – a kind of language academy – on lexical innovations and acquisitions in the 1970s does not contain one single reference to the women's movement as a source of lexical innovation in Germany. If authors (e.g. Carstensen 1983) do mention neologisms and other lexical innovations linked to feminism and the women's movement, these have been extracted from mainstream publications whose use of such words is often in stark contrast to that found in feminist publications. Yaguello (1978) notes for French that words like *sexisme*, *femme-objet*, *phallocrate* were only to be found in the Larousse *Dictionnaire des mots nouveaux dans le vent* (dictionary of new words) despite fairly widespread use in the community. In Australia, Morris (1982: 89) notes that even if dictionaries (e.g. the Australian *Macquarie Dictionary*) do include linguistic creations and concepts of the women's movement (sexism, feminism) their definitions obscure rather than centre around the meanings which women and feminists attached to them:

> While it is true that the usages accepted by the *Macquarie* are stand-ard liberal currency today, the point is that the concepts developed by feminists are not even marginalised into second place, but rather omitted altogether.

Sexism is also found in the actual definitions of words, espe-cially those relating to women and men. Without exception *woman* is primarily defined as a sexual being. For example, the definitions found in English, French, Japanese, Dutch, German and Spanish dictionaries stress her biological features, i.e. her reproductive capa-city or her capacity to engage in sexual activity. Brouwer (1991a: 15) notes for Dutch that the *Van Dale's Groot Woordenboek der Nederlandse Taal* (Dutch dictionary) defines woman as a female person who is no longer a virgin. Other recurring main features of the definition of *woman* are her (dependent) relationship to the male member of the human race, e.g. as spouse, or as companion and her marital status, i.e. as adult female who is (not) or has been married. This is in sharp contrast to the definitions given to the word *man* which seldom mentions biological features or includes reference to *woman*.

Well-documented for a variety of languages is the sexism rampant in the exemplary sentences illustrating the meanings of a particular word. Luise Pusch's (1984b) essay 'Sie sah zu ihm auf wie zu einem Gott – das DUDEN-Bedeutungswörterbuch als Trivialroman'[6] in which she 'deconstructed' the entries under the letter A in the authoritative German dictionary *Duden* as a *Trivialroman* (trash novel). She found that the recorded meanings were not only often sexist or male-biased but also that the examples illustrating mean-ings revealed a very stereotyped picture of the sexes. For example, women were and are primarily portrayed as caring about children, involved in household chores, concerned about their looks, troubled by emotions and feelings of fear, interested in culture and, finally, devoted to a man, men or 'him'.

Somewhat earlier Gershuny (1973) had constructed a similar stereotyped picture of the sexes on the basis of the illustrative sentences of the American *Random House Dictionary* (English). Hampares' (1976) work on sexism in Spanish lexicography, García's (1977) study of linguistic sexism in Spanish dictionaries as well as Brouwer's (1991a) investigation of the Dutch dictionary *Van Dale*, have all made the observation that examples illustrating word usage are often sexist, thus not only reflecting sexist attitudes in society but also perpetuating such attitudes.

In descriptive as well as prescriptive grammars sexist practices have not only been located in illustrative examples but also in explanations of linguistic and grammatical rules. For English, Baron's (1986) comprehensive study of grammar and gender discusses the sexism of some early and more recent descriptions of grammatical gender, of the relationship between natural and grammatical gender, and of marking referential gender. Other investigations of English (e.g. Bodine 1975, Stanley 1978) have looked at the discussion of the gender versus number agreement with reference to third person pronouns (singular *they*, *he*, *she*). The androcentrism of grammars will be taken up again later in this chapter when the category of gender is discussed.

The language practices promoted by handbooks on correct usage or by style manuals have often been a major source of discontent from a feminist perspective.[7] Especially in the English-speaking world, feminist language commentators have argued that such manuals have halted if not stifled the process of language change towards a more equal treatment of the sexes in language. For example, until recently various American style manuals or handbooks regulating the language practices of the printed press prescribed the masculine generic pronoun *he* as the only correct use for generic reference and did not recognise the title *Ms* for women. They also advocated asymmetrical naming practices for women and men (see, e.g., Miller and Swift 1991). Handbooks of style are also quite influential in the tertiary education sector in the United States where they regulate the language practices adopted by students and provide guidance to first-year students, so-called 'freshmen'.

Sexism in the mass media

The linguistic portrayal of women in the mass media has also been a crucial point of focus because of the alleged importance of the mass media in shaping and/or influencing people's attitudes (Tuchman 1978). Although advertising has been subjected to intensive scrutiny with regard to its visual representation of the sexes, *linguistic* sexism has been primarily researched in newspapers and some current affairs and general interest magazines focusing on articles, features and job advertisements rather than on commercial advertising. Major newspapers from a variety of countries including Australia, Britain, Canada, Germany, Italy, Japan, Norway,

Thailand and the United States[8] have been analysed for features of linguistic sexism such as referential gender, gender-stereotyping and the (in)visibility of women. Specific attention has been paid to gender-inclusiveness in job advertisements. Most investigations again pinpoint the gender bias against women in such texts because of the prominence of gender-stereotyping both in content and language use.

In Norway, for example, Toril Swan undertook a diachronic study of the linguistic portrayal of women in Norwegian newspapers throughout the twentieth century (Swan 1992): she found that women were and are largely invisible in newspapers because they are not regarded as 'newsworthy' items. In the first period (1911–13), women mainly appeared either in advertisements or in death and other personal notices. Their main description focused on their status as 'wife of'. There was only the occasional mention of women in professional capacities, usually restricted to the arts. In the second period, from 1945 to 1946, the visibility of women in the newspapers was often restricted to female collaborators of the German enemy or to women in the resistance. However, this period was also a time of change with the use of female honorifics in decline and the emergence of new compounds with -kvinne (woman) to denote women in a professional capacity. In the third period, covering the years 1989 to 1991, Swan (1992) noticed only a half-hearted attempt to improve the image of women in newspapers: there was some increase in gender-neutral occupational nouns to refer to women and men; however, pronominal reference to such nouns was still predominantly achieved by means of the masculine generic pronoun *han* (he). Swan (1992: 52) concluded her analysis with the observation that the media have helped spread some changes and innovations but that

> with respect to the general visibility of women, . . . they have been less than acceptable, and do not reflect Norwegian society very accurately. Indeed, as this remains true in present-day papers as well, one might well conclude that there is some degree of symbolic annihilation, and certainly not equality.

Anamaria Beligan examined the linguistic consequences of the 1989 revolution in the Romanian press and the representation of women, ethnic and other minorities (Beligan 1993). She described how the sudden liberation from press censorship in Romania led to an orgy of linguistic abuse often directed at ethnic and other minorities, including women. Scrutinising ten issues of top selling

Romanian newspapers,[9] Beligan found that gender bias and xeno-phobic language characterises the current Romanian press, irrespect-ive of political orientation. In terms of gender-bias and linguistic sexism, Beligan noted not only an immediate reinstatement of the pre-communist honorific titles *domn* (Mr), *doamnă* (Mrs) and *domnişoara* (Miss) but also a derogatory misuse of titles for women. The term *domnişoară* was sometimes used to question a woman's virginity. Sometimes the term *madam* was used to discredit women because of its connotation in Romania with servants and lower-class women. Further features of linguistic sexism in Romanian newspapers include the gratuitous specification of gender in articles, images of women as witches or shrews (especially if they are engaged in a male-dominated profession) and as sexual commodities, and the increased use of words denoting women which have derogatory or trivialising connotations (e.g. *cucuoana, coana, duduia, duduca*). An interesting phenomenon in Romanian is the process of femin-isation and ethnicisation of names as a means of derogation: in order to derogate or vilify a male opponent or referent, his name is subjected to a process of feminisation and often to a process of ethnicisation (either germanisation/slavisation or magyarisation).

In an exploratory investigation of the representation of women and men in two Japanese newspapers[10] Masahiko Nakayama found that there were no substantial quantitative or qualitative differences in the use of sexist expressions between the national and regional newspapers. Her main observations regarding the portrayal of women and men in these newspapers concern the asymmetrical use of honorific titles, the predominantly gratuitous marking of femaleness in occupational nouns, the exclusion of women from generic nouns as well as some common gender-stereotyped de-scriptions. For example, Nakayama (1993) found that the gender-neutral honorific title -*san* was used in a sex-specific way through the practice of using -*san* in connection with male names and -*ko-san* in relation to women: -*ko* is a popular suffix of women's first names. However, the corresponding male suffix -*o* is not used in a similar way in connection with the honorific title -*san*. Similarly, generic expressions such as *kaishain* (company worker) are used primarly, if not exclusively, for male workers whereas female com-pany workers seem to be referred to by the English loan 'O.L.' or *office lady*. The gender of female agents and referents is made much more explicit than those of men. When describing teachers, students and bosses, the newspapers always marked the occupa-tional nouns for gender if female agents were involved but not in the case of male agents or referents: for example, *joshi-daisei* (female university student), *joshi-kyooshi* (female teacher) and the loan creation *onna bosu* (female boss). The physical appearance of women is much more likely to be described than that of men, as well as women's marital status – for example, *shufu* (housewife), *o sono tsuma* (and his wife), *yome* (someone's wife).

Sexism in the language of the law

Another major area of concern is the linguistic sexism found in legislative and legal documents. Danet (1980: 448) states that 'words are obviously of paramount importance in the law; in a most basic sense, the law would not exist without language'. People's rights and obligations are therefore intricately interwoven with linguistic expressions. Some sources (e.g. Guentherodt 1984 for German; Bosmajian 1977, Collins 1977, Driedger 1976, Miller and Swift 1991, Ritchie 1975 and Scutt 1985 for English; and Verbiest 1990 for Dutch) have shown that the ambiguity of androcentric language use has severely hampered women's legal rights, including women's access to some professions and women's right to vote. Miller and Swift (1991: 91) quote an example of a woman who could not be admitted to the bar in Virginia, USA, because the term 'woman' was not legally considered to be a 'person'. Verbiest (1990) reports that in The Netherlands in 1883 Aletta Jacobs requested to be placed on the electoral list because the law concerning electoral rights referred to those with voting rights as *ingezetenen* (residents), a term (adjectival noun) which does not linguistically exclude women. However, it was decided by the *Hoge Raad* (the High Council) that this gender-neutral term was not meant to include women. Guentherodt (1984: 243) reports a similar case of androcentric language barring Swiss women from the right to vote (women did not obtain the right to vote in Switzerland until 1971). In 1957 some Swiss women in the French-speaking canton of Vaud challenged their exclusion from voting rights by pointing out that 'according to contemporary legal and common usage which interprets the French masculine plural to include the feminine' (Guentherodt 1984: 243) the expression *tous les Suisses* (all Swiss people) as used in Art. 23 concerning suffrage in Vaud would have primarily a gender-neutral interpretation. Their challenge, which was quashed by the Swiss Federal Supreme Court, exposed the myth of masculine genericness. This was confirmed by the linguistic modification undertaken at federal level when women were finally granted the right to vote in 1971: in Art. 74 of the *Bundesverfassung* (Federal Constitution) the reference is to *Schweizer und Schweizer- innen* (Swiss men and Swiss women). Guentherodt (1984: 241) comments that

> masculine forms which in one context of legal language are supposed to be neutral and include women, may exclude women in another con- text if it serves male interests.

Sexism in the language of religion

Feminist theologians have been instrumental in exposing the lin- guistic sexism found in the domain of institutionalised religion.[11] Investigating and exposing linguistic sexism in the domain of reli- gion is considered critical because of the importance of language in religion and religious experience. Greene and Rubin (1991: 81) speak of religion as a 'verbal construction':

> language is so central to humans' experience of the supernatural that sacred language itself often takes on the same sanctity and taboos that are associated with the spiritual entities to which language refers.

In this domain of language use a great variety of sexist language practices is found, although the main focal points of analysis are usually the male terminology and imagery used to refer to God and religious experiences. Miller and Swift (1991: 76) comment that

> religious thinkers are forced to depend on symbols, particularly meta- phors and analogies, to describe and communicate to others what is by nature indescribable except in terms of human experience.

Being couched in a patriarchal world view, it is not surprising that the major Western religions have used male-biased metaphors cul- minating in the linguistic and visual portrayal of God as the supreme spiritual being whose features and characteristics are best repres- ented by those of male human beings. In the words of James Harris working on figurative gender attribution: 'the Supreme being is, in all languages, masculine, in as much as the masculine sex is the superior and the more excellent' (Harris [1751] 1765: 54). In fact, male imagery is used throughout religious texts to portray all spiritual matters, whereas female imagery is used predominantly in reference to earthly (nature) matters such as sexuality (positive sexuality – the image of the virgin, and negative sexuality – the image of the whore). Although 'the apologists' – a term used by

Miller and Swift (1991) – of Western religions have downplayed the symbolisation of God as male, the male imagery of God has been used to keep women from entering the priesthood (e.g. Myers 1972). Gender-biased translations of religious texts, especially of the Bible, have further strengthened the 'God = Male' imagery.

The work of the American feminist theologian Mary Daly (e.g. Daly 1973, 1978) has made a significant contribution not only towards exposing the linguistic sexism pervading religious writing and thinking but also towards changing sexist practices in religious language. Furthermore, Trible (1973, 1976), a theologian and expert of Hebrew scriptures, points out that some female imagery of God was present in Hebrew scriptures but that this imagery was often ignored in (English) translations of those passages.

Wegener et al. (1990) pinpoint sexism in the language of German prayers, of German translations of the Bible (especially by Luther) and in the language used in church services and religious rituals (e.g. christenings, weddings). Like their English-speaking sisters, they notice the dominance of male imagery associated with God:

> Gott ist der Vater der Väter, ein Hirte des Volkes, ein machtvoller Krieger («Herr der Heerschaaren»), ein König über alle Götter und ein Richter über alle Völker. [God is the father of fathers, the shepherd of people, a powerful fighter, Lord of heavenly hosts, a king of all kings and a judge of all peoples.] (Wegener et al. 1990: 86)

Women in both the Old and the New Testament are largely invisible: for instance, Jacob's daughters, Rebecca, Lea, Rachel and Dina, are not given a mention in relation to Jesus's ancestors. Another example mentioned by Wegener (1990) is the pseudo-generic use of words like Bruder/Brüder (brother/brethren), Sohn/Söhne (son/ sons) and even Vater/Väter (father/fathers). If women are mentioned in the texts, they are portrayed as the property of a man or men: e.g. in Genesis 2:25 Adam and Eve are spoken of as 'der Mensch und sein Weib' [man (=human being) and his wife]. In Exodus 20:17 women are considered the property of men on a par with animals (and slaves): 'Du sollst nicht begehren deines Nächsten Weib, Knecht, Magd, Rind, Esel noch alles, was dein Nächster hat' [thou shalt not want/desire your neighbour's wife, manservant, maid, cattle, ass/donkey or anything your neighbour has]. Both this verse from Exodus and the formulation of the tenth commandment 'Du sollst nicht begehren deines Nächsten Weib' leave no doubt about the androcentric perspective in the formulation (see also Pusch 1984a).

Investigating linguistic sexism in religious domains has not been limited to those predominantly found in the Western world: Ng and Burridge (1993) note that the Chinese cosmology involving the principles of *Yin* and *Yang* also shows traces of sexism: the *Yin* principle is closely associated with women, nature, emotion, ignorance, passivity and physicality. The *Yang* principle, on the other hand, has an association with men, culture, reason, assertiveness, creativity and intellect. The superiority of the *Yang* principle over the *Yin* principle is taken for granted. This is also reflected in the language associated with *Yin* and *Yang*. *Yin* compounds are more likely to have negative connotations whereas compounds involving *Yang* attract neutral, if not positive, connotations. The authors illustrate this with examples such as *yin'an* (dark and gloomy), *yindu* (insidious and sinister), *yinshi* (shameful secret), *yinbu* (genitals), *yingi* (presence of evil spirits). Ng and Burridge (1993: 79) not only state that 'in all aspects, *Yang* is equated with reason and control and *yin* with emotion and chaos' but also that

> the associations attached to *Yin* have quite clear damaging repercussions for women in China today. . . . The alignment of women with the *Yin* principle and the chimera of *Yin–Yang* harmony is costing Chinese women significant opportunities in life.

Sexism in other texts and domains of language use

Other domains and texts in which linguistic sexism has been noted (but not always formally described) include the field of business writing (memos, reports, business correspondence, manuals) and the domain of public administration and communication (e.g. circulars, invitations, forms requesting personal information). It is not unusual to find adult female job applicants described as 'girls' in widely publicised job advertisements or to find the female clerical staff referred to as 'the office girls' or 'the girls in the office' in internal memos.

Invitations, circulars and other forms of general correspondence still exhibit male-biased formulations in that they assume that the 'normal' or 'standard' addressee is male. Trömel-Plötz (1982) comments that the exclusion of women in job advertisements, taxation forms, and general correspondence is a recurrent problem in German. She presents a particularly poignant example of the wording in a formal invitation which leads to the exclusion of female (married) academics:

So lädt der Rektor der Rheinischen Friedrich-Wilhelms-Universität Bonn «die Hochschullehrer mit ihren verehrten Damen zu einem Professorium in Form eines Winterfestes mit Tanz für Freitag, den 16. Januar 1979, ab 20 Uhr in die Aula der Universität ein». [The 'rector' of the Rheinische Friedrich-Wilhelm University of Bonn invites the professors with their wives to a 'Professorium' in the form of a winter party with dance on Friday . . .] (Trömel-Plötz 1982: 31)

Also, many invitations (usually to formal occasions) in English seem to be directed at men as the following expressions illustrate: 'Dress: Black Tie' or 'Dear colleague, you and your wife are invited to attend . . .' or 'To Mr X and wife . . .'. Male partners or spouses accompanying female academics to conferences are often not acknowledged in conference forms. Until recently, the announcements of the conference programme for accompanying persons were (even in the case of linguistic associations!) cast in sexist language: such programmes were (are) often labelled 'ladies' programmes'.

On forms requesting information, appropriate title choice for women is often problematic. Takahashi (1991), for example, examined the title choices given to people filling in coupons from general interest magazines (*New Women, Good Housekeeping, Real Woman* and *Sunday Times Magazine*) and found that 57 per cent of coupons did not provide titles and only 1 per cent provided symmetrical title choice for men and women (i.e. Mr/Ms). My own observations of forms produced by financial institutions and insurance companies in Australia confirm that a majority of forms do not offer a symmetrical title choice for the sexes or do not list 'Ms' as an alternative for women. In receiving circulars it is also not a rare instance for women to find themselves addressed as *Dear Sir* or *Mr X*. Like many of my female colleagues who have the academic or professional title of 'Dr', I regularly receive circulars and some personal mail addressing me as *Dear Sir, Dear Mr Pauwels, Sehr geehrter Herr* (Dear Sir), *Lieber Kollege* (Dear (male) colleague), *Cher* (Dear (masculine)). As an aside, the regularity with which this occurs makes me think that there must be an (un)written rule or a computer (merge) programme which automatically equates 'Dr' with 'Mr' and other male titles (!!).

A final remark I wish to make before moving on to a description and discussion of common features of linguistic sexism in languages relates to the phenomenal growth in the last ten years of studies exploring and exposing linguistic sexism in a great variety of languages. Whereas the 1970s and early 1980s were dominated, if not monopolised, by researchers working on English, descriptions of linguistic sexism in most other European languages have appeared since the mid-1980s. Later, studies in linguistic sexism were undertaken for some Asian languages (e.g. Japanese, Chinese, Thai) and even African languages as well as for the artificial language, Esperanto.[12] This growth in studies not only widens the international database on linguistic sexism, but also prompts some comparative research between typologically different languages (e.g. Japanese and English).

Common features and issues in linguistic sexism across many languages

The investigations of the linguistic portrayal of women and men in texts and discourses across languages have revealed common sexist practices. This is not to deny the fact that there certainly are differences (sometimes substantial) between languages in terms of the mechanisms that are used to express sexism and in terms of the prevalence of sexism in linguistic practices. This commonality is not surprising if one accepts the belief that there is a close relationship between language and social reality. It is argued that, since the social reality in most societies is one of gender inequality, the language and linguistic practices will in part reflect this inequality. Common elements in the linguistic representation of women and men across languages include:

1. The man (men or the male) is portrayed as the benchmark for all human beings; he is seen as the norm or reference-point. The woman (or women), on the other hand, is subsumed to be included in any linguistic reference to the man. The generic function for human agent nouns, including pronouns, is mainly expressed through nouns, pronouns and other linguistic practices which coincide with those referring to male human beings.
2. As a result of the above practice, the woman is largely invisible in language. However, if she is visible, her visibility is predominantly of an asymmetrical nature. She is made linguistically visible to show her 'deviation' or 'exception' from the male norm.
3. The linguistic portrayal of women is also one of dependence: grammatical and other features of language often contribute towards a view of linguistic dependency or derivation of the female element on (from) the male (e.g. derivation of feminine forms from masculine forms).

4. The linguistic representation of both sexes is often highly stereo-typical. Women are primarily portrayed as sexual creatures (e.g. the 'madonna–whore' polarity) whereas men are more likely to be portrayed as 'rational' creatures.

In one of the first major works comparing the portrayal of women and the feminine across a variety of European languages (Danish, Dutch, German, Greek, Italian, Norwegian, Spanish), Hellinger (1985a) similarly observes common features in the ways in which these languages express sexism. She extrapolates three main regularities.

- The first regularity is that terms used in reference to women are always gender-specific whereas terms referring to men can have two functions: gender-specific and generic.
- The second regularity is the semantic (both denotative and con-notative) asymmetry between human agent nouns, specifically occupational nouns, referring to men and to women. The fem-inine occupational nouns are often derived from masculine nouns and/or their meaning is trivialised *vis-à-vis* the masculine = generic noun.
- The third regularity concerns comparisons of women to men ('she is a second Mozart') and men to women ('Peter cries like a girl'). Whereas the former comparison is mostly considered to be a positive evaluation, the latter is always seen to be denigrating, illustrating the innate inferiority of women *vis-à-vis* men.

In the following sections I shall discuss common features in the linguistic representation of women and men found in a variety of languages. This will include a critical look at the grammatical cate-gory of gender and its relationship to the category of (biological) sex; a review of gender-marking practices, especially in relation to human agent nouns; a discussion of semantic asymmetries between terms for women and for men; a report on naming conventions; and an examination of stereotyped descriptions of the sexes, including proverbs and idioms. Furthermore, some evidence is provided of sexism in orthographic systems (notably Chinese).

Sexism and the category of gender

The introduction of Corbett's (1991: 1) authoritative work on gender in languages reads

> Gender is the most puzzling of the grammatical categories. It is a topic which interests non-linguists as well as linguists. . . . In some languages gender is central and pervasive, while in others it is totally absent.

This fascination with the category of gender also applies to the many linguists and non-linguists exploring and analysing the portrayal of the sexes in language. Their particular interest in the categories of sex and gender concerns the relationship of this grammatical category to the extralinguistic category of sex. The study of grammatical gender and linguistic sexism is one that has created considerable controversy among linguists and non-linguists, feminist and non-feminist language commentators alike. Before I discuss the problems of gender and its role in the portrayal of women and men as seen from a feminist (linguistic) perspective, a brief clarification of the concept of gender and of gender systems in languages is appropriate.

Gender, gender labelling and gender systems in languages

Gender is a grammatical category affecting nouns. It is considered a system for classifying nouns into various groups. These groups or classes then behave differently with regard to concord and agreement of other parts of speech/language. For example, it can have an impact on adjectives and verbs, on the choice of determiner (definite or indefinite article) and the replacement of a noun by a pronoun. Although gender is far from universal in language, there are nevertheless a substantial number of languages which display this category. Corbett (1991), for example, discusses aspects of gender assignment and gender marking in more than 200 languages, although he mentions that languages from almost every language family have gender systems. Notable exceptions are some of the major language families found in Asia.

Although the term 'gender' is certainly widespread (derived from the Latin *genus* meaning 'sort' or 'kind') to indicate this grammatical category, there are other terms used to denote this category including 'class' or 'noun class'. The number of genders or noun classes can vary substantially from language to language. There are many languages which have a two- or three-gender system, and others with up to twenty different genders and/or subgenders. The labels given to these different genders also vary considerably. Although the labels *masculine*, *feminine* and *neuter* are very common in many languages, there are other labels including *animate*, *inanimate*, *human*, *non-human*, *strong*, *weak* (see Corbett 1991 for a more detailed description). In some cases the genders are numbered rather than labelled (e.g. in the Australian Aboriginal language, Dyirbal).

Corbett (1991) distinguishes between two major types of gender systems: semantic and formal. The latter can be further subdivided into morphological and phonological systems. In semantic systems gender is assigned on the basis of the meaning of the noun. These systems are also referred to as 'natural gender' systems. In these languages nouns are categorised into classes which reflect, or are based on, 'natural' or 'inherent' features or distinctions found outside language. In many of these languages the genders labelled 'masculine' and 'feminine' have a relationship with the extralinguistic category of sex with regard to classifying male and female humans. With very few exceptions, male humans will be found in the masculine class and female humans will be found in the feminine class. It is also interesting to note that in most semantically-based systems female and male humans will be put in different classes, even if these are not labelled feminine or masculine. The current English gender system is said to be essentially one of 'natural gender' based on the inherent *sex* characteristics of the noun. Nouns referring to male humans and animals are classified as masculine, those referring to female humans and animals are classified as feminine, whereas objects and other inanimates are classified as neuter. However, there is some 'irregularity' with regard to the inanimate class: inanimates (objects and concepts) are sometimes classified as masculine or feminine (e.g. hurricanes, cars, planes, boats, countries) with the allocation to the masculine or feminine gender being based on some metaphorical reference to 'maleness' or 'femaleness' – a phenomenon that is sometimes referred to as 'metaphorical gender' (e.g. Baron 1986). Although the feature of sex is important in many natural gender systems, this is not always the case; for example, Proto Bantu is assumed to have had a natural gender system based on inherent qualities of animacy, shape, size and other features (for more examples, see Corbett 1991).

In morphological systems, nouns are assigned a gender on the basis of a morphological feature (e.g. noun inflections or derivations). According to Corbett (1991: 34) 'there is no purely morphological system . . . they always have a semantic core' and 'they may also overlap with semantic rules'. In other words, nouns are seldom solely classified on the basis of morphology: often semantic features or criteria contribute towards their classification. For example, the classification of a noun as either feminine or masculine will not only be determined by its form (e.g. suffix, prefix) but also by semantic information (e.g. male human, female human). It is also interesting to note that semantic criteria overrule morphological ones in case of discordance. Corbett (1991: 38) provides the example of the Russian word *djadja* (uncle) which belongs to the second declension: the second declension is feminine but the word *djadja* behaves like a noun of the masculine gender.

In phonological systems[13] nouns are assigned to a gender/class on the basis of a single form. A hypothetical example could be that all nouns ending in *-us* are masculine and all nouns ending in *-as* are feminine. Semantic criteria again take precedence over phonological ones in cases of discordance. Corbett's (1991: 61) example comes from French where 'nouns ending in /m/ are predominantly masculine but *femme* (/fam/) "woman" is feminine'.

Languages with a morphologically and/or phonologically-based gender system are also referred to as grammatical gender languages.

There are also languages without a grammatical gender system, such as Hungarian and Finnish. They often mark the sex of a person lexically; for example, in Finnish the difference between a widow and a widower is expressed as **nais**leski (widow) and **mies**leski (widower).

Problems with the category of gender from a feminist linguistic perspective

In many descriptions on linguistic sexism the category of gender is mentioned as a major stumbling-block for the linguistic equality of the sexes. Of course, the problems with the gender category vary across languages, as languages vary in how they express and mark gender. The main problems raised from a feminist linguistic perspective concern European languages with gender systems (semantic and formal) which incorporate the genders of 'masculine' and 'feminine'. Criticisms have been directed at the so-called arbitrariness of grammatical gender systems *vis-à-vis* the extralinguistic category of sex, and at the predominant use of the masculine gender as the gender for generic and epicene nouns denoting humans.

The arbitrariness of grammatical gender systems, especially the sex-gender type

Many representatives of modern-day linguistics assert that grammatical gender systems which classify nouns into 'masculine', 'feminine' and/or 'neuter' bear little or no relationship to the extralinguistic category of (biological) sex (e.g. Herbert and Nykiel-Herbert 1986, Hjelmslev 1956, Ibrahim 1973; Kallioinen *et al.* 1987, Lyons 1969). For example, Herbert and Nykiel-Herbert (1986: 57) state that

> Systems of grammatical gender, on the other hand [*as opposed to natural gender systems – author*], classify objects arbitrarily, i.e. there are no inherent similarities or connections between objects in any single category.

Kallioinen *et al.* (1987: 378) claim that the grammatical opposition masculine/feminine 'is a linguistic convention, which is essentially arbitrary and which could be replaced by a more abstract terminology'. Corbett (1991) agrees in essence with this view, although he does acknowledge the impact of (biological) sex in assigning female and male humans to the feminine and masculine gender classes.

Feminist-oriented scholars such as Baron (1986), Cameron (1985), Pusch (1984a), Violi (1987) and Yaguello (1978) have reacted primarily against the denials by some modern linguists that the grammatical gender categories of 'masculine' and 'feminine' bear no relationship whatsoever to the categories of 'male' and 'female'. They claim that there has not only been a semantic and symbolic link with the extralinguistic categories of maleness and femaleness but they also provide evidence of this link in the works of respected 'forefathers' of linguistics. Baron (1986: 90) notes that

> The most blatant attempts to connect linguistic form with stereotyped characteristics of the sexes are not found in the pseudobiblical theories of pronoun origin, . . . but in the study of the phenomenon of grammatical gender.

Cameron (1985: 64–5) traces the origin of the category of grammatical gender to the Greek grammarian, Protagoras, who classified nouns into 'masculine', 'feminine' and 'inanimate' (neuter) according to the sex, or lack of sex, of the referents. Protagoras thus based a grammatical category on biological sex differences. He even attempted to change the gender of some Greek words (*menis*, anger and *peleks*, helmet) from feminine to masculine because of their closer connection to maleness. Cameron also mentions that Jakob Grimm, the authoritative German grammarian and Germanic philologist in the nineteenth century, believed that grammatical gender was a later stage of natural gender, which occurs in languages 'when their speakers pass from mere recognition of male and female creatures to the postulation of abstract male and female principles in whose terms everything and anything could be classified' (Cameron 1985: 64–5).

Baron (1986) devotes a chapter of his book on grammar and gender to the origins of gender in language. Like Cameron, he also finds evidence in older treatises on gender which points to a link between grammatical gender and biological sex categories, a link which is now (vehemently) denied by some linguists as mentioned above. The German philosopher Johann Gottfried Herder [1772] (1966), for instance, compared grammatical gender categories with human genitals. Baron (1986) furthermore shows that early works on gender consider masculine to be the primary gender both in creation and in importance (Lepsius 1880, Brown [1851] 1880; Harris [1751] 1765, Beattie [1788] 1968). The idea of the primacy of the masculine gender – the doctrine of the 'worthiness of the genders 'according to Baron (1986) – is still found in more recent works such as Joly's (1975) theory of gender in modern English.

Yaguello (1978) confirms a linkage between natural gender and grammatical gender in French works on this subject. Houdebine (1988: 47) provides some evidence that the metaphorical reference to masculine and feminine nouns has a sexual base, as illustrated in this quotation:

> On parle en France de la Tour Eiffel comme symbole de Paris, et ce mois-ci (mars 1989 [sic]) elle est souvent citée sur les ondes: *la vieille dame va fêter son centenaire. La vieille dame?* La métaphore sexuelle a été produite par le genre. [In France one speaks of the Eiffel Tower as a symbol of Paris, and in this month (March 1989 [sic]) it is often cited . . . : the old lady is going to celebrate her centenary. The old lady? This sexual metaphor is brought about by the gender of the noun *Tour*.]

This procedure of sexual metaphorisation is seen as evidence of a linkage between grammatical gender and natural gender.

The masculine gender as the dominant or the more 'worthy' gender

In semantic and formally based gender languages[14] which distinguish the masculine/feminine (sometimes neuter) classes of gender, it is mostly the masculine gender which dictates patterns of agreement in the case of epicene, generic nouns or complex noun phrases involving male and female human agent nouns. For natural gender languages like English this translates into the use of the masculine pronoun for common gender nouns in generic contexts. For example, in a sentence like 'the traveller is responsible for his own luggage', the generic noun which could indicate either a male or female traveller triggers a masculine possessive in 'his luggage'. In cases where English marks gender in nouns (e.g. actor–actress), it is the masculine noun which acts as the generic noun in almost all cases. For grammatical gender languages it is the masculine human agent noun which acts as the generic noun. For example, *le directeur* (French, masculine, director), *der Bürger* (German, masculine, the citizen), *el profesor* (Spanish, masculine, the professor), *il maestro* [Italian, masculine, the teacher]. Grammatical gender languages with a common gender[15] (e.g. Danish, Dutch, Norwegian and Swedish) behave in a fashion similar to English, i.e. they select the masculine gender (pronoun) in generic contexts.

This 'masculine dominance' is also expressed in languages which require gender concord with nouns in adjectival and verb endings, e.g. Italian, French and Spanish. If adjectives or verbs referring to two nouns of different gender in a coordinate noun phrase require gender concord, it is generally the noun(s) with the masculine gender which will determine the gender concord. For example,

French: Pierre (male name) et Jeanne (female name) sont allés (masculine plural ending) seuls (masculine plural ending). [Pierre and Jeanne went alone.]

Italian: Mario (male name) e Paola (female name) sono arrivati (masculine plural ending). [Mario and Paola have arrived.]

Also notice the practice of putting male names first.

Feminist linguists have further noted that, in cases of sex-gender incongruence in nouns with human referents, sex concord is more likely to override gender concord[16] if the incongruence is between a male referent and feminine gender than if it is between a female referent and masculine gender. Polish is a case in question. Herbert and Nykiel-Herbert (1986: 60) mention that

> male referent nouns are permitted sex-determined concord (male sex is stronger than grammar) if they are grammatically Neuter and are *obliged* to display sex-determined concord if they are Feminine. On the other hand, the agreements for female referent nouns are always grammatically determined; the language system (and its users) tolerate Neuter and Masculine concords for female referent nouns without difficulty. (my *italics*.)

Herbert and Nykiel-Herbert (1986: 60–1) illustrate this with the following examples: 'm' stands for masculine and 'f' for feminine.

1. A feminine noun with an exclusive male referent obtains sex-determined agreement in demonstrative, adjectival as well as verb endings (notably the past tense):

   ten$_m$ stary$_m$ chłopina$_f$: that old man

   ten$_m$ stary$_m$ chłopina$_f$ tánczył$_m$: that old man danced

2. Masculine or neuter nouns with a female referent obtain grammatical agreement:

   ten$_m$ sympatyczny$_m$ podlotek$_m$: that pleasant teenage girl

   ten$_m$ sympatyczny$_m$ podlotek$_m$ tánczył$_m$: that pleasant teenage girl danced

   tó$_n$ sympatyczne$_n$ dziewczę$_n$: that pleasant girl

The Polish gender system displays another interesting feature which could be seen to stress the dominance of the masculine gender and the link between gender and sex. In the plural, Polish distinguishes only between two categories, coined the 'Virile' and 'Non-virile' categories. The Virile category contains nouns with exclusive male human referents and so-called generic human referents. In the non-virile category we find the non-male human referents, i.e. exclusively female referents and animate non-human referents as well as inanimates. Herbert and Nykiel-Herbert (1986: 64) provide the following remark:

> Thus, it is clear that the two plural genders, Virile/Nonvirile, are hierarchically ordered and the Nonvirile is less valued than the Virile. Thus, one could argue that the sexist bias of the language is evident in two facets of this dichotomy: 1) females are included in the more highly valued category (Virile) only in the presence of accompanying males; exclusively-female references are always Nonvirile, and 2) males can be 'demoted' to Nonvirile, i.e. to the category of women, animals, and inanimates for the purpose of semantic derrogation [*sic*].

Feminist linguists across languages have commented that this practice[17] of using the masculine for generic purposes and the primacy of the masculine gender in determining grammatical concord make women invisible in language and relegate women to a secondary position dependent on the man.

Gender marking in human agent nouns

An integral part of the problems surrounding gender is the gender-marking practices in human agent nouns, especially occupational nouns found in various languages. Many languages have gender-marking practices in human agent nouns which treat women and men differently: they are discriminatory practices in that they often make women invisible, treat them as secondary or have a trivialising effect on the linguistic portrayal of women. Women's invisibility with regard to human agent nouns is caused by using masculine nouns generically. This is often the case when there are lexical gaps for female human agent nouns. The view that women's status is not only dependent on that of men but also secondary to it is linked to the derivative nature of many female human agent nouns from male ones. This 'morphological' asymmetry in male and female human agent nouns is said to have a semantic impact: women's occupational terms are often derived from masculine ones by adding a 'feminine' suffix to the 'masculine' base. This suffixation process often results in a trivialising of the meaning of the female derivative. An example for English is the use of the suffix -*ette* to create such words as *majorette* and *suffragette*. Sabatini (1985: 72) provides a poignant example of this for Italian. An Italian female senator who raised the issue of asymmetrical naming practices in the Italian Parliament, and who was concerned about sexism in language and its effect on women, nevertheless preferred to describe herself in a newspaper article by means of the masculine 'Sono *un* Sena*tore* famoso' because of the trivialising effect of the feminine version. This connotation of triviality has also stopped women in other language groups (e.g. French, Dutch, German, Spanish and the Scandinavian languages) from using the female-specific job title, especially in the case of more prestigious occupations and professions.

Furthermore, feminist language commentators have criticised both the practice of subsuming female human agent nouns under 'masculine generic' ones and of explicitly marking female human agents by means of derivational suffixes. The writings of feminist critics on gender-marking practices in a variety of European languages show two main areas of concern: *lexical gaps* and *morphological asymmetry*. Lexical gaps refer to the absence of many words for women incumbents of professions/occupations. Morphological asymmetry concerns the process of deriving women's forms of occupational nouns from those of men's, either via compounds or feminine suffixes (the latter often coincide with suffixes marking diminutives).

Lexical gaps

Feminist language critics comment that the existence of lexical gaps in relation to human agent nouns contributes to the invisibility of women. This is especially the case for nouns indicating professions and occupations. Despite considerable changes in women's participation in the paid workforce, this participation is not yet (fully) reflected in language. In other words, the lexical gaps usually concern the representation of women in professions rather than of men. The latter type of invisibility does exist, although it is rather rare in languages. Lexical gaps can cover a range of practices.

In languages with productive feminine suffixes or with a tradition of marking female agent nouns through suffixing, lexical gaps concern the absence of female-specific forms. Sabatini (1985: 68–9) comments that in Italian – a language in which female agent nouns are frequently formed through suffixing – there are no female equivalents for words like *medico* (medical doctor), *architetto* (architect), *sindaco* (mayor), *ministro* (minister) and there are no female terms for *ingegnere* (civil engineer), *finanziere* (financier), although there are female equivalents for many words ending in *-ere*: e.g. *infermiere/-a* (male/female hospital nurse); *portiere/-a* (doorman/doorwoman); *cameriere/-a* (waiter/waitress). Similarly, some masculine words ending in *-ore* have no female forms (e.g. *assessore*, municipal official). Yaguello (1978: 121) finds for French that masculine words like *docteur* (doctor), *professeur* (professor/teacher) and *ingénieur* (civil engineer) do not have female equivalents, although there are productive feminine suffixes for the masculine *-eur*, e.g. *-euse* as in *vendeuse* (female shop assistant), *chanteuse* (female singer). In German, the feminine suffix '*-in*' is still very productive. When compiling one of the first sets of German guidelines for non-sexist language use, Guentherodt *et al.* (1980) noticed that, in German, female equivalents for terms such as *Pilot* (pilot) and *Passagier* (passenger) were missing. In Polish, there are no female terms corresponding to *szofer* (chauffeur-driver), *murarz* (bricklayer), *marynarz* (sailor), *oficer* (officer) and *kominiarz* (chimney sweep).

Some linguists have put forward explanations that these lexical gaps affecting the formation of the feminine forms are due to phonological constraints (see, e.g., Klemensiewicz 1957, for Polish) or because words already exist which use the 'feminine' suffix in one of its other functions. Herbert and Nykiel-Herbert (1986) comment that in Polish the common feminine suffix *-ka* is also used for functions other than marking feminine gender. The suffix *-ka* has already been used for another function in relation to *szofer*, *murarz*, *marynarz* and *kominiarz*, i.e. *szoferka* (drivers' booth), *murarka* (masonry/brickwork), *marynarka* (jacket, navy), *oficerka* (officer's boot), *kominiarka* (type of hat). Consequently, the *-ka* suffix cannot be used to form the female equivalents, female driver, female bricklayer, female sailor, female officer, female chimney sweep. Yaguello (1978) and Sabatini (1985) mention similar arguments for lexical gaps in French and Italian respectively.

Besides 'linguistic' explanations for these lexical gaps it is also important to note the impact of social factors. It is noticeable that the absence of female counterparts is primarily found in relation to occupations with high social prestige (doctor, lawyer, judge, professor) to which women could not get access easily or occupations with strong male associations (pilot, bricklayer, officer, sailor), or from which women were sometimes legally barred.

Another type of lexical gap is found in the Germanic languages. In these languages there is a range of occupational and other human agent nouns which contain the controversial free morpheme *-man* (or its equivalents *-man* in Dutch and Swedish, *-mann* in German and Norwegian, *-mand* in Danish). Many feminist language critics dispute the generic nature of human agent nouns containing *-man* or its equivalents and expose them either as exclusively or predominantly referring to a male person and conjuring up male images. In other words, *-man* words are considered sex-specific. Although all these languages have a female equivalent morpheme available, i.e. *-woman* in English, *-kone* in Danish, *-vrouw* in Dutch, *-frau* (German), and *-fru* in Swedish, this is seldom if ever used to form the female equivalent of occupational and other nouns ending in *-man*. For example, there is no *fisherwoman* in English or no *timmervrouw* (female carpenter) in Dutch. There are no *helmswomen*, *stuurvrouwen*, *styrkvinder* or *Steuerfrauen* respectively in English, Dutch, Danish or German (female equivalent of helmsman) or no *fagkvinne*, *Fachfrau*, *vakvrouw* respectively in Norwegian, German or Dutch (female equivalent of expert).

The category of common gender nouns whose etymology shows that the agent suffix was originally masculine could be seen as a type of lexical gap. However, feminist critics have seldom taken up this issue. Baron (1986: 126ff) mentions that some early male grammarians and philologists argued that suffixes like *-er* in English should not be used for women as they can only refer to males.

Lexical gaps also affect male incumbents in some professions that have been open to men but which have not attracted many men. For example, there are no male equivalents for midwife in Italian (*levatrice*), Dutch (*vroedvrouw*), French (*nourrice*), German (*Hebamme*) and Norwegian (*jordmor*). In Norwegian, the word for secretary (meaning office clerk) is gender-specific *kontordame* (literally, office lady). In Danish, nurse (*sygeplejerske*) has no male equivalent (*sygeplejer* means a psychiatric aide). Feminist critics have pointed out, however, that the opening up of female jobs to males has usually had different linguistic consequences to women's entry into male domains. Whereas the dominant practice expected of women is to adopt the masculine title or noun, the presence of men in predominantly female jobs is much more likely to lead to new job titles, also for women. For example, when men took up the practice of midwifery in Germany, the title *Entbindungspfleger* was developed. The creation of *Entbindungspfleger* led to the formation of a feminine equivalent by means of suffixing – *Entbindungspflegerin* (female assistant in birthing) – which is starting to replace the original *Hebamme*. In addition, the form *Entbindungspfleger* is used as the generic noun, leading to the following paradigm:

Generic: Der Entbindungspfleger
Masculine: Der Entbindungspfleger
Feminine: Die Entbindungspflegerin

In other words, the 'male' lexical gap has not only been filled but has also changed the way women are referred to: they are now made secondary to the masculine term which doubles as the new generic term.

Morphological asymmetry in masculine and feminine human agent nouns

Whereas lexical gaps contribute to the invisibility of women, the process of deriving female referent terms from those referring to men contributes to the view that in language the feminine/female element is treated as secondary and as having a dependent status. Researchers have established that in many languages in which gender marking through suffixing is common, the feminine suffix is often added on to the (masculine) base. The following are examples from a range of languages:

Danish: The suffixes *-inde* and *-ske* are added onto masculine words ending in *-er* to form the feminine. For example, *lærerinde* (female teacher), *arbejderske* (female worker). Gomard (1985) mentions that the use of feminine suffixes is decreasing. It is very seldom that a new word forms the feminine by suffixation.

Dutch: Dutch has seven suffixes to indicate female referents: *-a*, *-euse*, *-trice*, *-es*, *-in*, *-e*, and *-ster*. The first three are mainly used with foreign words of Latin or French origin. The others are almost always added to the masculine base; for instance, *lera(a)r-es* (teacher), *boer-in* (farmer), *agent-e* (police officer). According to Brouwer (1985a, 1985b) the '-ster' is used most, although feminine suffixes are seldom used in relation to new coinages.

English: Similar to Danish and Dutch, feminine suffixes in English are no longer (very) productive. The suffixes *-esse*, *-ette* were added onto masculine (gender-neutral) base: *manager–manageress*; *poet–poetess*; *major–majorette*; *usher–usherette*.

German: The most common feminine suffix in German is *-in*, which is added on to a masculine base. For instance, *Lehrer-in* (teacher), *Autor-in* (author), *Köch-in* (cook), *Tänzer-in* (dancer). There are some other feminine suffixes including *-euse* (e.g. *Friseuse*, female hairdresser), although they are not used very often.

Italian: Italian has a number of feminine suffixes, e.g. *-a*, *-trice*, *-essa*. The *-essa* suffix is added to the masculine noun as illustrated in *professore/professoressa* (professor); *avvocato/avvocatessa* (lawyer); *studente/studentessa* (student); *presidente/presidentessa* (president).

Norwegian: The two main feminine suffixes in Norwegian are *-inne* and *-ske*, which are added to masculine words usually ending in *-er* (also *-or*). For instance, *amerikaner-inne* (American); *lærer-inne* (teacher); *skiløper-ske* (person who skis); *arbeider-ske* (worker).

Polish: Polish has multiple feminine suffixes, most of which are added on to a masculine base form (with or without minor alterations). Herbert and Nykiel-Herbert (1986) list as examples: *pan–pani* (terms of address for men and women); *student–studentka* (student), *dozorca–dozorczyni* (caretaker). In Polish gender-marking also occurs in surnames: the suffixes *-owa* (to indicate wife of) and *-ówna* (to indicate daughter of) are attached to a man's surname, e.g. *Wójcik–Wójcikowa–Wójcikówna*.

Russian: Although the current trend in Russian is for 'gender-neutral' terms, in the early days of the communist regime when separate terms for male and female practitioners were advocated, the feminine terms were

derived from the masculine ones via derivational suffixes such as *-ka, -nitsa, -ixa, -sa*. For example, *trak-
toristka* (female tractor driver), *izdatelnitsa* (female
publisher), *vracixa*[18] (female doctor) and *diktorsa*
(Martynyuk 1990b).

The fact that some suffixes used for marking female referents are
also used for other purposes (especially that of marking diminutives) has attracted some criticism. English and Polish are cases in
point: the *-ette* suffix was a popular suffix to form diminutives in
the nineteenth century (Baron 1986). One of the functions of the
-ka suffix in Polish is to mark diminutivisation when attached to
a grammatically feminine base form: for example, *dziewczyna* (girl),
dziewczynka (little girl) (Herbert and Nykiel-Herbert 1986).

In many Western societies criticism of gender-marking practices
affecting human agent nouns came into prominence when antidiscrimination laws covering the employment of women and men
were introduced, especially in the 1970s and early 1980s. The
debate about the appropriate occupational nomenclature for women
is not unique to this period. In fact this issue had been raised
before. For example, as a result of the First World War and the
October Revolution of 1917, significant changes occurred in the
make-up of the paid workforce in the former USSR: many women
entered into professions and occupations previously dominated by
men. This had an impact on occupational nomenclature. Whereas
the pre-revolutionary intelligentsia had opted for a single-term
approach, the initial post-revolution official policy was for separate male and female titles because women were, in the name of
sexual equality, entitled to their own professional titles (Herbert
and Nykiel-Herbert 1986). For English, Baron (1986: 131) mentions that the presence of women in male-exclusive and male-
dominated work areas during the Second World War not only led
to discussions about appropriate nomenclature for women but
also to a proliferation of *-ette* coinages for women in the professions. Brouwer (1985b) documents the opinions of some male
Dutch grammarians (e.g. de Vooys 1967, Meijers 1952 and Van
Haeringen 1949) who comment on the desirability of female occupational nouns in reaction to greater female participation in the
workforce. That these opinions were not always based on 'grammatical arguments' can be seen from the following extract of Meijers
(1952) as quoted in Brouwer (1985b: 136–7).

(...) man kann zwar ausdrücken und am benutzten Wort sehen lassen, dass die betreffende Person eine Frau ist, aber vielen wäre es vielleicht noch angenehmer, aus dem Wort abzuleiten, ob sie jung oder alt, schön oder hässlich oder was auch immer ist. Mit anderen Worten: die Wirklichkeit ist stets so reich und vielfältig differenziert, dass wir sie nie in einem Wort erfassen können: das hyperkorrekte Streben, koste es was es wolle in einem Wort auszudrücken, dass die betreffende Person eine Frau ist (...) setzt die Uhr der Sprachentwicklung wieder ein ganzes Stück zurück. [(...) one can try to express and try to show in the used word that the person in question is a woman, but many would prefer perhaps to be able to derive from the word, whether she is young or old, beautiful or ugly, or whatever. In other words, reality is always so rich and diverse, that we can never express all of it in one word: the hypercorrect urge, to express in one word, whatever the cost, that the person in question is a woman sets the clock of language change and development back substantially.]

Authors like Yaguello (1978) and Pavlidou (1985) mention similar debates for France and Greece which followed the entry of women into local government and national parliament. In France, the mass entry of women into local governments in March 1977 as (Lord) Mayors, caused the French some linguistic worries as they did not have a name for their newly elected mayors. Should they be called *maires* (mayors) or *mairesses* (mayoresses)? When the first woman entered parliament in Greece in the 1950s, Triandaphyllidis (1963), a prominent linguist and proponent of Dhimotiki, also raised the question of nomenclature for women in parliament.

Some of the earlier debates concerning separate or common terms for men and women in occupations were also triggered by (male) discontent with women entering territories considered exclusive to men. Baron (1986: 132) credits Mamie Meredith (1930) with being 'the first language authority to trace gender suffixation not to the women who were entering roles formerly occupied only by men, but to the masculine *reaction* against this increase in the sphere of women's activity'. Having separate terms for male and female incumbents allowed men to distance themselves from women in their professions. This was especially true if the female agent nouns were formed by means of suffixes. This argument is similar to the reaction noticed by Stannard (1977) in relation to the dominant naming practice for married women in the nineteenth and early twentieth centuries, i.e. 'Mrs John Smith'. In the eyes of some men this naming practice was degrading for men because male names could now be used by women.

Semantic asymmetry: sexual woman and generic man

Of major concern to feminist language critics is the semantic asymmetry that exists between nouns and terms referring to women and to men. This is especially the case for the terms 'man' and 'woman' and their equivalents in other languages as well as for other human agent nouns. This asymmetry is to a large extent caused by the different features determining the meaning of words referring to male and female persons, appropriately illustrated by the labels *sexual woman* and *generic man*. In the section covering sexism in dictionaries I mentioned that a fundamental characteristic of any definition of 'woman' is her sexual nature (for women, sex is destiny), whereas this feature has little or no importance in the definition of 'man'. An important semantic feature in the definition of the word 'man' and its equivalents in other languages is its capacity to represent or stand for the entire human race (even if there exists a separate word to denote a human being without sex reference). The word 'man' thus obtains generic qualities and is regarded as the norm against which to judge humanity. In Brouwer's (1991b: 30) words:

> De man is de standaarduitvoering, terwijl het lichaam van de vrouw extra wordt benadrukt. [The man is the standard model whilst the body of woman receives special attention.]

In fact, words like 'man' and its equivalent in other languages often have a dual meaning: it denotes the male of the human species *and* allegedly refers to the human species *per se*. Feminist language critics have commented that this dual meaning of 'man' has the effect of establishing 'man' as the linguistic norm, of de-emphasising the fact that 'man' like 'woman' has the semantic feature of sexual being, and of reducing women to the status of 'dependent other'. In addition they have shown that this duality of meaning leads to semantic confusion or to a deliberate or unconscious (depending on one's point of view) portrayal of humanity as 'male'. This is especially so in languages in which the word 'man' coincides with that for human being (e.g. *uomo* in Italian, *homme* in French, *hombre* in Spanish). Among the often quoted examples to expose this false genericness in English are the following:

> To survive, man needs food, water and female companionship.
> As for man, he is no different from the rest. His back aches, he ruptures easily, his women have difficulties in childbirth.

This fundamental semantic difference in the words 'woman' and 'man' affects the semantics of the entire field of human agent nouns at different levels. Word pairs like English *queen–king*, Dutch *vrijgezel–oude vrijster* (bachelor–old spinster) and German *Junggeselle–alte Jungfer* (bachelor–old spinster), French *compère–commère* (mate/accomplice–chatterbox), and Spanish *patrono–matrona* (employer – a madam) demonstrate more than a sexual difference. They are also indicative of a process of semantic derogation affecting the female terms.

This semantic asymmetry is also found in word pairs which are not lexically marked for sex (e.g. common gender nouns like secretary, professional or tramp). For instance, it is very likely that native speakers of English attach different meanings to the following gender-paired phrases:

He is a professional; i.e. he is a member of a respected profession.
She is a professional: i.e. she is a member of the 'oldest' profession (prostitute).

He is a secretary: i.e. he works for an organisation.
She is a secretary: i.e. she does typing and general office work for a person.

He is a tramp: i.e. he is a homeless person, drifter.
She is a tramp: i.e. she is a prostitute.

This phenomenon has not only been noticed in European languages but also in Asian ones. For Japanese, Hiraga (1991: 52) remarks that many parallel phrases describing men or women obtain a sexual connotation when they are applied to women. Examples include,

Yogoreta otoko: a dirty man, i.e. a man who is physically unclean.
Yogoreta onna: a dirty woman, i.e. a promiscuous woman.

Kegare-nak-i seinen: a pure young man, i.e. pure of mind.
Kegare-nak-i otome: a pure young maiden, i.e. pure of body (a virgin).

In the case of morphologically marked male–female pairs, I have already shown in a previous section that the addition of a feminine suffix to masculine human agent nouns usually does more than simply change the gender reference of the word: it often attaches a meaning of triviality, of lesser status or dependence to the term. In fact, in a range of languages the female derivative of professional terms can mean both 'wife of . . .' and 'female incumbent'. In some instances, the process of pejoration affecting the female terms has led to the terms acquiring quite different meanings. In

Spanish, *un reo* means a criminal whereas *una rea* refers to a poor prostitute; in French, *maître* means 'teacher and/or expert' whereas *maîtresse* has as its main meaning a man's paramour.

As a consequence of the centrality of the 'sexuality' feature in defining female persons, terms referring to women have been more susceptible to a process of pejoration or debasement than those referring to men. This process has been referred to as *the semantic derogation of woman* by Schulz (1975: 64), who claims that

> Again and again in the history of the language, one finds that a perfectly innocent term designating a girl or a woman may begin with neutral or even positive connotations, but that gradually it acquires negative implications, at first only slightly disparaging, but after a period of time becoming abusive and ending as a sexual slur.

This process of pejoration and of semantic shift affecting words such as 'woman', 'wife', 'lady', 'mistress', 'queen', 'girl', 'madam' has been documented for a number of languages including English (e.g. Schulz 1975, Stanley and McGowan 1979), German (Koch-skämper 1991, Ott 1989), Jordanian Arabic (Abd-el-Jawad 1989), Japanese (e.g. Cherry 1987, Nakamura 1990, Takahashi 1991), French (Sautermeister 1985). Researchers have shown that the dominant form of debasement in female terms is caused by the term acquiring sexual overtones, thus making it unsuitable for use in its original sense. Consequently, the term is avoided in its original context and new terms are needed to express the original meaning. This is usually done by means of euphemisms and/or through the process of semantic shift to another term indicating a female person. The current use of 'lady' is an example in English according to Lakoff (1975). Other researchers have shown for a variety of languages that the asymmetrical use in such word pairs as 'girl–boy', 'gentleman–lady', 'man–woman' is often a result of con-notations of triviality, sexuality, 'contactability' and 'immaturity' present in the female word which are absent or less obvious in the male word. For example, the word 'girl' and its equivalents in many other languages is often used to refer to an adult woman in contexts where the word 'boy' cannot refer to adult men. In the word 'girl'[19] the semantic feature of [+ young] or [− adult] does not have the same importance as in the word 'boy'. Feminists have commented that this practice in language contributes to a view of women as 'immature' and 'childlike' who do not have to be taken seriously (see, e.g., Frank and Anshen 1983, Trömel-Plötz 1982). Similarly, the word 'lady' is used in many more contexts than its male equivalent 'gentleman' (e.g. Baron 1986, Kramer 1975, Lakoff 1975). Trömel-Plötz (1982: 93) comments as follows about the use of *Dame* (lady) in German:

> *Damen* [*my emphasis*] tun nichts Ernsthaftes, Wichtiges und Bedeutendes, verlangen keine gleichen Löhne für gleiche Arbeit und wollen auch sonst nicht gleich behandelt werden wie Männer. [Ladies do not engage in anything serious, of importance or significance, they don't demand equal pay for equal work and they don't want to be treated equally with men in any other areas.]

In Japanese there are four major terms to denote female persons *onna, zyosi (joshi), zyosei (josei), huzin (fujin)* and three for males *otoko, dansi* and *dansei*. There is no male equivalent for the female term *huzin* which refers to a married woman (usually a house wife) with possible connotations of elegance. Both Nakamura (1990) and Takahashi (1991) comment that the term *onna* has sexual connotations which its male equivalent *otoko* lacks. Depending on the context, the words *zyosei, zyosi* and *huzin* are used to avoid the sexual overtones found in *onna*.

Sexism, sex and the sexes

The vocabulary around sex and sexual activity demonstrates better than any other field in language that a woman's primary status is that of a sexual being, if not a sex object. This field of the lexicon also testifies to the fact that men rather than women are the principal namers and meaning makers. The sexual act is primarily described from a male perspective. To date there are (very) few words to describe women's sexual experiences from a female perspective: her sexual behaviour is portrayed through a male perspective, i.e. as a function of men's needs, desires and dislikes. Investigations of the vocabulary of sex in languages such as English (e.g. Farmer and Henley 1965, Schulz 1975, Stanley 1977b), French (e.g. Guiraud 1978, Yaguello 1978) and German (Bornemann 1971, Werner 1983) have commonly found that words, phrases and metaphors designating women engaging in (promiscuous[20]) sexual activity far outnumber those for men. For English, Farmer and Henley (1965) recorded more than 500 terms which are synonyms for a (female) prostitute. Schulz (1975) located approximately 1,000 terms and phrases which describe women in sexually derogatory ways. For (white) American English, Stanley (1977b) found 220 terms designating a sexually promiscuous woman as opposed to

20 for men. Similar imbalances have been noted by researchers for other languages. The actual labels for sexually promiscuous women are mainly derogatory, reducing women to an object of pleasure and a product for sexual consumption by men.

Werner (1983) categorised the terms and metaphors for prostitutes and other sexually promiscuous women found in Bornemann's German dictionary of sex into three main groupings. Although they were based on German, these categories also seem to apply to other languages.

1. *Metaphors involving references to other female persons.* Werner (1983) considers this group to be the least denigratory because at least women are compared to other women. Words in this category are often euphemisms and include for German *Freuden-mädchen* (pleasure girl), *Stundenbraut* (Bride for an hour), *Nacht-schwester* (night nurse). For English we could include such terms as *lady of the night, painted lady, corner girl* (Am.), *callgirl*. In French there is *concubine* (concubine).

2. *Metaphors comparing prostitutes to animals.* For German, Werner (1983) lists words like *Bettwanze, Drossel, Kellerassel, Lusthase, Mieze, Reitpferd, Sau, Schnecke.* French has the words *gibier d'amour, lièvre, grenouille*, among many others. Words for English include *fox, bitch, bedbug.*

3. *Metaphors involving reference to objects.* This is by far the largest category of words in most languages. Here we can distinguish between terms which stress the fact that women are objects providing sexual relief and pleasure for men and terms which compare women to container-like objects which act as the receptacle for the male (penis). Examples from German, English and French are *Amüsiermatratze* (mattress of pleasure), *Ausziehpuppe* (dress up doll, literally doll to undress), *Pissoir, pisseuse* (pisspallet), *sac de nuit* (night sack), *pot de chambre* (chamber pot), *bedpan, dose* (box), *Pfanne* (pan), *Schlitz* (slit), *jar*, etc.

Another important class of metaphors for 'sexual' women is that of food, especially fruit. Hiraga (1991: 45) comments that the 'women are food for men to eat' metaphor is common and strong in Japanese, as is illustrated in the following sentences:

> 'Ano onna-was tabe-goro da: That woman is in the best season to eat.'
> 'Ano onna-wa ure-ure da: That woman is fully ripe.'
> 'Oisisoo-na onna de: She (the woman) looks delicious.'
> 'Taroo-wa onna-no karada-o musabot-ta: Taroo devoured a woman's body.'

Allan and Burridge (1991) note that in African languages 'to eat' is often used as a euphemism for 'to copulate'. Other sources[21] have indicated that in African languages women are usually portrayed as 'the food' and the men as 'the eaters of the food'.

Feminists have drawn attention not only to the fact that the discourse around (hetero)sexual activity reflects primarily a male point of view but also that women's (hetero)sexuality is both obscured and negated in current expressions and metaphors. Many words and phrases describing heterosexual intercourse leave no doubt about the role of woman in sex: she is often the (passive) object of 'man's desire'. Both the (pseudo)scientific and colloquial terminology portray sexual intercourse as something that *a man does to a woman*. This can be illustrated by the fact that most languages do not have a female equivalent for the word 'penetrate' and its many colloquial expressions: a woman's perspective is simply presented by the passive form, i.e. she is penetrated.[22]

A female perspective on coitus/sexual intercourse or orgasm is equally under-represented in language. Yaguello (1978) examined Guiraud's work on the language of sex and finds that, of the terms designating coitus, only a few define it from a female perspective. She writes (p. 160):

> Le vocabulaire érotique souligne ainsi le contraste entre la femme passive et l'homme actif. Sur 1300 synonymes de *coït*, environ 80 le définissent du point de vue féminin. Et encore, tous ces mots ont-ils un sens passif. [The erotic vocabulary thus stresses the contrast between the passive woman and the active man. Of 1300 synonyms of *coitus*, about 80 define it from a female point of view. Furthermore, all these words have a passive sense.]

Other feminists have commented that words like 'foreplay' and 'mature orgasm' (referring to vaginal orgasm) are the result of the idea that penetration is the ultimate in sexual fulfilment (e.g. Brownmiller 1977, Rich 1977, Spender 1980).

Not surprisingly, scientific discourse about sex and sexuality shows a similar male bias. Spender (1980: 175) quotes research by Scully and Bart (1973) which found that in medical textbooks up to the 1970s

> it was common to state (contrary to the findings of . . . which were available) that the male sex drive was the stronger and that procreation was the major function of sexual intercourse for females.

The language and discourse of sex and sexual activity is said to be a clear testimony to the fact that it is men who have the power to name and define in language.

The politics of naming and address: names, titles and other terms of address

Naming practices involve a whole range of issues: the selection of a personal name (also known as 'first' or 'Christian' name in Western societies); the identification through a family/tribal, kinship or group name; the use of nicknames and other special names (often derogatory); dealing with taboo names, honorifics and other ways of addressing people. Names, titles and other terms of address are a powerful means of identifying and describing people. Depending on the society and the language, names can reflect and/or be determined by, for example, a person's sex, age, occupation/profession, social status, geographical, linguistic, religious or tribal affiliation.

Perhaps more importantly, forms of address are used to express social relations between people. According to Poynton (1985: 80) the issue of address 'undoubtedly provides the most elaborate resource for the linguistic realisation of social relations'. Usually two parameters are distinguished to characterise systems of address in languages which express social relations between people: they are the parameters of *power* and *solidarity*. Poynton (1985), working within a systemic linguistic framework, breaks up the dimension of solidarity into a contact dimension (a continuum from social distance to intimacy) and a dimension of affect (dealing with the positive or negative attitude or emotion of the speaker towards the addressee). Further in this section I show that the asymmetry found in the ways of addressing men and women can be linked to the social inequalities that exist between the sexes in patriarchal societies.

Furthermore, the act of naming has great symbolic value in most societies: those bestowed with the task or the power to name are therefore considered to be the powerful group in society. Feminist criticism has focused on the fact that the act of naming is a predominantly male prerogative in patriarchal societies and that names and naming conventions for women in such societies reflect, contribute to and perpetuate the social inequalities between the sexes.

Le droit de nommer est une prérogative du groupe dominant sur le groupe dominé. Ainsi les hommes ont-ils des milliers de mots pour désigner les femmes, dont l'immense majorité sont péjoratifs. L'inverse n'est pas vrai. [The right to name is a prerogative of the dominant group over the dominated group. That is why men have thousands of words for designating/naming women, of which the majority is pejorative. The opposite is not true.] Yaguello (1978: 150)

Let us now look at some of the criticisms feminists have raised in relation to some naming conventions and ways of addressing people.

Personal names: symbols of femininity and masculinity?

In many societies the act of naming a newborn baby is an important event marked by various kinds of traditions and rituals. Often the conventions characteristic of a particular family, social group, society or historical era are either reflected in, or reacted against, in the process of naming the newborn. Most communities attach great importance to marking the child's sex when choosing a name.

Children and adults with androgynous names may try to gender-mark their name or may find that others try to do this for them (e.g. by means of truncation, diminutivisation, compounds, nicknames, new names or by using their other name(s), if possible). Besides marking the sex of the child, personal names for girls and boys often reflect stereotyped features of femininity or masculinity prevailing in a particular culture or society. For example, boys are often given names associated with strength, power, heroism whereas girls have names reflecting grace and other 'feminine' virtues. Examples from the Slavic languages are *Wladimir* (master of the world), *Igor* and *Oleg* (war heroes) for boys and *Vera* (verity/faith), *Nadejda* (hope), *Lioubov* (charity) for girls. Similar examples can be cited for English. The naming conventions of the Puritan era gave rise to the girls' names of *Patience, Grace, Charity, Hope, Prudence.* In Japanese, both male and female names have a reference to flowers, plants or trees. However, many female names are taken from names for flowers which stress beauty and elegance. For male names derived from the plant world (e.g. peaches, plums and chrysanthemums) the *symbolic meanings* relating to flowers in Japanese culture are stressed rather than their actual physical characteristics such as beauty. Hiraga (1991) lists the following names for women: *Hanako* (flower child), *Hanae* (flower prosperity), *Hanayo* (flower world), *Sakura* (cherry), *Sakurako* (cherry-child), *Yuru* (lily), *Yuriko* (lily child) *Sayuri* (little lily), *Momoko* (peach child), *Momoe* (peach prosperity). In Jordan girls are often given 'beautiful and attractive' names whilst this is not so evident in the naming practices for boys. Abd-el-Jawad (1989: 309) explains that this goes back to the naming practices of ancient Arab tribes 'who used to give their sons ugly names but their daughters and slaves beautiful names' because they were motivated to do so by their belief that sons were named to frighten the enemy, while daughters and slaves were named to please their parents or tribe. Sons used to fight the enemy so their names should be ugly, tough or frightening, while women and slaves were used for entertainment and service so they were given beautiful names to please their masters.

Reflected in the choice of personal names for girls and boys are also the cultural and religious taboos and practices affecting a society. In Spanish-speaking communities, devotion to catholicism was/is often expressed through naming one's daughters after important Christian religious festivals, e.g. 'Asuncion'. In the Islamic world, on the other hand, it is boys who are given religious names. Abd-el-Jawad (1989) mentions that religious names for boys/men containing /abd/ (worshipper) and /hamd/ (gratitude and thankfulness) are considered the most precious. According to Abd-el-Jawad (1989: 310) 'women in Jordan seem to be excluded from this practice'.

It is also claimed that parents' wishes and desires for their newborn baby are often reflected in their naming practices. An extreme example is provided by Abd-el-Jawad (1989: 310) who notes that the preference for having boys instead of girls in Jordan is expressed in the naming practices:

> Unwanted baby girls are often given expressive names which indicate the parents'wish to stop having more. Female names such as /kafa/ 'enough', /xitaam/ 'conclusion or the end' or /nihaaya/ 'the end' are quite common among parents who have only baby daughters and no sons. Once a boy is born, he is also given a name expressing the joy of the parents and their gratitude to God, e.g. /ata/ 'gift from God/ or /sihdi-ishaadi/ 'begged from God'. Moreover, if the family has sons but no daughters, names indicating a wish to stop having sons are never given to males.

Another common practice found in languages is that of giving girls names which are diminutives of men's or boys' names. In French, this practice has given rise to such names as *Pierrette* from *Pierre*, *Georgette* from *George*, *Paulette* from *Paul*. In English similar patterns can be found in the names *Georgina*, *Pauline* among many others.

Girls and women are also much more likely to keep the diminutive form of their personal name for much longer than boys (sometimes for life). Poynton (1985: 82) states for English

'These suffixed forms [*e.g. the -y suffix, my comment – author*] along with other diminutive suffixes such as *-kin(s)* and *-poo(s)* are commonly used to children of both sexes, but boys come to see them, sometimes at a very early age, as 'girls' names' and reject them. Thus four-year-old *Robbie* at fourteen insists on *Rob* and six-year-old *Nicholas* has already rejected *Nicky* in favour of *Nick* or the full form *Nicholas*.

This practice of using diminutive names for adult women is also extensively found in Dutch-speaking countries, especially The Netherlands: Anne*ke*, Annemie*ke*, Henk*je*, Mie*ke*, Klaar*tje*, Maar*tje*, Wille*ke* (*-ke* and *-(t)je* are diminutive suffixes in Dutch).

'Family' names[23]: in the name of the father and the husband

A majority of (modern) industrialised societies operate with a patrilineal system of naming and of marking ancestry. The male line of ancestry is carried on through the naming process. In other words, children are given their father's name and women adopt their husband's name upon marriage. It is sons who can carry on the (father's) 'family' name whereas daughters lose this capacity upon marriage. Feminists have criticised this practice for various reasons. Women's lives and achievements are more difficult to trace through history, their identity is obscured, if not denied and it stresses the portrayal of women as the property of men, passed from father to husband (and possibly to son). Despite the fact that many societies no longer have legal requirements for women to adopt their husband's names upon marriage, women who do not conform to this practice still face many practical and attitudinal obstacles.

Titles: Mr Man and Mrs/Miss Man

Another naming practice which treats women differently from men concerns courtesy titles or honorifics. There is quite a range of languages (especially European) which distinguish women's courtesy titles on the basis of marital status, but not those of men. This discriminatory practice is said to mark the availability of women in terms of marriage (sex) and reinforces the view that a woman is the property of a man (either her father or her husband). For example, in European languages such as Danish, Dutch, English, French, German, Italian, Norwegian, Spanish and Swedish common courtesy titles for women mark the woman's marital status. If she is married (or considered of an age that she *should/could* be married), a woman will be addressed as *Fru* in Danish, *Mevrouw* in Dutch, *Madam* (or *Mrs*) in English, *Madame* in French, *Frau* in German, *Signora* in Italian, *Frue* in Norwegian and *Señora* in Spanish. If she is not married, she will be called *Fruken* (Danish), *Juffrouw/Mejuffer* (Dutch), *Miss* (English), *Mademoiselle* (French), *Fräulein* (German), *Signorina* (Italian), *Froken* (Norwegian) or *Señorita* in Spanish. This practice is not only restricted to European languages. In Jordanian Arabic the equivalent to 'Mrs' is /sayyida/ and to 'Miss' /ʔaanisa/.

From a feminist perspective, Spender (1980: 27) has commented that

> The practice of labelling women as married or single also serves supremely sexist ends. There is tension between the representation of women as sex objects and the male ownership rights over women and this has been resolved by an explicit and most visible device designating the married status of women.

Although there are courtesy titles for young unmarried men (e.g. *Master* in English and *Jonge Heer* in Dutch), these are not frequently used and, if they are used, they are more clearly markers of age than of marital status (i.e. for boys). Spender (1980: 27) attributes this to the fact that

> as women do not 'own' men, and as men have many dimensions apart from their sexual ones in a patriarchal order, it has not been necessary to make male marital status visible. On the contrary, it could hinder rather than help male operations in the world so it has never appeared as a 'logical' proposition.

The impression that married women are the property of their husbands and that women have no linguistic identity of their own after marriage culminates in the practice, still adopted in some societies, in which the woman is simply identified as 'the wife of (i.e. Mrs) of a man': in English *Mrs John Citizen*, in French *Madame Jean* (male personal name) *Dupont* and in Dutch *Mevrouw Lodewijck* (male personal name) *De Baert*.

In languages which do not mark gender in their courtesy titles (e.g. Japanese), asymmetrical use is nevertheless observed with regard to men's and women's honorifics. Takahashi (1991) remarks that the three major honorific titles (suffixes) in Japanese (*-san*, *-sama* and *-shi*) do not mark marital status but levels of politeness, formality and social status. She notices asymmetry in the use of these honorific titles for women and men of equal social rank:

For example, when the participants in a panel discussion are introduced on paper, it is very likely that male names are followed by -*shi* and female names by -*san*, even though the social status of female panelists is the same or higher than that of their male counterparts. (Takahashi 1991: 290)

In many Slavic languages the marital status of women is marked mainly through derivational suffixes attached to male surnames. For example, the Polish language has only one major courtesy title for women, *Pani* (*Pan* for men), but the marital status of women is often expressed through the suffixes -*owa* (Mrs) and -*ówna* (Miss) attached to male surnames. In Lithuanian, a married woman's surname is derived from the stem of her husband's name unto which the suffix -*iene* is added. In the case of an unmarried woman, her name is based on her father's surname to which one of the following suffixes is added -*aite*, -*yte*, -*ute* or -*te*.

Asymmetrical use of professional titles is a very common practice in many languages. In the language of the media, women's professional titles (e.g. Dr, Professor, Prime Minister, Senator) regularly disappear and are replaced by the courtesy titles Mrs, Miss or Ms (e.g. President Reagan and Mrs Thatcher). In The Netherlands there is the asymmetrical practice of marking female professionals by means of the phrase *Mw* (Mrs) followed by their professional title, e.g. *Mw Drs A.B.E. Jansen* (Drs = doctorandus) whereas men are simply marked by their professional title *Drs E.B.A. Jansen*.

The entry of women in a variety of professions, public offices and occupations has not only created problems with regard to occupational nouns but also professional titles. In some languages, like German, a woman will also adopt her husband's professional title upon marriage, e.g. *Frau Professor, Frau Doktor*. Now that many more women have professional titles in their own right, there is some confusion as to the exact meaning of such titles. The presence of married women in public offices such as premier, prime minister, mayor, etc., has also created problems for the naming conventions of their spouses. In Australia, female mayors' (possible) objections to the title 'Lord Mayor' are not heard or taken seriously, whereas many men and women commiserate with the fate of her husband who really should be referred to as 'Lady Mayoress'. Of course the serious use of such a term for men is unthinkable, as the men have made abundantly clear (they are referred to as Mr X). Yaguello (1978: 177) mentions a similar incident in France with the husband of a minister in the French government claiming 'Je ne suis pas le mari de Simone Weil, c'est elle qui est ma femme.' [I am not the husband of Simone Weil, it is she who is my wife.]

Addressing women and men

Asymmetry and non-reciprocity also characterise the ways men and women (can) address each other. Since relations between the sexes are marked by differences in power and (social) status, it is not surprising that these are reflected in forms of address, being the linguistic realisation of social relations. Some critics also claim that their existence obstructs changes in power relations.

Asymmetrical power relations between the sexes lead to non-reciprocal forms of address. This has been observed particularly in work situations[24] where it is not uncommon for a male boss or superior to address his female secretary, assistant or office clerk by means of her first name or even an endearment, such as *sugar*, *darling*, *sweetie*, *girlie* in English, *Schätzchen* (darling/treasure) in German, *schat* (darling/treasure) in Dutch, and *ma petite* (my little one) in French. It need not be said that the female worker cannot reciprocate in similar terms to address her male superior.

Although some sociolinguistic commentators remark that this asymmetry is primarily a matter of power and status differences rather than of sex/gender differences, there is nevertheless some evidence that when the status of the sexes is reversed (i.e. female boss vs male assistant/clerk or secretary) women in positions of power are still more likely than men to attract asymmetrical forms of address. Indeed, comments made by female bosses indicate that their male assistants often initiate or determine the forms of address to be used between them (usually a prerogative of the more power-ful) and occasionally address them by an endearment. Similar comments have been made by women in gatekeeping positions (e.g. doctors, lawyers, social workers) who find themselves addressed by their (predominantly male) clients by their first names and endearments (e.g. *honey*, *liebe Frau Karsten* (dear Mrs Karsten), *liefje* (dearie)).

Another domain marked by asymmetry is address in service encounters. Wolfson and Manes (1980) found that many female customers were addressed by means of an endearment by male and female shop assistants alike. In their observation men were never addressed as such in the United States. In other English-speaking countries, as well as in continental Europe, similar patterns have been observed, although men are also exposed to such endearments in some settings (e.g. pub, market stalls).

The fact that women are addressed more frequently by strangers and non-intimates (usually male) by means of endearments is explained by Poynton (1985) and others as resulting from the greater 'contactability' of women (and children) in Western cultures. This in turn is linked to the underlying belief that relations between men and women are primarily sexual, which is characterised by 'contact' and 'affect'. Men's wolfwhistles, as well as their calls to attract the attention of a woman often unknown to them, mainly focus on women's physical or sexual features (e.g. 'gorgeous', 'sexy legs', 'big tits', etc.).

Other asymmetrical practices observed in a variety of cultures include restrictions put on women but not men in relation to addressing and referring to male members of the family. Abd-el-Jawad (1989) reports that among the Circassians and the Chechens, two minority groups in Jordan, women cannot use the real names of the male members of their husband's family because it is considered better for a woman to die rather than mention her husband's first name. In other cultures (e.g. some Australian Aboriginal cultures) this restriction also affects men.

Trudgill (1974) and Kramer (1975) observed similar conventions among the Zulu and Caffre women in Africa. In Japanese, Cherry (1987) noted that a common way for men to address (married) women is to refer to them in terms of their allotted spatial domain (the home) i.e. *okusan* or by the more formal *okusama*, meaning 'Mrs Interior/Indoors'. The term (which has no inherent marker of sex) cannot be used to refer to a man, because men are not seen to have the home as their main domain. Furthermore, Japanese husbands call their wives *kanai*, which means 'house-insider'. The wives, on the other hand, call their husbands *goshujin* or *dannasan*, which mean 'honourable master' or sometimes the informal *teishu* (master of an inn or teahouse).

Linguistic stereotyping of the sexes

The portrayal of the sexes in a stereotyped[25] manner has been found in the use of all languages that have been examined for sexism. It affects all forms of discourse and language domains: e.g. the media, academic and scholarly discourse, religion, legislation, the language of public administration, education, proverbs and idioms. Although sex-stereotyped images can be equally restrictive and detrimental for both sexes, it is women who seem to suffer more under these images. This is not surprising as many stereotyped images for men in patriarchal cultures express values which are highly regarded in such cultures: physical strength and force, intellectual superiority, rationalism, aggression, sexual prowess, independence, mastery over other beings and things. Women's images, on the other hand, are based on features considered desirable in women by men but not highly valued in the patriarchal world: dependence, physical beauty, sexual attractiveness, emotionality, sensitivity and caring.

Although gender relations and gender roles vary among societies and cultures, the stereotyped images of men and women in their languages are remarkably similar. Here I compare stereotyped images of women in English-language societies with those of women in Japanese society. In English, women are frequently described as 'gorgeous blondes', 'stunning brunettes', 'glamorous sex symbols', 'well endowed', or as 'mother of X number of children', as 'wives' and 'daughters of (famous) men', as 'looking after husband and children', 'devoted to a husband', 'occupied with caring for men and children', and even 'having limited brains', 'leaving the thinking to the husband/men'. They are treated like a piece of property alongside other goods.

Stereotyped descriptions of women in other patriarchal societies and cultures are remarkably similar: stereotypes of Japanese women stress physical beauty, submission, being a commodity, and/or focus on sexuality. The importance of physical beauty as a female attribute is noticed in the practice of attaching the word *bijin* (literally 'beauty person') to female incumbents of certain occupations: *bijin anaunsa* (beauty-announcer), *bijin hosutesu* (beauty-hostess), *bijin henshusha* (beauty-editor). Job descriptions for women often specify physical traits: *yoshi tanrei* (graceful figure; Cherry 1987). Cherry also mentions words for women who do not show themselves as submissive: e.g. *otoko masari* (male surpasser), *sukeban* (boss girl). Both Cherry (1987) and Hiraga (1991) provide examples of women being described as a commodity (sexual and otherwise) and as a sales product (especially unmarried women): the phrase 'Hanaka-wa *hakoiri* musume da' (Hanako is a daughter in a box) can only be said of women and not of men. Cherry (1987: 119) reports that a woman who engages in sexual intercourse prior to marriage is referred to as 'damaged goods', *kizumono*. Hiraga (1991: 40–1) lists a number of expressions indicating that women are sales products which can be bought, be for sale, be put on the market, or remain unsold.

Taroo-wa yuube onna-o *kat-ta*: Taroo bought a woman last night.

Ano ie-ni-wa *uridasi chuu*-no musume-ga ir-u: There is a daughter for sale in that house.

Sinseki-juu-de uchi-no musume-no *urekuci*-o sagasi-te i-ru: All the relatives are looking for a market for my daughter.

Atira-no o-joo-san-wa *urenokot-te* i-masu: Their daughter has remained unsold.

Proverbs, idioms and other formulaic and fixed expressions about the sexes and gender relations are also a source of stereotyping: they portray women as 'idle chatterboxes', as 'weak', 'jealous', 'stupid', 'possessive' and as 'concerned with physical beauty' or 'trivial things'. Women's sexuality is sometimes portrayed as dangerous to men. Webster (1982: 176) mentions that 'women are thought to possess power through sexuality, power not only to control but to damage a man'. Studies of proverbs[26] relating to the sexes not only pinpoint stereotyped images of the sexes in proverbs but also reveal a high degree of misogyny expressed in them. Here are some examples of misogynous proverbs derived from a variety of languages:

It is only a woman that can make a man become a parody of himself [French]. (Thiselton-Dyer 1906: 2)

A thousand men may live together in harmony, whereas two women are unable to do so though they be sisters [Tamil]. (Thiselton-Dyer 1906: 5)

A woman's hair is long, but her sense is short [Russian]. (Thiselton-Dyer 1906: 8)

A woman's tongue three inches long can kill a man six feet high [Japanese]. (Thiselton-Dyer 1906: xii)

A woman is like a goat – if she is not in harm she is coming out of it [Irish]. (Williams 1984: 84)

Where the devil cannot cause a mischief, there he sends an old woman, and she does [Serbian]. (Canciani 1913: 92)

The woman's sexual lust is seven times the man's [Judeo–Iraqi proverb]. (Khayyat 1974: 945)

Clearly this brief description of the linguistic stereotyping of the sexes represents the mere proverbial 'tip of the iceberg'. I refer the reader to the many studies quoted in the first part of this chapter. These contain many more examples of stereotyping.

Sexism in ideographs and characters

More recently, some investigations have examined the sexism present in writing systems, notably the Chinese writing system (e.g. Xu 1988, Wong 1991, Ng and Burridge 1993). It is alleged that the female/feminine radical *nü* [女] is used in many characters representing behaviours, actions and states of being that have negative connotations or are considered bad. For example, verbs expressing illicit sexual relations or behaviour contain the feminine radical: *pin* [姘], to cohabit or have illicit sexual relations. The feminine radical is also used to refer to other forms of negative or bad behaviour: e.g. *dù* [妒], to be jealous; *dú* [妕] to slander or humiliate; *xián* [嫌] to quarrel, hate, suspect; *xiè* [媟] indecent; *wàng* [妄] absurd, outrageous, ignorant, stupid; and *lán* [婪] covetous, greedy. Wong (1991) also points out that there is no masculine radical in Chinese, only a feminine and human radical. The character for male (*man'nán*) does not contain a masculine radical. He suggests that the absence of a specific masculine radical is due to the fact that 'Chinese men in ancient times might think that only men were the human beings, so they could just use characters with the human radical to represent meanings related to men'. Whatever the exact source of the absence of a specific radical for man, its absence results in a gender asymmetry similar to that found in other languages (man is the norm, i.e. equated with human being, woman is different from the norm).

Documenting reactions to linguistic sexism

An important aspect of the documentation stage in language planning is to explore people's reactions to the alleged language problem. Ensuing proposals for change will be influenced by the community's reactions to the problem. If there is widespread recognition that a language issue is problematic and that change is needed, proposals might be accepted more easily and the implementation stage may run smoothly. However, in the case of strong opposition to the existence of a language problem, the language reformers may experience considerable difficulty in having their proposals accepted and implemented.

Here I focus on the reactions of the speech community to the allegation that language is sexist. The issue, however, will be raised again in the context of people's reactions to non-sexist language proposals in Chapter 6.

In addition I shall present some evidence put forward by feminist language reformers to substantiate some claims of sexism. They include laboratory-type tests and experiments as well as attitudinal studies.

The alleged existence of a male bias in language (use) and its discriminatory and detrimental effect on women as language users are not (at all) unanimously acknowledged or accepted by the speech community at large. Obviously, the allegations made by feminist language critics about the sexist nature of languages are challenging deeply-rooted views about language as a semiotic system, as a means of human communication and about the relationship between languages, their users and societies.

It is not surprising then that a major reaction coming from both professional and lay sectors of speech communities was (and still is) one of *denial*: denial that sexism in language(s) exists and denial that it has detrimental effects on the position of women and the relationship between the sexes in society.

Language teachers, linguists, editors, authors, media commentators, philosophers, self-appointed guardians of language, journalists, the 'man' and the 'woman' in the street among many others expressed their opinions (sometimes with great vehemence) against what they considered to be 'absurd' claims by feminists against language. Their refutations of the feminist claims of linguistic sexism varied considerably in sophistication and were shaped by the nature of their knowledge of language and by their attitudes towards (deliberate) language change. Some common threads, however, do run through their arguments criticising feminist claims of sexism in language.

The first one is to discredit or question the feminist critics' knowledge and understanding of language, suggesting that the latter lack the necessary linguistic knowledge to make such claims and judgements. This argument is common among more linguistically expert opponents, although lay 'experts' also use this argument (for details, see Chapter 6).

A second common thread is one which criticises the feminist critics' view of the relationship between language and society. A more elaborate discussion of this issue is found in Chapter 3.

A third point found in many refutations is a warning to people that feminist critics have hidden motives and are radicals who are intent on destroying all forms of society and all forms of communication for their own benefit (for details, see also Chapter 6).

It is interesting to note that few, if any opponents of the 'language is sexist' claim ever attack or refute *ALL* features of linguistic sexism as described earlier in this chapter. Rather, they concentrate on refuting a particular feature of feminist criticism of language. Nevertheless, their conclusions are formulated in such a way that they deny the existence of any form of sexism in language.

Denial of the claim: language is not sexist

Feminist claims about the gender bias in structural aspects of language(s) have come under intense scrutiny, especially from linguists and other language experts. They argue, with varying degrees of intensity, that feminist language critics have naive, confused or misguided ideas and knowledge about the relationship between the grammatical category of gender and the non-linguistic, social and biological category of sex. In their view feminists' deliberate or misguided confusion of these categories has affected their interpretations of such issues as the genericness of masculine nouns and pronouns in certain languages, the so-called 'superiority' of the masculine gender, gender-marking practices and the concept of markedness in languages.

In the section on sexism and the category of gender I have already made reference to the problematic relationship between biological sex and grammatical gender and linguists' theories of the origin of gender in languages. Opponents to the 'language is sexist' claim categorically deny any connection or even overlapping between the two categories. In their view, grammatical gender is a mere linguistic convention and not a linguistic expression of the category of sex. For example, Kallioinen *et al.* (1987: 378) claim that the grammatical opposition masculine/feminine 'is a linguistic convention, which is essentially arbitrary and which could be replaced by a more abstract terminology ("gender A/gender B") if the use of the terms "masculine" and "feminine" was not so enshrined'.

Commenting on Trömel-Plötz's (1978) article on sexism in German, Kalverkämper (1979a: 60) articulates clearly that feminist language critics are mistaken about their views of gender and sex:

> Hier liegt neben . . . ein weiterer Mißgriff in der Argumentation von Frau TRÖMEL-PLÖTZ. Sie vermischt die außersprachliche Kategorie 'Sexus' mit der sprachlichen Kategorie 'Genus', indem sie von Gegebenheiten beim Genus auf Gegebenheiten des Sexus schließt. [Here we find besides . . . a further mistake in the argumentation of Ms TRÖMEL-PLÖTZ. She confuses the extralinguistic category 'sex' with the linguistic category 'gender', as she derives features of gender from features of sex.]

Concerning the related issue of linguistic markedness affecting gender-marking practices and genericity in many languages, opponents again stress the *arbitrariness* of the fact that in many languages the masculine gender or masculine noun is the unmarked form. They also provide examples of some languages in which the feminine gender is unmarked (e.g. the language of the Tunica Indians, and of the Irokese Indians). Furthermore, they point towards the fact that if one considers the entire lexicon and not simply human agent nouns, one would find that the masculine noun is not always the unmarked one. Kalverkämper (1979a: 59) provides the example of the French word *la poule* (chicken): *la poule* (feminine gender) is the unmarked noun in the word pair **le** *coq* (cock, rooster) and **la** *poule* (hen, chicken). It belongs to the feminine gender thus denying the claim that the masculine gender or masculine noun is unmarked.

The Department of Linguistics at Harvard (USA) based its reactions against a proposal to ban *Man, man* and *he* as generics by two students from the Harvard School of Divinity also on the claim of arbitrariness of marked and unmarked nouns in English:

> Many of the grammatical and lexical oppositions in language are not between equal members of a pair but between one of which is more 'marked' than the other (to use the technical) [. . .] For people and pronouns in English the masculine is the unmarked and hence is used as a neutral or unspecified term. This reflects the ancient pattern of the Indo-European languages [. . .]. The fact that the masculine is the unmarked gender in English (or that the feminine is unmarked in the language of the Tunica Indians) is simply a feature of grammar. It is unlikely to be an impediment to any change in the patterns of the sexual division of labor toward which our society may wish to evolve. There is really no cause for anxiety or pronoun envy on the part of those seeking changes. (*The Harvard Crimson*, 16 November 1971, p. 17)

Nor have lay people shied away from exposing feminist language critics' apparent lack of linguistic knowledge. Unlike their 'learned' colleagues who refer to formal linguistic theories and concepts to discredit the 'language is sexist' claim, the lay 'experts' cite (folk) etymological arguments to deny the claim. A classic example is the case of the origin and meaning of -*man* in compounds of the kind *chairman, statesman, postman, countryman*. Lay experts claim that the -*man* in words like *chairman* does not have an etymological, historical or formal link with the word 'man' but with the Latin word 'manus' (hand). A further argument used by experts against the claim that language is sexist is that of the deliberate or naive confusion by feminist linguists between language as a system and language in use. In other words, the language system itself is neutral because it is an abstract system, 'a "mental" organ, an aspect of the functioning of the mind' (Lepschy 1987: 160), and can therefore not be accused of being sexist. It is, however, the *use* of the language system (the 'parole') by people with sexist attitudes that leads to sexism in language.

Similar views are also expressed by those who show some sympathy or understanding for the feminist claims of male bias in language, as illustrated by the quote from the work of two Russian linguists, Dorodnykh and Martynyuk (1990: 178):

> One major methodological error of the feminists is lack of discrimination between language and the use of language units in speech. Language serves all social classes equally well and cannot by itself be an instrument of social oppression.

Linked to this argument of the need to distinguish between language as a system and language use is sometimes the belief that there is no (direct) relationship between language and society. In other words, inequities between men and women in society, sexist practices and patriarchal structures cannot or do not mirror themselves in language. The evidence provided for this point of view usually consists of references to languages like Turkish, Hungarian or Finnish which do not have sex-specific third person pronouns and yet the societies in which these languages are used are not free from sexist practices.

Evidence in support of the claim that language is sexist

Feminist reactions to these arguments have consisted mainly of three strategies. Firstly, feminist *linguists* have sought to clarify their position by making their use of linguistic concepts and terminology more explicit and by providing further critiques on the grammatical concepts or features such as markedness in language, gender and gender marking (see, e.g., Cameron 1985, Hellinger 1990, Pusch 1984a). Secondly, they have repeatedly stressed their rejection of the criticism that language is a neutral medium. Thirdly, there has been a concerted attempt to provide research evidence that female and male language users experience sexist language structures and practices differently and that there is a link between language use and other societal behaviour.

Experimental research evidence

Most research evidence in support of the claim that language is sexist has focused on the meaning and understanding of generic nouns and pronouns in English. Experiments and tests undertaken primarily by social psychologists and psycholinguists[27] in the 1970s and 1980s provide some proof that people's perception and understanding of masculine generic nouns and pronouns in English is not as 'generic' and 'unambiguous' as linguists claim.

PERCEPTIONS AND IMAGES OF *Man* AND *-man* COMPOUNDS

Studies by Kidd (1971), Bem and Bem (1973), Schneider and Hacker (1973), Pincus and Pincus (1980), among many others, all investigate aspects of informants' interpretation of *man* and *-man* compounds allegedly used in a generic sense. A common finding in these projects is that children (in some cases also adults) had difficulties interpreting the word *man* and *-man* compounds as generics. Both adults and children call up predominantly male images with those words. For example, Schneider and Hacker's (1973) research showed that the use of gender-neutral language in titles and headings in history and social studies textbooks reduced the male imagery associated with such titles: when children were asked to supply illustrations and pictures associated with titles such as *Industrial Man*, 64 per cent of the pictures selected only showed men. This was reduced to 50 per cent when gender-neutral titles were used.

Bem and Bem (1973) also showed that gender-biased language can influence whether or not women and men pursue certain employment options. They found that if job advertisements used gender-biased language only 5 per cent of women and 30 per cent of men were interested in applying for opposite-sex jobs. In the neutral job ads 25 per cent of women and 75 per cent of men were willing to apply for opposite sex jobs. Finally, in sex-reversed job advertisements, 45 per cent of women and 65 per cent of men were willing to consider applying for opposite-sex jobs.

DOES HE INCLUDE SHE?

Findings similar to those on masculine generic nouns were noted for investigations relating to the so-called generic use of the masculine pronoun *he*. Mackay (1983: 40–1)[28] states that 'a long line of experiments . . . have tested and conclusively refuted the pronominal surrogate assumption'. By 'pronominal surrogate assumption' he means

> the assumption that pronouns simply stand for their antecedents and that prescriptive *he* [i.e. *generic* he – *author*] designates a sex-indefinite antecedent, such as *person* or *pedestrian*, without excluding women or adding new meaning of its own.

Soto *et al.* (1975) commented that people were more likely to perceive the pronoun *he* in its generic function as referring to men rather than women. Mackay and Fulkerson (1979) surveyed American college students on the interpretation of generic uses of *he*: 87 per cent interpreted the pronoun as referring exclusively to males. Mackay (1980) found that students who read textbook paragraphs containing masculine generic pronouns with neutral (generic) antecedents assumed that they referred to men in 40 per cent of the cases.

The study by Moulton *et al.* (1978), in which two groups of subjects were shown one-sentence statements containing either masculine generic pronouns (*he*) or gender inclusive ones (*he or she*) before writing an essay on a related topic, revealed a significantly greater tendency to write essays describing males as a result of being exposed to masculine generic pronouns.

Wilson and Ng (1988) found that masculine generic pronouns invoked sex-specific images and Hamilton (1988) reported similar findings about masculine generic pronouns and male-biased imagery in the mind of the user.

One of the experiments reported in Martyna (1978) revealed that the generic use of *he* is seldom interpreted as meaning *he and she*. She also found some gender differences in the perception of pseudo-generic usage of *he*: the imagery reported by males for sentences using generic *he* was predominantly male. Women, on the other hand, often reported an absence of imagery relating to sentences containing generic *he*. Martyna (1978: 138) noted

> Unfortunately, even those who clearly intend 'he' as a generic term can't guarantee that their usage will be understood that way. In fact explorations of our understanding of the generic masculine have demonstrated that 'he' is an ambiguous term which often allows a specifically male interpretation to be drawn from an intended generic usage.

Wheeless *et al.* (1981), on the other hand, found no gender differences in their investigation of generic *he* pronoun usage.

Whether or not these research findings made any impact on their opponents, feminist language critics nevertheless used the evidence to push for language reform by promoting non-sexist alternatives to masculine generic pronouns (see Chapter 4).

Gauging women's and men's attitudes towards sexism in language

Questionnaires and interviews can also be used in the documentation of linguistic sexism. They can examine people's awareness and understanding of the issue at stake as well as their attitudes towards it. An insight into people's understanding and attitudes aids language planners in their approach to language planning and in their selection of solutions and strategies for implementation. For example, if a speech community is relatively uninformed about a problematic language issue, or does not easily recognise the issue, then language planners will need to pay particular attention to raising people's consciousness before they can turn to proposing and implementing reforms. On the other hand, if a speech community is very aware of a language issue (e.g. choice of a national/official language), then language planners need not concern themselves so much with consciousness raising as with formulating and evaluating proposals for reform.

Unfortunately there have been few studies to date which have systematically sought to investigate people's awareness of linguistic sexism, their views on sexism in language as well as on proposed changes. The few systematic studies that have been conducted are all rather small-scale done on a relatively homogeneous population (usually white, middle class, college or university educated) in relation to English, French and German (e.g. Bate 1978, De Silva 1992, Goh 1994, Hellinger and Schräpel 1983, Henley and Dragun 1983, Houdebine 1988, Houssami 1994, Jaehrling 1988 and Schafroth 1993). Most, if not all, studies do not ask the informants to identify forms of sexism in language; rather they either provide a definition of sexism or list of examples/categories of sexist language practices. Informants are then asked to react to these. I believe this approach to be largely a result of people being unable to pinpoint sexism in language without some form of explanation being provided, which indicates the subconscious nature of the phenomenon. If asked to identify forms of sexism in language without further explanations, people tend to identify either forms of linguistic stereotyping or derogatory labelling of women but not the other issues identified in this chapter. However, if the various forms of sexist language practices are identified, informants show a certain level of awareness of them.

Hellinger and Schräpel (1983) surveyed a group of 162 German-speaking women and men to gauge their awareness of sexist language and their reactions to proposed reforms of sexist language. The authors provided the informants with a definition of sexism and then probed their awareness of the issue by asking if they had encountered sexist language practices in a variety of domains. They found that more than 50 per cent of their sample showed awareness of sexist language practices in a variety of domains, especially in the media and in official language (the language of bureaucracy and public administration). Women's awareness of sexist language was (substantially) higher than that of men for all the named domains (school; profession/workplace; media; official language; leisure).

Jaehrling (1988) surveyed 150 German and Australian (English-speaking) informants in relation to their attitudes to sexist language and to sexist language reforms. She found that, on average, about two-thirds of the informants agreed with the fact that a number of language practices in both German and English were sexist: blatant as well as more subtle forms of stereotyping (e.g. portraying women as chatterboxes, the weaker sex) were almost unanimously acknowledged as being sexist. Around 90 per cent of German and English informants considered such expressions sexist. The -*mann* and -*man* compounds in German and English which were used in a generic sense were also overwhelmingly identified as sexist (approximately 75 per cent) in both language groups. Asymmetrical naming practices such as *salesmen* vs *salesgirls* in English and *Skimädchen* (literally ski girls, i.e. female skiers) vs *Skimänner* (literally ski men, male skiers) in German were also considered sexist by approximately 70 per cent of informants. Lower scores for sexism were given in German to the use of the indefinite pronoun *man* (one) which requires agreement with the masculine gender (40 per cent) and to the distinction between *Miss* and *Mrs* for women in English (46 per cent). It is interesting to note that there was no substantial difference between German and English language users. However, there was a difference in relation to age combined with gender. Younger people (especially women) were more willing to accede than older people (and men) that certain practices were sexist. Jaehrling (1988) also asked her informants whether they would like to see a non-sexist alternative used in place of the sexist description or expression. The overwhelming majority of German informants were in favour of replacement (in most cases more than 70 per cent). They were most eager to see a replacement for the *-mann* compounds and were least inclined to change the use of the indefinite pronoun *man*. For the English speaking informants a similar picture emerged: the highest support came for the replacement of *-man* compounds (91 per cent) and the generic use of *he* (93 per cent). The lowest support (44 per cent) came for the replacement of honorific titles for women.

Goh's (1994) small-scale survey of 40 Australian students' reactions to sexist language found that 65 per cent of the female students and 35 per cent of the male students agreed with the statement: 'the English language is sexist: it is too male centred.' Houssami's (1994) survey of the use and attitudes towards sexist and non-sexist pronouns among 60 Australians (including high school and university students and professional people) revealed that almost all informants conceded that generic *he* was sexist and only 8.3 per cent preferred to use generic *he*. De Silva (1992) questioned twenty editors in commercial publishing houses in Australia regarding their awareness and understanding of sexist language use. Her results indicated that all editors were aware of sexism in language practices and most were willing to change them, provided they could do so without sacrificing style or altering content.

In addition to these surveys, there is a wealth of anecdotal evidence about people's reactions to, and people's experiences with, sexism in language. Many feminist authors and scholars have commented on the often painful but liberating process of becoming or being made aware of sexism in language. In her introduction to *Das Deutsche als Männersprache* [German as a men's language], Luise Pusch (1984a: 9–10) writes of her discovery of sexism in language:

Nächtelang war ich wütend über vergewaltigende und prügelnde Ehemänner, über die systematische Benachteiligung der Frau im Beruf, über den alltäglichen Sexismus in Lehrbüchern und in den Medien. Aber Sexismus in der Sprache – nein, das war für mich kein Thema, obwohl ich von den «Laiinnen», gerade als Sprachfachfrau, ständig darauf angesprochen wurde. Das neue Pronomen, *frau*, das ich in feministischen Texten nun allenthalben las, fand ich lustig, schön frech und aufsässig, aber nicht eigentlich wichtig – weil ich die Supermaskulinität von *man* auch nicht so wichtig fand ... Es bedurfte wohl radikalfeministischer Verve, Unbekümmertheit, Subjektivität und entschlossener Parteilichkeit, um zu dieser Auffassung über Sprache zu kommen. [For nights I was fuming about husbands who rape and beat, about the systematic discrimination against women in the workplace, about the everyday sexism in textbooks and in the media. But sexism in language – no, that was not an issue for me, although I was often approached by 'laywomen', in my capacity as female language expert about this matter. I found the new pronoun, *frau*, which I read in feminist texts, funny, cheeky and contrary, but not particularly important . . . It needed radical feminist verve, carelessness, subjectivity and determined partiality to arrive at this view of language.]

Since I started teaching and researching the issue of linguistic sexism in the mid-1980s I have occasionally kept notes on students', colleagues', friends' and acquaintances' comments on the portrayal of the sexes in language and on their discovery of sexist patterns in their own and other people's language use. My impressions, based on these notes and discussions with people, are that alertness to and awareness of sexism in language often come as a direct result of discussions with someone aware of linguistic sexism or from reading about it in connection with books on feminism (see also Chapter 6). If questioned about the portrayal of sexes in languages, most people would mention that they had noticed forms of gender-stereotyping in the language of the media and school books. When they were not given further information of what is meant by sexism in language, only a few of them mentioned or recognised other aspects of linguistic sexism. For example, two Italian women and one French woman commented on gender agreement with the masculine in the case of a multiple noun phrase including feminine nouns. A Russian-born woman mentioned the Russian practice of addressing a male or female person by his or her first name, followed by the father's first name. A Chinese student reported that he felt that some Chinese characters were denigratory to women. Quite a few women found that courtesy titles in English (*Mrs*, *Miss*) were discriminatory because they revealed marital status whereas the title *Mr* does not.

Women who described themselves as feminists or who (including some men) were involved in the women's movement were usually more aware than others that there was a male bias in language, although they could not always describe exactly what it entailed. Comparing levels of awareness across language groups, I found that there was a substantial difference between English speakers and speakers of other languages (including Danish, Dutch, French, German, Polish, Turkish, Chinese, Thai, Italian, Spanish). However, since these impressions are not based on systematic observations over a longer period of time, they should not be interpreted as marking a significant difference in levels of awareness and of concern. At best, they reflect the fact that the issue of linguistic sexism has received more public attention in English-speaking countries than in others.

Once (made) aware of sexist practices in language, women were usually more eager than men to pursue the topic and to relate their experiences. Reactions to the discovery of sexist practices in language were often quite complex: some women had felt cheated because 'even language let them down', others said they felt relieved at finally having the term 'linguistic sexism' to describe the feelings that they had had about men's and women's relationship to language. Trying to deny or play down the existence of sexist structures in language was another early reaction of some people. A variation on this reaction was the response by mainly older men and women: they agreed that some languages were discriminatory with regard to the sexes but their language certainly was not (in most cases they were speakers of European languages). Quite often men had been made aware of sexism in language by women close to them: they claimed to have accepted that language was sexist but admitted that they had no real personal experience of the issue. However, they were prepared to change their language habits in solidarity with women.

Both the anecdotal evidence as well as evidence gathered through small-scale surveys leave us with the impression that increasing numbers of people are becoming more aware of the fact that linguistic sexism is a problematic issue. Furthermore, a growing number of people agree that such sexist language practices treat women in a discriminatory fashion and that they are in need of change. In other words, they are in favour of language planning, or language reform.

In this chapter I have discussed the documenting or fact-finding stage relating to feminist language reform. This included (a) a documentation of the extent of sexist practices in language, (b) a discussion of the types of sexist practices and (c) a short overview of (i) the reactions to the claim that language is sexist and (ii) research evidence in favour of the claim.

In the next chapter I move on to the next stage in language planning (LP), referred to as *the planning stage*.

Notes

1. The comments made by Jespersen (1922) are a classic example. Baron's (1986) overview on grammar and gender provides many more instances.
2. For example Cohen *et al.* (1983) contains an extensive bibliography on sexism and stereotyping in children's books (especially English).
3. The study of English as a second language is commonly abbreviated as ESL and English as a foreign language as EFL.
4. Some examples of analyses include Cochran (1992), Gupta and Lee (1990), Hellinger (1980), Porecca (1984), Pugsley (1992), Sunderland (1992), Talansky (1986).
5. Examples of analyses of sexism found in dictionaries include for English: Gershuny (1974, 1975, 1977), Hennessy (1993), Kaye (1989b), Kramarae and Treichler (1985), Morris (1982), Schulz (1974), for German Pusch (1984b), for French Sautermeister (1985), Yaguello (1978), for Spanish Bierbach (1989), García (1977), Hampares (1976), for Chinese Wong (1991).
6. Translation: She admired him as if he were a god. The Duden dictionary as trash novel.
7. See, for example, the analysis of style manuals undertaken by Cameron (1995).
8. Examples of studies include Akkramas (1989), Beligan (1993), Davis (1985), Lee (1982), Luebke (1985), Nakayama (1993), Sabatini (1986), Stirling (1987), Sutton (1978), Swan (1992).
9. These included issues of the *Evenimentul Zilei*, the right-wing *Romania mare*, the left-wing weekly *Academia Catavencu* from the period January 1990 until December 1992.
10. The newspapers which were examined by Nakayama (1993) included the *Yomiuri* newspaper, which is one of Japan's leading daily newspapers, and the *Kanagawa* newspaper, which is the local newspaper in the Kanagawa prefecture. A total of 30 issues were investigated in the period 15–30 March 1993.
11. Most analyses have been concerned with religions based on Judaeo-Christian beliefs. For more detailed analyses see, e.g., Gonzalez (1978) for English and Spanish, Adams-Smith (1987), McFague (1982), Myers (1972), Russell (1976), Spears (1978), Pusch (1984a), Wegener *et al.* (1990) for German.
12. See, for example, Lee (1976), Pusavat (1981).
13. Corbett (1991) points out that the distinction between morphological and phonological gender systems is not always very clear and in many instances these two types of formal systems are closely interconnected.
14. As indicated earlier in the chapter, semantic systems are also referred to as natural gender systems in many cases, and the morphological/phonological gender systems are labelled grammatical gender systems.

15. Common gender is the name used for the gender which treats masculine and feminine nouns in a similar fashion with regard to some qualifiers or agreement markers. For example, in Dutch, a language with common gender, masculine and feminine nouns are not distinguished in terms of definite articles: **de** *man* (the man), **de** *vrouw* (the woman).

16. Corbett (1991) discusses the fact that semantic criteria are likely to override morphological or phonological criteria, especially in the case of human agent nouns which are classified into masculine/feminine and/or neuter categories.

17. This practice has also been linked to the concepts of markedness in languages (see Cameron 1985, Hellinger 1990). The masculine gender has the status of being the unmarked gender category in many languages (exceptions quoted are the language of the Tunica Indians (Cameron 1985), the language of the Irokese Indians (Yaguello 1978).

18. Martynyuk (1990b) asserts that the terms *vracixa* (female doctor) and *diktorsa* (female announcer) are restricted to use in colloquial, highly informal Russian.

19. Girl has also overt sexual connotations in certain contexts, i.e. that of a synonym (euphemism for a prostitute).

20. The evaluation that the sexual activity is promiscuous is also defined from a male perspective.

21. Personal communication from Yisa kehinde Yusuf and Arua E. Arua.

22. For more recent work, see, e.g., Patthey-Chavez and Youmans (1992), Patthey-Chavez *et al.* (1996).

23. Family names are by no means a universal phenomenon. In many societies, there is no need or desire to identify a family, kin or tribal group by means of a name similar to all members. Here we shall only look at some Western societies and their naming practices, as these have been the subject of feminist criticism.

24. The asymmetrical addressing practices of course vary from workplace to workplace (e.g. large company vs small business, public vs private organisation), from culture to culture (in some cultures the workplace situation is one marked by great social distance where only formal forms of address are considerate appropriate) and from individual to individual. Nevertheless, despite these variations, address forms between women and men are often asymmetrical and non-reciprocal.

25. A stereotype is a generalised and relatively fixed image of a person or persons belonging to a particular group. This image is formed by isolating or exaggerating certain features – physical, mental, cultural, occupational, personal and so on – which seem to characterise the group. Stereotypes are discriminatory in that they take away a person's individuality. Although they may reflect elements of truth, these are usually misinterpreted or inaccurate due to oversimplification.

26. For example studies by Mieder (1982), Canciani (1913), Degh *et al.* (1976), Delano (1979), Dundes (1976), Jordan and de Caro (1986), Khayyat (1974), Lewis (1974), Nwachukwu-Agbada (1989), Oduyoye (1979), Thiselton-Dyer (1906), Webster (1982) and Williams (1984) discuss the image of women in proverbs in European, African and some Asian languages and dialects and report a prevalence of misogynous descriptions.

27. For a good summary of studies on people's perceptions and interpretations of masculine generic nouns and pronouns, see Pearson *et al.* (1985).

28. Mackay (1983) is a comprehensive overview of the arguments and evidence for and against the use of 'he' as a generic pronoun.

3 Should sexist language be changed?

Introduction

After identifying and documenting sexist practices in language use, language planners enter into the language planning (LP) stage. Here issues about the desirability and the viability of the types of reform are considered. In this chapter I focus on these issues by addressing the question 'Should sexist language be changed?'.

Although the 'documenters' of sexist practices in language share the view that linguistic sexism is a reality not to be denied, they do not necessarily share the same views on whether or not to reform, or on how to eliminate the problem. The documenters, and indeed some planners, may hold very different views on the aims of language reform. For example, the main intention of some documenters of linguistic sexism is to *expose* yet another area in which women face discrimination. For others, on the other hand, the documentation of linguistic sexism is firmly linked to a series of detailed proposals to eliminate this form of discrimination against women. There are also those who see their role as furthering the discovery of sexist practices in texts or languages which have not yet been subjected to analysis. An important factor in the question 'whether or not to reform sexist language' is the documenters' (language planners') view of the relationship between language and reality.

Views on language and reality

A range of views exist about the nature of the relationship between language and reality. One view posits that there is no particular relationship between language and reality. Those adhering to this view argue that language is an arbitrary system of signs which is used to represent reality. In relation to the sexist language reform (LR) debate, this view is held, implicitly or explicitly, by those who deny the existence of sexism in language. The discussion in Chapter 2 around the possible influence of the extralinguistic category of sex (gender) on the grammatical category of gender (especially of the 'feminine–masculine' type) illustrated the different views on this issue. Those who defended the view that there is no relationship between sex and gender subscribe to this view of language and reality. Adherents of this view are also keen to point out that if there was a particular relationship between language and reality and between language and social practice, then languages associated with societies in which women are very much oppressed should be more heavily marked by sexism than those associated with communities in which women are treated less oppressively. The fact that analyses of linguistic sexism in different languages have not been able to confirm such direct correlation is taken as sufficient proof for their view on language and reality and their negative stance *vis-à-vis* LR.

The other views assume some interrelationship between language and reality. These views are important in the debate on feminist language reform. In Chapter 1 I discussed that feminist LP or LR was couched in a sociolinguistic framework of LP which recognises language as a resource that can improve social life (Fasold 1984). This approach to LP thus assumes a relationship between language and reality.

The first view affirms the existence of a relationship between language and reality and subscribes to the belief that *language reflects reality*.[1] In other words, language structures, patterns and use are influenced and inspired by non-linguistic reality including social structures and organisations, physical features and phenomena. The way in which languages are used and structured has been influenced by the institutions, social constructs and ideologies of the communities and societies with which they have become associated. This would account for the differences between languages in how they encode reality. An example would be the differences in the use of German (especially in the meanings of words, but also in aspects of syntax and in the use of particular language varieties) between the former Federal Republic of Germany and the German Democratic Republic. They can be explained as resulting from their association with divergent political ideologies affecting the institutions in the respective societies. This view is widespread among linguists (especially sociolinguists) and anthropologists studying language in culture and society. For example, the work of such renowned sociolinguists as William Labov, Peter Trudgill and Lesley Milroy and of the anthropological linguist Franz Boas is done in this framework of language reflecting reality.

A second view of the relationship between language and reality is often referred to as *linguistic determinism, linguistic relativity*[2] or the *Sapir–Whorf hypothesis*. According to this view, *language influences*, or even stronger, *determines, how an individual constructs and views reality*. This view is usually associated with the works of the anthropologists Edward Sapir and Benjamin Whorf. Whorf's work on Amerindian and other languages led him to believe that thinking occurs (primarily) through language and that language therefore structures one's thinking. Consequently, language determines how we construct and view both the physical and the social world:

> We dissect nature along the lines laid down by our native language. The categories and types that we isolate from the world of phenomena we do not find there because they stare every observer in the face; on the contrary, the world is presented in a kaleidoscopic flux of impressions which has to be organized in our minds – this means largely by the linguistic systems in our minds. (Whorf 1956: 213)

In other words, it is likely that people with different native or first languages construct reality in different ways and therefore have different views of that reality.

Although it is beyond the scope of this book to critique the concept of (Whorfian) linguistic determinism and to discuss the empirical evidence surrounding it, it is important to distinguish between the two versions of the Sapir–Whorf hypothesis which have developed over time. The 'strong' version of the hypothesis posits that language *determines* thought whereas the 'weak' version takes the view that language *helps construct* thought. The support for the strong version of the hypothesis has generally waned in the face of substantial (empirical) evidence and by arguing that in a system of absolute determinism translation would be a sheer impossibility. The weak version, on the other hand, has received considerable support among researchers of language and social practices, especially those working on language and gender.

The third view of the relationship between language and reality is a kind of synthesis between the first and the second views. It posits that *language not only reflects reality but also helps to construct it*. This view does not focus on determining the direction of influence or effect between language and reality but stresses the act of

mutual influencing between the two. This view is sometimes referred to as the *interactionist* view (e.g. Pauwels 1989a, 1993c)
and is often held by linguistic researchers whose work on language
and social practice has been influenced and inspired by critical
theory and discourse studies. Some feminist scholars have referred
to this view as constituting 'a weak version of the Whorfian hypothesis' (e.g. Frank and Treichler 1989). Others have referred to it
as a dialectical position involving language, the individual and
society, 'a synthetic view in which language both helps construct
sexual inequality and reflects its existence in society' (Graddol and
Swann 1989: 165).

In the context of feminist LR the weak version of the Sapir–
Whorf hypothesis will be aligned with the interactionist view on
language and reality.

Is linguistic action necessary or desirable?

All views on language and reality have been used to argue in favour
of or against LR in discussions about the feasibility and desirability of linguistic action to eliminate sexist practices from language.
The view that argues against a relationship between language and
reality will not be elaborated as it posits that there is no sexism in
language and therefore no need for reform. The view that language
merely *reflects* reality is the one most often used to argue against
the viability of LR. The *determinist* and *interactionist* views, on the
other hand, are used to argue in favour of LR.

Although I present these views *vis-à-vis* LR as separate positions,
it should be clear that in reality proponents or opponents of change
sometimes combine elements of other positions to argue their case.
This is especially so for those who adopt an interactionist view of
language and reality. Therefore, the association of particular authors
or researchers with a position does not imply that they merely argue
their case from that position.

Arguing against language reform: do not change language, change society!

The supporters of the 'language reflects reality' view are less strongly
inclined to call for linguistic action since they doubt that language
change would be able to bring about desired social change. They
argue that sexist practices in language mainly result from prevailing
sexist attitudes of their users who are living in communities which

do not promote the equal treatment of women and men. In their view, the discriminatory treatment of women, women's oppression or women's subordinate status are not *caused* or *determined* by oppressive language practices but are merely *reflected* in them. Propagating linguistic reform is therefore seen as relatively futile in the struggle for the equality of the sexes. Instead they would like to see a more concerted effort in promoting social change and at making attempts to change sexist attitudes to obtain equal treatment of the sexes. They argue that, over time, these social actions will lead to linguistic change. Robin Lakoff's (1975: 47) stance on the desirability on LR illustrates this point of view:

> But it should be recognized that social change creates language change, not the reverse; or at best, language change influences changes in attitudes slowly and indirectly, and these changes in attitudes will not be reflected in social change unless society is receptive already.

Alla Martynyuk, a Russian linguist who has undertaken some contrastive studies of linguistic sexism in Russian and English (Martynyuk 1990a, 1990b), expresses not only a similar view about the relationship between linguistic and social change but also criticises feminists for their simplistic view of the relationship between language and social reality:

> Feminists' compliments to Russian [*regarding its so-called frequent use of gender-neutral occupational terms – author*] probably come from their simplistic view of the relations between language and social phenomena. Language is rather sluggish compared with social development and even revolutionary events cannot revolutionize a language overnight. . . . It is obvious that the attempts of the feminists at reforming a specific language will remain a sort of intellectual exercise until and unless there is enough social urgency and awareness to alert lay language users. (Martynyuk 1990b: 109)

Arguing in favour of change

Language change lags behind social change

The 'language reflects social reality' view does not completely exclude the desirability of, or even necessity for, linguistic action. In fact, a substantial group of proponents of official guidelines for nonsexist language use subscribe to this view and nevertheless argue in favour of change because *language change lags behind changes in social and cultural practices*. In other words, they claim that the current portrayal of women (and men) is outdated and does not reflect the changes in the position and roles of women in society. An example often quoted to illustrate this linguistic lag, for English, is the continued discriminatory practice of differentiating titles for women according to their marital status (i.e. *Mr* vs *Mrs* and *Miss*) in view of legislation barring discrimination on the basis of marital status as well as in view of the changing patterns in cohabitation, and the lack of appropriate occupational terms for women. A more international example relates to the continued lack of appropriate occupational nouns for women which reinforces their invisibility and secondary status despite their ever-increasing presence in a great variety professions and occupations.

Among the best-known proponents of the linguistic lag argument are the American freelance editors Casey Miller and Kate Swift, authors of *Words and women, new language in new times* and *The handbook of nonsexist writing for writers, editors and speakers* who believe that language needs a bit of a push to catch up with changed times.

Another well-known author of non-sexist guidelines, Bobbye Sorrels (1983), lists ten reasons why people should use non-sexist communication patterns. Among the more prominent reasons are those stressing the point that sexist language is outdated and no longer relevant in today's society:

> Whereas in the past society virtually restricted males to certain roles and females to others, such restrictions no longer exist. Therefore, communication symbols based on past roles simply do not portray current conditions properly. Instead they distort reality. They constitute an anachronism in the course of human events. Cannot and do not women work as police officers, deliver mail, practice law, and serve in the army? Yet, the words *policeman, mailman, lady attorney,* and *infantryman* deny that they can and do perform these roles. (Sorrels 1983: 2)

Sexist language is the cause of women's oppression

A determinist view of the relationship between language and reality sees language as a dominant, if not central force in creating as well as maintaining the unequal treatment of the sexes in society. In the eyes of the proponents of the 'strong version' of the Sapir–Whorf hypothesis, women's oppression and women's subordinate status in society has a causal link to their treatment and representation in language. Dale Spender's views about language in *Man made language* illustrate this thinking about language and women. She expresses a determinist view when she interprets the Sapir–Whorf hypothesis as 'it is language which determines the limits of our world, which constructs our reality' (Spender 1980: 139). Furthermore, she asserts that

> language helps form the limits of our reality. It is our means of ordering, classifying and manipulating the world. It is through language that we become members of a human community, that the world becomes comprehensible and meaningful, that we bring into existence the world in which we live. (Spender 1980: 3)

According to Spender and others supporting this view, it is men who have control of language in a patriarchal society. They are the ones who can name, define, encode and change meanings. The result is a language which is literally *man-made* and which constructs and presents reality from a male perspective. Not surprisingly, many women feel alienated from this language, because it fails to express their meanings, their experiences and perspectives which in turn leads to their subordinate status in society.

For many supporters of this view language holds the key to women's liberation. Language is seen as both an instrument of oppression and liberation. Spender, as one of the more outspoken proponents of this view, believes that language can be reformed and changed in favour of women.

> It may not be easy to break out of the patterns of thinking and believing into which our society and language have led us, but it is possible. Language is a human product, it is something which human beings have made, and which can be modified. We can – with perseverance – posit alternatives which are readily available within our society. We can make the effort to formulate possibilities at the periphery of our cultural conditioning and to reconceptualize our reality: we can generate new meanings – and we can validate them. (Spender 1980: 3)

Spender advocates that women reject the male-only validated meanings, create their own meanings, label their experiences and validate them.

A place in language for women and 'writing the body'

Language also plays a central role in accounting for women's oppression and subordination in the works of feminist scholars and writers influenced by postmodern approaches to language, psychoanalytic theory and deconstruction. Work by French feminists Hélène Cixous, Julia Kristeva and Luce Irigaray, for example, has a clear focus on language as a key to understanding women's status in society. These writers have had a major influence on feminist scholarship in other parts of the world (especially the English-speaking world) in many disciplines of the humanities and some social sciences.

Although their ideas and theories have not yet had a major influence on the area of LP, including feminist LP, it is nevertheless important to acknowledge their stance *vis-à-vis* LR.

Unfortunately in the context of this book I cannot do full justice to the immensity and complexity of the theories of language and gender associated with these thinkers. I urge readers wishing to explore their theories to such excellent introductory texts as Marks and de Courtivron (1981), Moi (1985) as well as the works of the authors themselves.

My concern here is to identify whether or not their thinking about language and women's status supports the idea of LR.

The work of French feminists such as Hélène Cixous, Julia Kristeva and Luce Irigaray has been informed and influenced by Lacanian psychoanalytical theory which, in turn, was inspired by the work of Sigmund Freud. Lacan strongly believes in the centrality of language in the construction of the self (the individual, the subject). Lacan asserts that a child's development of its subjectivity (identity) occurs through the process of language learning and involves moving through various stages ('Orders' in Lacanian terminology). At first a child finds itself in the *Imaginary Order* (roughly speaking, this order corresponds to Freud's pre-Oedipal period). Here the child does not have its own identity as it seems to be part of the mother's body. Developing a sense of self involves moving out of this *Imaginary Order* and taking up one's place in the *Symbolic Order*. The *Symbolic Order* is Lacan's term for society including the social, cultural and other semiotic practices that regulate society. Taking up one's place in the Symbolic Order involves a process of both individualisation and socialisation of which language learning is a fundamental process. Through language a child learns to distinguish itself from others in various ways. The use of the word 'I' is evidence that a child can recognise itself as a separate entity from others expressed through words like 'you', 'he', 'she'.

Of importance to feminists is the fact that Lacan, building upon Freud's theories, claims that the *Symbolic Order* is ruled by the *Law of the Father* or by the *authority of the Phallus*, and that boys and girls enter the Symbolic Order differently. Consequently, they have a different relationship to language. This is due to the boys' and girls' different experiences of the castration complex – a Freudian concept which has been maintained in Lacanian psychoanalytical theory. Rosemary Tong, (1989: 221) writing from a feminist perspective, explains this as follows:

> Boys experience the process of splitting from the mother differently than girls do. In the Oedipal phase, the male child rejects identification with his mother . . . and identifies instead with his anatomically similar father, who represents the Symbolic Order, the word . . . On account of their anatomy, girls cannot fully accept and internalize the Symbolic Order.

Because the Symbolic Order is ruled by the Law of the Father, which women, because of their anatomy, cannot fully accept or internalise, they are in a way excluded from this Order or are marginalised within it. This marginalised position leads to their oppression. With regard to language, the Symbolic Order can sustain only one language. This language is characterised by binary oppositions ('presence of' or +, and 'lack of' or –). Since language is closely linked to sexuality in this theory, the binary oppositions involving terms and concepts like 'male' and 'female', 'masculine' and 'feminine' are constructed on the basis of the human genitals. Since the female genitals are described as lacking a penis, woman is thus described as the negative pole of the binary opposition 'male–female'.[3] Furthermore women's marginalised position in the Symbolic Order also means that they are deprived of a language which can express *their* feelings, experiences and subjectivity.

This view of language, sometimes referred to as *Lacanian linguistics*, is one of determinism. The determinism lies not only in the fact that language constructs the self but also the fact that a child's entry into the Symbolic Order involves taking up its place in a pre-existing order. The process of language learning involves the acquisition of a linguistic system in which meanings are fixed. Cameron (1985: 124) remarks:

> In fact it seems to me that despite all their disclaimers, despite their awareness of the contextuality of meaning, Lacan and the Lacanians do indulge in a covert Saussurean determinism, which allows meanings to be fixed (though liable to 'slippage') by the linguistic system. For the important concept in Lacanian accounts of language acquisition is the idea of *inserting oneself in a pre-existing order* and it is difficult to see how anyone could do this unless the order, and the meanings it made available, were fixed and stable, produced outside the individual and enjoined on her as the price of entry into human society.

The Lacanian account of the development of the self or a person's subjectivity has been used by some feminists to account for women's oppression. However, it is difficult to see how such a deterministic approach to language and the place of women allows for any changes, let alone linguistic change.

However, some feminist thinkers whose work was inspired by Lacan have moved beyond the stifling determinism found associated with Lacan's interpretation of the relationship between language and the sexes. In particular, Luce Irigaray and Hélène Cixous believe that language change is feasible and they advocate some forms of linguistic action which would benefit women. Here I'll briefly review Kristeva's, Cixous's and Irigaray's main ideas regarding language and the possibility of language change.

Julia Kristeva's work, which was influenced by Derrida's criticism[4] of Lacan, challenges the 'anatomy is destiny' view inherent in Lacan's theory. She argues that the position a child takes up in the Symbolic Order is not one determined only or mainly by its sexual anatomy but by its identification with the mother or the father. In other words, girls do not necessarily have to identify with the mother and boys with the father: there should therefore not be an equation between 'female' and 'feminine', between 'male' and 'masculine'. Men can take up a feminine position in the Order and women a masculine position. Kristeva also postulates the existence of a semiotic order in the pre-Oedipal phase which is linked to a child's oral and anal drives (i.e. Lacan's *Imaginary Order*). These drives are suppressed upon entry into the Symbolic Order but they are sometimes 'discernible in linguistic discourse through rhythm, intonation, gaps, meaninglessness and general textual disruption' (Cameron 1985: 126). According to Kristeva, the feminine subject position in the Symbolic Order is linked more strongly to the pre-Oedipal phase which will be marked in the person's language. For her, some form of liberation could come for women if there was a greater acknowledgement of the interplay of the semiotic and Symbolic Order. Nevertheless, this interpretation does not fundamentally challenge the phallologocentric Symbolic Order.

Hélène Cixous, whose work also shows substantial traces of Derrida's criticism of Lacanian theory, sees linguistic action as an important step to freeing women from the oppressive masculine, phallologocentric Symbolic Order. Like Derrida, Cixous objected to the binary oppositions that characterise the language of the Symbolic Order which she calls *masculine (writing)*. In this theory of language the most fundamental opposition is the one between man and woman, which defines the man as the self and the woman as his other. Cixous believes that women cannot express themselves in a phallologocentric language. She advocates radical linguistic action on behalf of women which would involve women *writing themselves out of the language constructed by men* and creating their own *feminine writing*. This type of writing will be able to express what was classified as unthinkable or unthought in masculine writing. According to Cixous, *feminine writing* closely resembles female sexuality which is open and multiple and is not bound by the traditional rules of syntax. Finally, Cixous believes that this style of writing contains 'the very possibility of change, the space that can serve as a springboard for subversive thought, the precursory movement of a transformation of social and cultural standards' (Cixous 1981: 249).

Luce Irigaray's critique of Lacanian linguistics, like Derrida's, challenges Lacan's refusal to accept a plurality of language/sexuality in the Symbolic Order. Irigaray postulates that women have their own language which is fundamentally different from that of men's (parading as the universal language in a patriarchal system) but that this language is not simply *repressed* (as is the semiotic order in Kristeva's theory) but *suppressed*, actually denied any existence in a patriarchal system, the Symbolic Order which is phallologocentric.

> The question of language is closely allied to that of feminine sexuality. For I do not believe that language is universal, or neutral with regard to the difference of the sexes. In the face of language, constructed and maintained by men only, I raise the question of the specificity of a feminine language; of a language which could be adequate for the body, sex and the imagination . . . of the woman. A language which presents itself as universal, and which is in fact produced by men only, is this not what maintains the alienation and the exploitation in and by society. (Irigaray 1985: 62)

Because of this suppression of the feminine in the Symbolic Order, the only definition and description of the feminine we have is that of the *phallic feminine*, i.e. that of the feminine seen through the eyes of the male. Like Kristeva, Irigaray believes that the Imaginary Order which women never fully leave behind or with which women have a greater link (because of their different experiences of the castration complex) may hold potential for expressing the 'feminine feminine'.

Irigaray concedes that Western thought and culture are unlikely to embrace a theory of the self which defines the feminine in a positive sense, i.e. not as absence or lack of:

Where woman does not reflect man, *she does not exist* and, will never exist until the Oedipus complex is exploded and the 'feminine feminine' released from its repression. (Irigaray 1985: 74)

However, she does propose strategies which should enable women to experience themselves more positively than their marginalised place in the Symbolic Order allows them to. Two of the strategies involve language. Firstly, Irigaray encourages women to pay attention to the nature of language and to expose the myth of 'male = universal' language as well as to try to speak in an active voice rather than in the passive voice which characterises traditional science.

The other strategy advocated by Irigaray is that of extreme, exaggerated mimicry of patriarchal discourse in order to expose its effects. This strategy is not without its dangers because women might lapse back into 'real' phallocentric discourse.

Linguistic action is an integral part of women's liberation

Advocates of the interactionist view of language and reality are another group who firmly believe in the benefit of LR. Since language not only reflects but also helps to construct and perpetuate a sexist reality, taking linguistic action is not futile. Indeed it can contribute to change, especially by alerting people to the pervasiveness of sexism in all aspects of life, including language. If the aim of feminists and the women's movement is to eliminate all forms of discrimination against women, then it is imperative that action is also taken on the linguistic front. In my opinion the majority[5] of feminist language critics and language planners opting for 'linguistic intervention' can be aligned with this view: they do not assume that language holds the key to women's liberation nor do they believe that taking linguistic action alone will have a drastic effect in reducing discriminatory practices and oppressive situations in other aspects of life. They do believe, however, that linguistic action may give women an opportunity to express their perspectives and experiences, and that linguistic action can increase people's awareness that language is not a neutral medium for transmitting ideas and values.

This overview has shown that language reform is supported by a range of people speaking from different positions and holding different views on the relationship between language and reality. Their differences do not only affect their stance on the viability and the desirability of LR but also what types of LR they consider necessary or desirable to change the androcentric bias in language. The question of *how* to reform and change sexist practices in language is the subject of the next chapter.

Notes

1. For a more detailed account of how this view of language has arisen, see, e.g., Graddol and Swann (1989).
2. Some linguists (e.g. Hellinger 1990) dispute the synonymous nature of the terms *linguistic determinism* and *linguistic relativity*, both of which have been associated with the Whorfian hypothesis. Hellinger (1990: 46) claims that it is a misnomer to speak of linguistic determinism in relation to the Whorfian hypothesis because Whorf never claimed that the relation between language and thought was one of determinacy, rather one of mutual influencing.
3. For a critique of this interpretation, see, e.g., Cameron (1985).
4. In brief, Derrida's work criticised several aspects which characterised the Symbolic Order in Lacanian theory. These included the fact that Lacan only allowed one language (singularity) to prevail in the Symbolic Order as a result of its phallocentrism, the logocentric focus of the Order (i.e. its focus on the spoken rather than written text), and the dualist nature of the Order (i.e. its focus on binary oppositions). He wanted to replace the singularity of language and thought with a plurality and wanted to liberate language/thought from its binary straitjacket. Tong (1989: 222–3) mentions that 'he believed that the Symbolic Order can be resisted by showing how traditional interpretations of texts . . . have suppressed alternative interpretations of them' although he was pessimistic about the chances of reaching this goal because 'the only language he had available, was the logocentric, phallocentric, binary language that constricted his thought . . .'.
5. For example, the work by Frank and Treichler (1989), Hellinger (1990) and Yaguello (1978).

4 How should sexist language be changed?

The planning stage: selection and evaluation of alternatives

If the outcome of the previous stage (see Chapter 3) affirms the desirability of change, language planners need to turn their attention to the question of *how* to reform language to eliminate the problem at stake. Their concern in this stage is with the selection and evaluation of possible alternatives to replace the problematic forms. Finding and selecting viable alternatives is often complex as well as controversial. Although language planners may agree about the need for change, such consensus does not preclude considerable disagreement about the best ways to reform language.

Whereas some planners propose to eliminate sexist language practices by making minor amendments to existing linguistic forms, others suggest more substantial changes including semantic alterations (shifts and extensions of meanings), neologisms, more radical or extensive linguistic innovations such as the creation of an entirely new language and the development of alternative women-oriented discourses which are more capable of expressing a woman's perspective.

The selection of particular strategies for reform and the development of proposals for actual linguistic changes are influenced by a range of factors. In this Chapter I discuss these factors.

Who are the language planners and reformers?

Non-sexist language reform has been and continues to be a language planning activity with a strong grassroots character. It is mainly women from all walks of life with a shared concern about the linguistic portrayal of women (and men) in language and about women's relationship to language who have been responsible for initiating or undertaking language reforms.

Although many women share this concern, their individual experiences, their views on language and their ideological orientation, among other things, have an impact on their reform actions and strategies. For example, a feminist poet who feels she cannot express herself in 'man-made' language will probably opt for different language strategies from the feminist lawyer who seeks to rectify the linguistic exclusion of women in legal texts or from women in a consciousness-raising group trying to express their experiences of living in a patriarchy. In addition, their experiences with language reform may vary substantially: whereas some have considerable experience with forms of language reform, others have not. The level of personal commitment to the issue may also vary among language planners. For example, institutional reformers, e.g. EEO committees, terminology taskforces or language working parties, may not have the same personal commitment to the reforms as individual language planners. This can impact on the selection of reform strategies.

Another important factor which affects the selection of strategies and alternatives is the language reformers' view of language and meaning. People hold very different views on what language is, how it operates, how meaning is created and how linguistic change occurs. Proponents of linguistic change whose views of language have been shaped by specific forms of professional training (e.g. linguistics, literature, philosophy, psychology) will usually select strategies reflecting *their* understanding of language. For example, linguists recognise the existence of distinctive parts of speech (language) which work together to create meaning. Those trained in other disciplines may have different views of language which do not necessitate an examination of the same structural properties of language to study meaning. Proponents of change who believe that it is possible to create gender-neutral meanings by altering the form of words will select different strategies from those who believe all meaning is contextual and that meanings cannot be changed by amending or manipulating form.

In Chapter 3 I showed that one's view of the interaction between language and social reality was a main determinant in the decision to reform or not to reform language. These views of the relationship between language change and social change also influence the selection of strategies and planning of alternatives. Linguistic actions which are inspired by a belief that *linguistic change lags behind social change* are more likely to focus on strategies that will 'amend' the portrayal of the sexes in language so that it more adequately reflects the current status of women and men in a changed and changing society. Those who believe that *sexist language is the cause of women's oppressed status* in society, or that language as we know it is incapable of expressing a woman's perspective, may opt for strategies exposing sexism and may develop a woman-centred language.

Furthermore, the selection of strategies and alternatives to sexist language will also be influenced by the proposed goals of the language reforms. Although the proponents of change share the common goal of wanting to free language from sexism, they may differ considerably in what they consider to be of main concern in attaining this goal. Some are primarily concerned with drawing attention to the discriminatory treatment of women in language rather than with striving for linguistic equality of the sexes in language. Others are mainly concerned with remoulding or reforming language to reach an unbiased representation of both women and men in language. Yet others are mainly interested in creating a new language capable of expressing a woman's point of view. These different goals and concerns will clearly affect the choice of actions and strategies promoted by the party in question. For example, it is more likely that creative neologisms such as *herstory* or *himmicane* will be used by those whose emphasis lies in exposing discriminatory practices in language than by those striving for linguistic equality in the portrayal of the sexes.

Linked to the main goals of the reform is the issue of the target audience for the reforms. The audience also has an effect on the choice of strategies and the types of changes. Target audiences for linguistic change can range from oneself (i.e. the proposer or language planner), one's friends, the 'sisterhood', all women, to specific professional groups such as legislators, journalists, advertisers and publishers of educational materials, and to the entire speech community. Target audiences will vary substantially in their awareness and knowledge of the issue of linguistic sexism as well as in their attitudes towards the need for linguistic change: someone who is sympathetic to change and/or who has a good understanding of linguistic sexism, can be reached and convinced by certain linguistic actions which may be totally inappropriate or useless in the case of a target audience unaware of the issue or hostile to any linguistic change. For example, those concerned with reducing women's alienation from language and language practices primarily target the changes at women who may have experienced similar feelings.

In this case strategies of linguistic creativity and experimentation with word boundaries may not only be tolerated but also preferred by the target audience (e.g. readers of a feminist novel). If, on the other hand, the entire speech community is targeted for the promotion of linguistic equality of women and men, word puns, creative neologisms and other eye-catching innovative practices may cause too much linguistic disruption leading to their rejection.

In the following sections I discuss a range of strategies and types of linguistic changes proposed by feminist language planners and critics. Because many feminist language critics practice what they 'preach', and because many grassroots language reformers can only make their proposals known through personal use, it is not always easy or useful to distinguish between *proposals* for change and *actual changes*. Although I comment mainly on the strategies and types of language reform found in more formal or widespread proposals (e.g. manuals, guidelines and handbooks of non-sexist language), I also refer to some strategies and changes proposed or found in the language practices of feminist authors, speakers and in feminist publications.

My decision to focus primarily on feminist language reform as expressed in guidelines, manuals and other formal proposals is motivated by the fact that the more formal proposals are better documented, thus allowing for cross-linguistic comparisons. Also the adoption of changes proposed in a formal manner can be examined and evaluated more systematically than those changes made at individual levels.

I shall discuss the strategies for language reform and the types of changes proposed in light of the main goals of feminist language reform. These include

(a) a desire to expose the sexist nature of 'patriarchal' language;
(b) a desire to create a new language or reform language to suit the expression of a woman's perspective;
(c) a desire to create a language in which the sexes are treated in an equal and symmetrical manner.

Although I discuss the strategies and changes associated with the different goals separately here, it should be noted that in many planning proposals they are integrated.

The chapter closes with an assessment of the viability of the proposed strategies and alternatives in bringing about the desired changes.

Strategies and changes to expose sexism in language

Causing linguistic disruption

A widespread reaction to the discovery that language, like many other social practices, is affected by sexism is to expose it. This is done by drawing attention to sexist meanings and practices in one's own and other people's language use. Some believe that this type of linguistic action is effective in making the speech community aware of the many ways in which women are discriminated against in language.

The primary aim of this exposure is *to cause some linguistic disruption* to the system of patriarchal language in order to make people think about current language use and practices *vis-à-vis* women and men. Mary Daly, an English-speaking feminist theologian and philosopher, has stated this quite explicitly in some of her works: 'men have starved women's minds through transmitting a poor vocabulary, a shabby symbol system' (Daly 1978: 3). Women should therefore engage in

> breaking the rules of the games, breaking the names of the games, . . .
> letting out the bunnies, the bitches, the squirrels, the cows, the foxy
> ladies, the chicks, the pussy cats, the old bats and biddies so we can
> at least begin to start naming ourselves. (Daly 1978: 7)

Supporters of the linguistic disruption strategy argue that this strategy is necessary as linguistic sexism is often more difficult to combat than other forms of sexism because of its insidious nature. In practising linguistic disruption, speakers not only signal their awareness of sexism but also their rejection of it. Linguistic disruption is also seen as a necessary or inevitable step towards making language more women-centred (see further).

The strategies which are used to attain linguistic disruption tend to involve *linguistic creativity* and *experimentation* with all parts of speech. Some authors disrupt the grammatical system of a language by flaunting rules of gender and number agreement, by not using masculine generics, by reconstituting morphological boundaries in words, and by assigning different genders to words. Examples of these strategies in English include the use of 'singular they' in reference to generic nouns in the singular: according to prescriptive grammars this practice breaks the rules about number agreement. The generic use of the pronoun 'she' constitutes another infringement against grammatical rules which prescribe that the feminine pronoun cannot have generic function as it is always gender-specific.

An example of reorganising the morphological boundary of words on semantic grounds is found in the word 'herstory': although the 'his' in 'history' does not have (free) morpheme status and can therefore not be exchanged for another (free) one, the creation of 'herstory' made up of 'her' and 'story' assumes (free) morpheme status for 'his' and 'her'. Furthermore, the 'his' in 'history does not have etymological connections with the masculine possessive pronoun 'his'. The creation of 'herstory' in analogy with 'history' therefore disregards morphological rules of English. This creation is meant to expose the fact that in patriarchal discourse 'history' is equated mainly with the story of men and not with that of women.

A similar example can be found in German. The feminist author and linguist Luise Pusch creates the word *Maskulinguistik*, which is made up of the words *maskulin* (masculine) and *Linguistik* (linguistics) to refer to the discipline of linguistics as practised by those without a feminist orientation.

For grammatical gender languages such as German, Dutch, Norwegian, Italian and Spanish some women have proposed changes to, or have changed, gender concord rules. In German, words like *wer* (who), *jemand* (someone), *man* (one) are considered masculine for concord purposes. For example, the sentence '*Wer hat seine Tasche vergessen?*' (Who forgot 'his' bag), or the expression *Jemand, der* . . . (Someone, who (masculine)) require a possessive pronoun and a relative pronoun in the masculine gender, i.e. *seine* and *der*. Similarly the following sentence, which is semantically speaking restricted to women, '*man erlebt seine Schwangerschaft immer wieder anders*' (one experiences one's pregnancy differently every time) requires a possessive in the masculine gender, i.e. *seine*. Feminists frequently flaunt these gender concord rules and use the feminine pronoun, especially when the utterance refers to a (predominantly) female experience or group. In a group of women it is most likely to hear the first sentence as '*Wer hat **ihre** Tasche vergessen?*' in which the gender concord rules have been flaunted to reflect the fact that the question is posed to women. Similarly the sentence about pregnancy would be rephrased to eliminate the masculine pronouns, '**frau** *erlebt* **ihre** *Schwangerschaft immer wieder anders*'. This example also includes a lexical innovation *frau* to replace the normal indefinite pronoun *man* which is related to the noun *Mann* (man). Similar concord disruptions have been observed for Dutch in the language used in the feminist magazine *Opzij*, for Danish (Gomard 1985) and for Norwegian (Lunde 1985).

For Italian, Sabatini (1986) proposes to do away with masculine concord rules in cases where adjectives or verbs require concord with two or more nouns in a coordinate noun phrase. Instead of saying *Mario e Paola sono arrivati* (Mario and Paola have arrived), she proposes gender concord with the last noun *Mario e Paola sono arrivate* (feminine, plural) or where there are more than two nouns, gender concord should be ruled by the gender in the majority, e.g. *Carla, Maria, Francesca, Giacomo, Sandra sono arrivate stamattina* (Carla, Maria, Francesca, Giacomo, Sandra arrived this morning).

Luise Pusch and Daniel Eisenberg, the editor of a journal for Hispanic Philology, both propose substantial changes to the gender system of German and Spanish respectively. In response to a request regarding changes to occupational nouns in German, Pusch (1984a) suggests that occupational nouns should be given the neuter gender when they are used in generic function: e.g. *das Student* (the student), *das Lehrer* (the teacher), *das Dekan* (the dean) instead of the current practice of the masculine gender for the generic function. Eisenberg (1985: 193) makes a similar suggestion for Spanish:

> The most important move towards linguistic equality in Spanish would be to expand its vestigial neuter to all parts of speech with gender markers: nouns, adjectives, and pronouns. The neuter would be used when it was undesirable, unnecessary, or impossible to designate a gender; it, rather than the masculine would be the default.

Other writers disrupt spelling conventions and make alternative use of diacritics to pinpoint alleged sexism in language. Again Mary Daly's work *Gyn/ecology* (1978) illustrates this strategy very well for English. Other examples for English include the alternative spelling of the words 'woman' and 'women' as 'womyn' or 'womon' and 'wimmin' to protest against the fact that a woman is defined by men in patriarchal, sexist language and to obliterate its graphemic link with man. In German, feminist authors often spell the indefinite pronoun '*man*' [one] as '*mann*' to highlight its link with the noun '*Mann*' [man]. Similarly the strategy of gender-splitting (see section on linguistic equality) in German is accompanied by graphemic innovation: for instance, some new gender-inclusive generic terms are written in the following way, '*LeserInnen*' [male and female readers], '*LehrerInnen*' [female and male teachers], '*der/die Student In*' [the male/female student].

A strategy used sometimes in spoken English is the deliberate change in stress pattern in generic uses of words such as 'policeman', 'chairman' (i.e. secondary stress is placed on 'man' resulting in the pronunciation [mæn] rather than [mən]. This is done to mark the fact that these words are pseudo-generics.

Making metalinguistic comments both in speech and writing is another strategy to expose sexist practices in language use. In response to the sexist practice of using asymmetrical expressions to refer to women and men, e.g. 'men and ladies', 'the girls in the office', some women will make explicit comments pinpointing this asymmetry along the lines of 'Is woman a dirty word in English?', 'Are there only ladies and no gentlemen left?', 'Do you employ under age females in your office?'.

Another strategy which also has the effect of exposing the discriminatory treatment of women in language is that of inverting sexist expressions and practices so as to make them stand out more. This is usually done in jest, although the reactions by the 'offending' party to this reversal strategy often lack humour. An example of this strategy in German is the creation and use of the title *Herrlein* (little sir/ little mister) in analogy with *Fräulein* (little woman meaning 'Miss') to address unmarried men. This inverts the sexism found in the current address system for women in German which distinguishes between *Frau* (Mrs) for married women and *Fräulein* for unmarried women. Across language communities women have replied to correspondence which addresses them as *Dear Sir, Cher monsieur, Sehr geehrter Herr*, etc. with salutations such as *Dear Madam* or *Dear Ms . . .*, *Chère Madame, Sehr geehrtes Fräulein* irrespective of the addressee's sex to react against the sexist practice of using the masculine form of address generically. An earlier literary example of this strategy is the Norwegian novel by Gerd Brantenberg (1977) entitled *Egalias døtre* (Egalia's daughters) in which women are considered the norm and men are the exception, aberration or dependent on women. Brantenberg's language reflects this reversal by making female occupational nouns generic and by changing surnames to reflect women's primacy: the common surnames found in Norway (and other Nordic countries) consisting of a male first or given name followed by *-(s)sen* or *-(s)son* (meaning 'son of'), such as 'Johansson', are replaced by surnames consisting of a female first or given name followed by *-dotter* (meaning 'daughter of') such as 'Lisdotter'.

Other examples of the inversion strategy usually target the stereotyped descriptions of women and men and their behaviour.

The inverting of stereotyped descriptions of the sexes is seen to be an effective strategy to call attention to this discriminatory practice. One of the early discussions on women, sexism and language in Dutch was published under the title *Vrouwentaal en mannepraat* (The language of women and the chitchat of men) (Brouwer *et al.* 1978) which reverses the stereotype of women's speech as idle, nonsense and trivial talk and men's as serious. Phrases such as 'the new bridegroom was in tears after his unsuccessful dinner', 'Mr Jones, wearing the latest in Italian fashion attire and with immaculate make-up, collected his award for bravery', 'Ms Smith, a leading lawyer in the firm Coke and Coke, and her husband, John, a tall dark-haired beauty attended the charity ball' and 'Yesterday Mr Lamb, a father of four, became the new premier of . . .' invert stereotypes for women and men by describing men primarily in terms of their physical attributes (hair, etc.), their appearance (clothes, make-up, jewellery) as well as their family ties.

Reclaiming pejorative expressions about women by redefining them positively or by returning to older, more positive/neutral meanings is another powerful strategy which causes linguistic disruption and paves the way for a woman-centred language. It not only attracts attention to the sexist ways in which women are defined and described but it also gives women the opportunity to become 'namers' and 'meaning makers' (see section on woman-centred language). This strategy is found in the speech and writing of many feminists as well as in publications subscribing to feminist ideology. The work *Gyn/ecology* by Mary Daly (1978) again provides poignant examples for this strategy. In her work she rejects the negative meanings associated with words like 'hags', 'witches', 'crones' in patriarchal language and encourages women to use them in a positive sense, i.e. to refer to strong, independent and wise women. The word 'spinster' in some feminist writing is also used in a positive sense. In certain circles of the German women's movement the derogatory word *Nutte* (whore) has been reclaimed and used to mark a sense of strength and solidarity among prostitutes. This is especially clear in the compound *Nuttenbewegung* (prostitutes' movement). Similarly, the words *Weib(er)* (woman/women, pejorative) and *Hexe(n)* (witch(es)) are being used in a positive sense by members of the women's movement in Germany. Although this strategy can be effective in drawing attention to the systematic derogation of women's terms in sexist language and can have a liberating effect on female users, there is nevertheless always the risk that the 'uninitiated' wider community will maintain the patriarchal meaning of such terms. This in turn could lead to more women distancing themselves from women who call themselves 'hags', 'crones' or 'witches'.

Other forms of linguistic disruption include the creation of new expressions to air one's dissatisfaction with patriarchal language practices. Words like 'sexism' and its equivalents in many languages, 'pornoglossia', 'phallo(logo)centric', *'Maskulinguistik'* all aim to expose the fact that men control language (see also the section on naming). Yet other ways to mark one's dissatisfaction with sexist use of language is to extend or limit the use of particular words and expressions, hoping to bring about certain semantic changes. An example of semantic extension is the use of the words 'prostitute', 'prostitution' and 'to prostitute' in the context of marital sex and love. Hoffmann (1979) examined the language of the feminist movement in Germany and found that marital sex and the position of the wife *vis-à-vis* her husband in sexual matters was often described in terms of prostitution. In evidence he quotes from Alice Schwarzer's book *Der kleine Unterschied und seine großen Folgen'* (The tiny difference with its vast consequences):

> Auch Ehefrauen mit Kleinkindern müssen sich nicht in ungewollten Ehen prostituieren. [Wives with small children don't have to prostitute themselves either in unwanted marriages.]

An example of restricting the semantic range of a word would be limiting the use of 'girl' to female children and teenagers and to contexts where males could be addressed as boys.

Finally, another major strategy is that of exposing semantic cover ups or euphemisms which hide or downplay negative actions of men against women and children. Penelope (1990: 204) encourages women not only to reject words which are agentless or hide agency but also to expose this strategy by making the agents of crimes against women visible because patriarchal discourse does not:

> I've already discussed some of the structural properties of English that make it a superb patriarchal language: . . . the sentence patterns that allow men to suppress their agency (passives, impersonal verbs, psych-predicates); verbs converted into nominals, a process that makes actions in the world into abstractions; the sex-marked predicates, which describe men as the only actors who count heterosexually. There are, in addition, structural ambiguities inherent in compounds like *father rape* and *daughter rape*, descriptions which, despite the word *rape*, incorporate the idea of mutuality suggested by *incest*. Structurally, English makes it impossible to identify the perpetrator and his victim unless we make an effort to do so in every instance.

Creating a woman-centred language

Another important goal for many feminist language reformers is to create a language which is more capable than patriarchal language of expressing reality from a woman's perspective. In patriarchal or sexist language women's ideas, feelings, activities and values are either not expressed or expressed mainly from a male perspective. Language in a patriarchal society is seen to silence women, to treat them as secondary or appendages, to make them invisible. Proposed changes range from the creation of new woman-centred words and meanings, graphemic innovations to developing female discourses and creating an entirely new language. Since the creation of a woman-centred language, or at least of expressions highlighting a woman's perspective, often necessitate disrupting the existing linguistic system, many strategies and mechanisms of change described in the previous section also apply here (e.g. redefining/reclaiming, relabelling, graphemic innovations).

A radical example of the creation of a woman-centred language is the work by science fiction writer and linguist, Suzette Haden Elgin. She created the language Láadan 'for the specific purpose of expressing the perceptions of women' (Elgin 1988: 1). Her science fiction novel *Native tongue* (Elgin 1984) described the process of developing Láadan by women and dispersing it through the community of women. In 1985 she published the first edition of a dictionary and a grammar of Láadan (Elgin 1985) which was revised and extended in a second edition (Elgin 1988). Through her work on the dictionary and the grammar of Láadan, Elgin attempted to demonstrate that the structure of the lexicon and the structural properties of a language (grammar) are shaped by one's perceptions of the world. Women's perceptions of reality and the world are different from those of men and are therefore reflected in the lexicon and grammar of their language. In Láadan, trying to express inner sensory information (e.g. how one feels about something, one's position and attitude towards certain information, one's intentions) is as important as reflecting the material world. Láadan makes use of a large variety of morphemes expressing this inner sensory information, e.g. speech act morphemes, state of consciousness morphemes, repetition morphemes, evidence morphemes. Examining the vocabulary of Láadan, Penelope (1990: 227) points out that it does succeed in presenting a woman's perspective better than English but it is still too patriarchal:

There are words for jesus of nazareth, penis, and testicle, but none for clitoris or Lesbian. So, although the conceptual framework of Láadan differs in significant ways from that of English, what one can think about in it conforms snugly to the thinking of conventional folks. The end result is yet another language governed by patriarchal conceptual structures.

Other radical proposals for a woman's language have come from feminists adopting poststructuralist approaches to language. In the previous chapter I mentioned that French feminist writers Hélène Cixous and Luce Irigaray both believed that women's experiences and perspectives could never be expressed adequately in phallologo-centric discourse which rules the Symbolic Order. Cixous suggested that women write themselves out of the language constructed by men and create their own *écriture féminine* (feminine writing) in order to express what was considered unthinkable or unthought in masculine writing. *Écriture féminine* closely resembles female sexual-ity, which is open and multiple and is not bound by the traditional rules of syntax. Irigaray also speaks of the existence of a woman's language which is suppressed in the Symbolic Order: like Cixous, she believes this language is closely linked to the female body and female sexuality and thus reflects the features of the latter, i.e. plural-ity of meaning and is not structured according to the traditional rules of syntax (Irigaray 1977). Both writers, as well as others sub-scribing to this view of women and language, call for women to explore ways of writing which are in tune with their body rhythms and sexuality (*writing the body*).

Similar attempts at creating a woman-centred language have been undertaken by feminist novelists and poets such as Adrienne Rich (English), Monique Wittig (French and English), Verena Stefan (German) and Gerd Brantenberg (Norwegian): whereas some experi-ment primarily with new grammatical forms of language (new pro-nouns, morpheme boundaries, word order, etc.), others concentrate on lexico-semantic aspects of language.

Other important strategies to attain a woman-centred language include naming, renaming or relabelling, revaluation and changing syntactic structures. Some of these strategies overlap with those used to expose the sexist nature of language, e.g. the process of naming and labelling, revaluating old labels and names.

Naming is seen as one of the most crucial mechanisms to the creation of a language capable of expressing women's perceptions and perspectives. Adopting a predominantly Whorfian view of the relationship between language and reality, many women have been frustated by not being able to name what they experience or feel: not having a word seems to lead to the feeling of not having one's experience legitimated. This in turn often results in the experience being ignored. Spender (1980: 186–7) quotes a conversation from a feminist research group in London in 1976 which illustrates some of the frustration felt by women at not being able to name experiences:

> M: Often I find there aren't any words that can say what I mean.
> J: What's something you want a word for that there isn't a word for now?
> M: I'd like a word for the next time I complain about doing the cooking, and my husband says, 'But dear, you're so good at it.' I want a word that describes what he is doing. Getting out of something by flattering me. He wouldn't dare say 'That's women's work', because we have had that one and he knows he can be shown to be unreasonable. So he tries this one instead. But he's doing exactly the same thing. He's still being unreasonable. He's being *nice* and I'm being *nasty*. If I complain that he's not being fair, he says that I'm just irrational. There's nothing sexist about it, its [sic] just that sort of behaviour that puts me down by being so gracious and polite and leaves me in the wrong. Sometimes I think he's probably right and then I really get mad. And that's it, isn't it. He *is* right. I'm irrational.

Consequently, naming experiences from a female perspective is seen as a fundamental activity in the process of liberating women from patriarchal oppression. Ramsay and Stefanou-Haag (1991: 40–1) write

> Firstly, and most fundamentally, by naming an experience we regain control of our understanding of it and so throw off the internalized oppression which, in the case of sexual harassment, told us that any discomfort we might be feeling was surely our own fault. While an experience remains unnamed, it apparently does not exist except at the level of unverified, illegitimate, individual – and very lonely – response, its cause ignored and objections to its effects silenced. Secondly, by identifying and naming the experience we can share it with others, we can explore and discuss its causes and effects and increase our understanding of it as a social and not an individual phenomenon.

Major fields for naming are those dealing with female sexuality, with female experiences of the way in which men treat women, with female perspectives on life and living in a male-dominated world.

In the area of female sexuality, women not only give names to their experience of sexual encounters and of sexual feelings but also rename body parts, experiences and activities to reflect more accurately women's perceptions thereof. For example, Verena Stefan's book *Häutungen* (Shedding) and the book *Hexengeflüster* (Witches' whispering) have provided German women with a whole range of alternative labels for female genitals and physical experiences. The authors of *Hexengeflüster* (1975: 1) argue:

> Wir wollen uns nicht länger unserer Geschlechtsorgane schämen. Deshalb haben wir das Wort 'Scham' durch Venus ersetzt. Venus ist die römische Göttin des Frühlings, der Fruchtbarkeit, der Gärten, der Liebe und der Schonheit. [We no longer want to be ashamed of our genitals. That's why we have replaced the word 'shame' with Venus. Venus is the Roman goddess of spring, of fertility, of gardens, of love and of beauty.]

Consequently they rename *Schamlippen* (labia, literally shame lips) *Venuslippen* (lips of Venus'), and replace *Schamhaare'* [pubic hair, literally shame hairs] with '*Venushaare*' [hair of Venus). The clitoris is referred to as *unsere Perle in der Muschel* (our pearl in a shell), female genitals are named *Muschel* (shell). Stefan (1976: 107) refers to menstruation blood as *der rote Fluß* (the red stream).

'Sexism', 'androcentrism', 'phallocentrism', 'phallocratic', 'male chauvinism' and many other -isms (and their equivalents in other languages) are (well-known) labels with which women describe the patriarchal and sexist attitudes of men towards women, and refer to the sexist structure of society and institutions. Farley (1978) coined the term 'sexual harassment' to describe the experience many women had in the workplace where they were treated by their environment as sexual objects first and fellow-workers second.

In societies where legal obstacles to name changes are minimal, women are known to change their first names as well as their surnames: for example, the well-known American feminist linguists Cheris Kramer and Julia P.(enelope) Stanley changed their names to Cheris Kramarae, and Julia Penelope respectively. Other names include Birch Moonwomon, Judy Chicago, Olivia Freewoman (see, e.g., Kramarae and Jenkins 1987; Stannard 1977).

The strategy of reclaiming words has already been discussed in relation to exposing sexism in language (linguistic disruption). Commenting on the strategy of reclaiming, Penelope (1990: 215) warns of the dangers of overusing this strategy. Penelope believes that only certain words and expressions should be reclaimed:

The words we decide to reclaim should be those that name a behavior or attitude that enables us to move outside the world as men have named it. They should denote actions and ways of being that reflect a radical valuation of ourselves and of which we can be proud. We will reject words that denote behaviors and traits men believe are positive for women because they are the fetters of which Sapir spoke.

According to Penelope, words like *slut*, *whore*, *gash* and *cunt* should not be reclaimed whereas *bitch*, *dyke*, *crone*, *witch* and *hag* can be revaluated.

Wordplays, neologisms, graphemic experimentations and other signs of linguistic innovation are not only used as strategies to mark disruption from patriarchal language but also to create a woman-centred language. Other examples are 'malestream' for mainstream, 'she/volution' for a description of evolution from a women's perspective.

Although many of the changes proposed are at word level, most feminist language critics implicitly or, less frequently, explicitly state that changing sexist language to create a more woman-centred language also calls for changes at sentence and discourse level. Penelope (1990: 227), who undertook an in-depth analysis of sexism at a syntactic level in the English language, stressed the crucial role of bringing about change at the syntactic level in order to achieve a woman-centred language:

> To date, with the exception of Láadan, the focus of suggested linguistic change has been on new words, and new meanings for old words. While having new words can alter the semantic structure of a vocabulary, simply dropping them into existing syntactic structures doesn't radically change the way we organize our perceptions. Syntactic structures must change, too.

She suggests that, in a woman-centred language, women should appear more often as (active) agents rather than as topics or passive objects. Women must also encourage or urge people to take responsibility for their actions by acknowledging agency. She claims that in patriarchal discourse men select 'the contexts in which they acknowledge their agency' (Penelope 1990: 229). According to Penelope (*ibid.*), men have frequently hidden their agency in contexts where they are the perpetrators of negative actions:

> When men have beaten or raped a woman, they omit explicit reference to their own agency, leaving themselves in the background of their descriptions so that their responsibility isn't directly accessible to our conscious minds.

Striving for linguistic equality of the sexes

Perhaps the most widely publicised concern of feminist language planners is that of striving for linguistic equality of the sexes. The primary emphasis here lies on achieving a balanced and equitable representation of the sexes in language without causing major disruption or changes to the structures of language. Underlying this concern is the view that the language system as we know it is capable of expressing linguistic equality of the sexes provided some proposed changes are implemented. The main strategies to attain this goal are those of gender neutralisation (also called gender abstraction) and gender specification (sometimes referred to as feminisation).

Gender neutralisation

The aim of the gender-neutralisation strategy is to obtain linguistic equality of the sexes by minimising or discarding gender-specific expressions and constructions. The strategy of gender neutralisation entails that any morphosyntactic and lexical features marking human agent nouns and pronouns (or other parts of speech) as masculine or feminine are 'neutralised' for gender, especially in generic contexts. This strategy is sometimes also referred to as 'gender abstraction' because it occasionally recommends the use of an abstract term or word to avoid gender specification in relation to occupational and professional nouns for women and men.

If gender is marked morphologically in an asymmetrical manner (e.g. suffixes are used to mark one gender but not another), the implementation of the gender-neutralisation strategy calls for the elimination of gender-suffixes and proposes the use of one form to designate a person in all three contexts, i.e. in reference to a male, to a female or to a person whose sex is not specified (generic). This strategy has been proposed for, and applied to, most of the Germanic languages including English, Danish, Dutch and Norwegian.

In all these languages occupational and other human agent nouns for women and men are often marked by asymmetrical gender-suffixing practices: female occupational nouns are derived from male ones by adding a gender-suffix to the latter.[1] Examples for English include *poet–poetess, host–hostess, usher–usherette, hero–heroine, aviator–aviatrix*. Danish examples include *lærer–lærerinde* (teacher), *arbejder–arbejderske* (worker/labourer). In Norwegian we find similar examples, such as *lærer-lærerinne* (teacher), *kasserer–kassererske* (cashier). The Dutch language has a wide variety of gender-marking suffixes including -*es* as in *leraar–lerares* (teacher), -*in* as in *boer–boerin* (farmer), -*ster* as in *opvoeder–opvoedster* (educator).

In Chapter 2 I mentioned that many of these suffixed forms not only caused morphological asymmetry but also often had a trivialising effect on the female bearer of the occupational or professional noun, especially in relation to high(er) status professions and occupations. In the case of the languages mentioned above, the gender-neutralisation strategy involves the elimination of the suffixed forms for female professional and occupational nouns and the universal adoption of the masculine/generic form instead. The result of this strategy is said to be the creation of a truly 'gender-neutral' form which can be used in a non-discriminatory way for either sex, both in sex-specific and generic contexts. With reference to some of the examples cited above the impact of this strategy is the removal of the feminine forms, i.e. *poetess, usherette, aviatrix, lærerinde, arbejderske, kassererske, opvoedster*. If it is important or relevant to mark the sex of the person, this could be done lexically, for instance, by means of using the adjectives 'male/female' and their equivalents in the other languages.

The strategy of neutralising occupational and professional nouns for gender has also been suggested for some of the Romance languages; for example, French (e.g. Houdebine 1988) and Spanish (Olivares 1984). These languages, however, have a more complex gender-marking system (see Chapter 2) which involves the marking of gender not only in nouns but also in determiners and other parts of speech (e.g. adjectives). This complicates the implementation of the gender-neutralisation strategy.

People proposing the gender-neutralisation strategy believe and argue that the consistent extension of the masculine generic form to female referents will eliminate or erode any masculine or male connotation of this form and will make it a truly generic form.

The gender-neutralisation strategy can also incorporate the formation of new 'gender-neutral' nouns: this is especially the case where occupational and other human agent nouns have lexical or morphological features associated with maleness. In the Germanic languages mentioned above there is a considerable group of human agent nouns which incorporate the suffix -*man* (English and Dutch, also Swedish), -*mand* in Danish and -*mann* in Norwegian and also German. Examples from these languages include *salesman, chairman, businessman, policeman, formann* (Norwegian, president, chairman), *ombudsman* (Swedish), *formand* (Danish, president, chairman), *styrmand* (Danish, navigation officer), *stuurman* (Dutch, navigation officer), *zakenman* (Dutch, businessman), *Amtmann* (German, public servant). These nouns are seen to be inappropriate forms for generic use. Alternative generic forms are therefore proposed which eliminate the element *man* or its equivalents in other languages. This is partly achieved by creating new words or compounds involving the word *-person* or *-people* (and their equivalents in other languages) leading to nouns such as *salesperson, chairperson, businesspeople, laypeople, varaperson* (Norwegian), *tillitsperson* (Norwegian), *tillitsfolk* (Norwegian), *zakenmensen* (Dutch) or other gender-neutral forms such as *-medlem* (Danish, member of), *-assistent* (Danish/Dutch, assistant), *medarbejder* (Danish, co-worker), *-utøver* (Norwegian), *-valgt* (Norwegian, elected) and *-mitglied* (German, member).

In some cases the gender-neutral generic noun is arrived at by some form of truncation as in the word *chair* for *chairman*, or *ombud* for *ombudsmann* in Norwegian.

Another recommendation to obtain gender neutrality in the case of nouns containing *-man* is that of disposing of the words containing *-man* and replacing them with an existing gender-neutral synonym such as *president* or *head* for *chairman*, or *leder* for *formann*. This strategy is also used to replace the word *man* in the meaning of 'human being'. For example, both French and Spanish consider replacing *homme* or *hombre* with the French and Spanish versions of 'human being', i.e. *être humain* and *ser humano*.

Creating new words or selecting existing gender-neutral words is also proposed for eliminating the use of compounds involving *-lady* and *-girl* and their equivalents in other languages to designate female incumbents of a particular profession or occupation. For example, words like *salesgirl, saleslady, tea-lady, weather girl, cleaning lady, office girl, girl friday* do not have a symmetrical male equivalent. Male salestaff are not referred to as either *salesboys* or *salesgentlemen* but as *salesmen*. Similarly, we do not speak of *weather boys, office boys*, or *cleaning gentlemen*, let alone *tea gentlemen* when referring to men. In Danish, this situation mainly arises in relation to compounds with *-kone, -pige* and *-dame*, e.g. *rengøringskone* (cleaning woman), *kontorpige* (office girl), *kontordame* (office lady/secretary). This is also the case for Norwegian which has the formations *-kone, -pike* and *-dame* as in *vaskekone* (cleaning woman), *stuepike* (chambermaid), *kontordame* (office lady, secretary). For Dutch and German this is especially the case for compounds ending in *-meisje* (Dutch, girl), *-mädchen* [German, girl], and -*dame* [Dutch, German, lady]. Examples include Dutch *kamermeisje* (chambermaid), German *Stubenmädchen* (parlour maid/housemaid) and German *Bardame* (barmaid). Some proponents also wish to eliminate female compounds involving '-woman' and replace them with gender-neutral nouns. Others, however, prefer to keep such formations because they make women more visible.

Gender specification/feminisation

The strategy of gender specification aims at achieving equal treatment of the sexes in language by making the invisible sex (in most cases, women) visible in language through the systematic and symmetrical marking of gender. The strategy of gender specification is therefore often called feminisation. The process of gender specification or feminisation is achieved in a variety of ways depending on the language in question and on the particular type of linguistic invisibility of women. The outcome, however, is more or less identical: if reference is made to a woman, the feminine form is used; if reference is to a man, the masculine form is used. In generic contexts for the most part, both the masculine and feminine forms are used leading to an explicit mentioning of both sexes.

One way of achieving feminisation is the systematic use of the productive suffixes marking feminine gender to form all occupational, professional and other human agent nouns denoting women. This has been proposed for such languages as German, Italian, Spanish, French and Dutch. In the case of German and Italian, the gender-specification strategy has been promoted significantly more than the strategy of gender neutralisation. In the cases of French, Spanish and also Dutch, there has been and continues to be a situation of competition between both strategies in relation to gender marking in occupational nouns, although official guidelines lean more towards the strategy of gender neutralisation for Dutch and feminisation for French and Spanish.

In German the process of feminisation entails forming a suitable feminine equivalent for *ALL* masculine/generic human agent nouns through the use of the main feminine suffix -*in*, which is still very productive. In most instances, this means creating a new form not previously in existence as in *die Pilotin* (the female pilot), or seldom used such as *die Postbotin* (the female postal carrier). In some instances, another feminine gender-marking suffix – e.g. -*euse* is replaced by the *-in* suffix as in *Friseurin* rather than *Friseuse* (female hairdresser).

In Dutch, French, Italian and Spanish, there are a number of feminine suffixes which vary in the extent to which they are still productive and they are associated with connotations of triviality. In these languages proponents of the feminisation strategy tend to select those feminine suffixes which are still (partly) productive and which have no or few pejorative connotations to promote the visibility of women in language.

In Dutch, for example, the feminine suffixes of *-e*, *-ster* and *-a* (the latter for Latin loanwords) and to a much lesser extent the suffixes *-euse* and *-rice* are promoted to form (new) female occupational nouns. Examples of this include the formation *medewerk***ster** (female co-worker), *verslaggeef***ster** (female journalist), *pilot***e** (female pilot), *agent***e** (female police officer), *komponist***e** (female composer), *advokat***e** (female lawyer), *doctorand***a** (female doctoral candidate), *regiss***euse** (female film director), *redakt***rice** (female editor).

In French, the strategy of feminisation leads primarily to the promotion of dual articles for epicene nouns ending in *-e* as in *un*/*une architecte* (an architect), in *-iste* as in *le*/*la dentiste* (the dentist), in *-aire* as in *le*/*la bibliothécaire* (the librarian), in *-ologue* as in *le*/*la psychologue* (the psychologist). Furthermore, it leads to the promotion of a 'new' feminine suffix *-eure*[2] as in *auteure* (author), *professeure* (professor), *docteure* (doctor) and to the systematic use of other (existing) feminine suffixes to mark female incumbents of jobs whose titles only exist in the masculine: for example **la** *présidente* as the female equivalent of *le président* (the president), **une** *écrivaine* (a female author).

For Italian, ways of feminisation similar to those found in French are being proposed. They include the use of dual articles/determiners in front of so-called common gender (epicene) nouns as in *il*/*la presidente* (the male/female president = the president), *il*/*la generale* (the general), and the consistent use of the suffix *-trice* to form the feminine equivalent of masculine occupational, professional nouns ending in *-tore* – e.g. *dottrice* (not *dottoressa*) for *dottore* (doctor); *ispettrice* for *ispettore* (inspector). The extended use of the suffix *-a* for the feminine equivalents of masculine words ending in *-aio, -ario, -iere, -o, -sore* is another form of feminisation. Examples include *notai***a** (female notary) *segretari***a** (female secretary of . . .), *ingegnier***a** (female engineer), *medic***a** (female doctor). The promotion of words such as *avvocata* (female lawyer) and *professora* (female professor) also involves the process of replacing one feminine suffix, -*essa* with another one, -*a*. The forms *avvo-catessa* and *professoressa* are replaced by *avvocata* and *professora* respectively. The main reason for this replacement in Italian and, to some extent, in French is to avoid certain feminine suffixes which are seen to have particularly pejorative or trivialising connotations; they include -*essa* in Italian and -*esse* as well as -*euse* in French.

Suggestions for gender specification in Spanish have included some more drastic changes to the present gender-marking system. For example, Eisenberg (1985) suggests that all human agent and occupational nouns ending in -*o* should designate males whereas all such nouns ending in -*a* should refer to women. Those nouns ending in -*a* which refer to male incumbents should become nouns indicating female incumbents. An alternative form ending in -*o* should be created to denote male incumbents. Examples cited by Eisenberg include the newly formed *el pianisto* to denote a male pianist, and *astronauto* to denote a male astronaut. Those human agent and occupational nouns (ending in -*o*) for which only a masculine form exists, should also have a feminine form created by replacing the 'masculine' suffix -*o* with a 'feminine' suffix -*a*: *ministra* (female minister), *abogada* (female lawyer, and *ingeniera* (female engineer) are examples. For other nouns not ending in either -*o* or -*a*, Eisenberg (1985: 194) recommends gender neutralisation: 'However, most nouns not ending in -*o* or -*a* could become neuter: "un papel importante" would then be neuter in noun, adjective, and article. . . .'

Gonzalez (1985), writing about Puerto Rican Spanish, mentions a less radical form of gender specification for that variety of Spanish. She suggests that there is a tendency to achieve gender balance and women's visibility in Puerto Rican Spanish by means of creating feminine forms ending in -*a* for words which do not have a female equivalent. For example, *supervisora* (female supervisor); *conductora* (female driver). For Spanish Spanish, Nissen (1986) advocates a similar less radical form of gender specification: he argues that there is already a trend in Spanish towards gender specification.

As I mentioned earlier in this section, the strategy of gender specification aims to make women visible by creating parallel terms for male and female incumbents of professions. In contexts where the reference is non-gender specific or generic, this strategy requires the mentioning of both genders or terms for women and men. German feminist language planners have called this practice of mentioning both genders in a generic context gender splitting.

The following examples, taken from German and Italian respectively, illustrate the practice of gender splitting:

Jede(r) StudentIn muss seinen/ihren StudentInnenausweis immer vorzeigen wenn . . . [Each student must be able to present his/her student identity card when . . .]

In this German example, gender splitting has affected (1) the determiner *Jede(r)* – the bracketed form is the masculine, (2) the head noun *StudentIn*, which incorporates *Student* and *Studentin* in the graphemic innovation *StudentIn*, (3) the possessive pronoun *seinen/ihren* with *seinen* being the masculine form and *ihren* the feminine form, both referring to *StudentIn-*; and (4) the compound *StudentInnenausweis*, which incorporates the plural forms of *Student* and *Studentin*.

Marguerite Yourcenar è una delle più grandi tra scrittrici e scrittori viventi. [Marguerite Yourcenar is one of the greatest living female and male authors.] (Based on Sabatini 1986)

Eduardo De Filippo è stato uno die più grandi tra attori e attrici italiane. [Eduardo De Filippo was one of the greatest Italian male and female actors.] (Lepschy 1987: 167)

In these two examples from Italian, the gender splitting is observed in the respective phrases *scrittrici e scrittori* and *attori e attrici*. These examples, however, also show some changes in gender-agreement rules. In traditional Italian grammar dual noun phrases, including a masculine noun, will be treated as masculine thus requiring agreement in the masculine gender. The proposal put forward by Sabatini (1986) and quoted by Lepschy (1987) in his example entails gender agreement with the last-mentioned noun in the complex noun phrase. In the first example *viventi* agrees with the noun *scrittori* which is in the masculine plural triggering a masculine plural in *viventi*. In the second example we get the reverse: *attrici* is a feminine plural leading to a feminine plural ending in *italiane*.

Another example of gender splitting is the use of double (dual) third person pronouns in English *he or she* (and its many variations, e.g. *s/he, she or he*), in Dutch *hij of zij*, in Danish *han eller hun*, in Norwegian *han og hun* and in German *er oder sie*.

Before I move on from the *description* of various strategies and types of linguistic changes to an *assessment of their viability*, it is important to reiterate that the outlined strategies for change should not be seen as totally distinct and incapable of being integrated. In fact in my previous discussion there were already quite a few examples which showed that languages often integrate various strategies (e.g. Spanish, French, English and Dutch).

Assessing and evaluating the (proposed) strategies and changes

Linguistic viability and social effectiveness

Assessing the viability of any proposed strategies and changes is a very important task for language planners. This is especially so when these proposed changes are targeted at modifying the language behaviour of a speech community at large.

In the case of language reform which is motivated by social concerns rather than purely aesthetic ones, language planners should evaluate the reform proposals not only in terms of their *linguistic viability* but also in terms of their *social effectiveness*. In other words, the language planner should try to assess the linguistic and social soundness of the proposals.

Except in cases where the LP process is a carefully executed task in the hands of an expert LP agency, this assessment of the viability of particular reform proposals and changes is not always carried out, or not always at the *right* stage. Especially in cases of *ad hoc* LP this crucial stage in language reform is often overlooked or ignored, either because it is not recognised as important or the urgent need for change makes such an assessment unviable. In some instances, evaluation of the various proposals does take place but only after they have already been implemented which then makes it an evaluation of the entire LR or LP activity.

This observation also fits the description of feminist LP and its assessment of alternative proposals. For example, some proposals were debated in academic circles (e.g. the pronoun question in English), some were never formally evaluated (e.g. the elimination of stereotypes), whereas others were evaluated after they had been distributed and implemented through guidelines (e.g. the proposal to change titles for women in English).

Although the absence or lack of a thorough assessment of the proposed strategies and suggested alternatives can be considered a weakness in a 'textbook' approach to LP, there is very little evidence in the case of non-sexist LR to suggest that a more thorough approach to this stage would have resulted in a greater acceptance of the proposals. After all, non-sexist LR is a form of sociolinguistic LP closely linked to social issues which may not always be so amenable to manipulation. It may, however, have led to more fine-tuned proposals.

If strategies for linguistic changes as well as proposed changes *are* the subject of evaluation, they should be assessed in terms of their ability to reflect and/or bring about social change and in terms of their linguistic viability.

Elsewhere (Pauwels 1989a, 1991b) I have stressed that non-sexist language proposals whose main aim is the linguistic equality of the sexes and which are targeted at public language use in a speech community should be guided by the *principles* of *social effectiveness* and *linguistic viability*.

The proposed strategies should be capable of bringing about social change and of reflecting changes with regard to the status of women and men in society: i.e. they should be socially effective.

Proposed changes should, however, also be linguistically viable: an assessment should be made of the extent to which they affect the structure and use of a language. For example, changes that do not affect the structural properties of a language may be more easily accepted than those that do. Similarly, changes that run counter to 'natural' (uncontrolled or subconscious) language change may be more difficult to accept than those that are in line with the latter. Sometimes changes by means of neologisms are more difficult to implement than those by means of semantic shift. On occasions, the reverse may be the more successful scenario. Furthermore, the linguistic viability of a proposed change can also be influenced by other factors such as degree of linguistic prescriptivism: if an alternative is promoted which, despite widespread use throughout the community, is seen to violate deeply ingrained prescriptive rules, its introduction may be opposed vigorously.

Assessing the social effectiveness of a proposal

Psychological tests, psycholinguistic experiments and questionnaires have so far been the main tools used to gain insights into people's cognitive imagery associated with sexist and non-sexist expressions. These tests usually try to establish the extent to which a particular non-sexist alternative form or structure can reduce or avoid the biased (in most cases, male-biased) interpretation affecting the sexist form or structure. For example, if the mental or cognitive imagery associated with the non-sexist alternatives for human agent nouns (significantly) reduces the interpretation that the person referred to by the noun is male, then alternatives may be con-sidered socially effective: they manage to represent the sexes more equitably or make women (men) more visible, which is the main *social aim* of this type of language planning.

In Chapter 2 I quoted a number of studies which examined how people understood masculine generic nouns and pronouns. Although these examinations focused mainly on the impact of *sexist* forms, they nevertheless provided some information on people's interpretation of non-sexist alternatives. For example, Bem and Bem's (1973) early study on the use of the masculine generic and non-sexist generics in job advertisements found evidence that gender-biased generics can influence women's and men's pursuit of employment options. In particular, women's interest in applying for jobs was higher when masculine generics were avoided. Another early study is that by Schneider and Hacker (1973) which investigated the use of masculine generic *Man* in chapter titles in educational textbooks. They found that if the masculine generic *Man* titles were replaced with more gender-neutral titles, students were less likely to associate male-only mental imagery with the title: they collected more diverse pictures and images to illustrate a chapter when gender-neutral titles were used. Moulton *et al.* (1978) examined the use of alternatives to the masculine generic pronoun (he) in English by sentence completion tasks followed by essay writing. They found that if students were given prompts which used *he/she* rather than masculine generic *he*, they were less likely to write essays about males only or predominantly males. Stericker's (1981) study showed that women's interest in jobs was encouraged by the use of the dual pronoun *he or she* in job advertisements and descriptions. Hellinger (1990) mentioned a similar finding for German as a result of gender-splitting practices in job advertisements.

Although there have been some useful studies of this kind, as illustrated by those mentioned above, it is nevertheless important to point out some limitations of these and other similar studies. Firstly, most of the studies have been conducted on English, especially in the American context leaving us with little or no information about other languages. Secondly, the main topics of examination have been the use of alternative forms for masculine generic nouns (especially those containing -*man*) and the masculine generic pronoun *he*. Admittedly, these examples of sexist language use are considered to be among the most controversial and the most difficult to change, yet they are only a small proportion of the sexist and non-sexist language use issues. A third limitation is that of methodology: many of these studies used American college or university students and college staff. Students are known to be quite a distinctive group (i.e. different from the community at large) when it comes to social, political and other related issues. They are therefore perhaps not the best group to use to establish possible trends or attitudes in the community. Although most researchers take great care of having a numerically representative sample, the sample universe from which they draw is usually not characterised by great diversity: for example, students' ages and educational achievements tend to be the same. A lack of diversity can reduce the overall validity of the findings for a population which is much more diverse than that tested. Furthermore, the 'laboratory type' setting and the experimental nature of the task may also make it more difficult to transpose the findings to people's behaviour in everyday language settings. This is not to say that these studies are unreliable or flawed: on the contrary, most of these are very rigorous studies with sampling and processing techniques appropriate to the discipline. However, assessing possible alternatives involves gathering opinions, views and information from a wider range of people and on a greater range of topics via a variety of methods. This may provide some interesting topics for aspiring researchers!

Assessing the linguistic viability of a proposal

Assessing the linguistic viability of proposed changes has been predominantly the domain of linguists and language planners with linguistic training. Usually such evaluations involve gathering information about past attempts at linguistic reform and change as well as studying natural language change involving the lexico-semantic as well as morphosyntactic levels of language. Furthermore, it investigates whether the adoption of the alternative proposal would lead to a likely disruption of the language system or could be integrated into it without 'major' changes. Linguistic assessments of an alternative also focus on such issues as the functional equivalence and the stylistic range of the alternative form *vis-à-vis* the form it is going to replace.

Linguistic assessments of non-sexist proposals have sometimes taken the form of debates between linguists arguing in favour of or against the proposals from a primarily linguistic angle (see section on the replacement of the masculine generic pronoun *he*). In other cases linguists have gathered historical evidence (e.g. Bodine 1975 in relation to singular *they*) or presented phonological and grammatical information (Bolinger 1980) in favour of or against proposed changes.

It is unfortunate that there have been few assessments which have thoroughly examined *both* the social effectiveness and the linguistic viability of the alternative proposals. This is partly the result of feminist language reform being mainly a grassroots reform movement in which assessments were often undertaken *ad hoc* or 'after the facts'. Another reason could be that the examination of each of these issues requires specialised expertise a combination that is not usually found in researchers.

In the following sections I nevertheless try to bring together information on the linguistic viability and the social effectiveness assessments of three proposals that have received much attention. I present them as case studies illustrating various aspects of the evaluation process which should form part or has formed part of the *planning* stage. The first case study is concerned with the selection of appropriate alternatives for masculine-generic occupational and human agent nouns in Dutch and German. The second case study concerns an assessment of the alternatives to masculine generic *he* in English. The last case study assesses the proposed strategies to rectify the gender imbalance in courtesy/honorific titles for women and men in English.

Case study 1: Non-sexist alternatives for occupational nouns and titles

The assessment of non-sexist alternatives for occupational nouns and titles has received more attention than any other aspect of linguistic sexism. This is largely because of its link to the introduction of anti-discrimination legislation, especially in the area of employment. Such legislation has had an impact on language, especially in relation to the language used in job descriptions, job advertisements, and other job selection procedures (including interviews) which had to be free from gender bias. Consequently, terminology commissions and other agencies regulating occupational nomenclature were asked to examine occupational nouns and titles for gender bias and, if necessary, to redress any such bias by changing the terminology. Usually such agencies or commissions then sought advice from language planners regarding appropriate gender-inclusive and non-sexist occupational designations. In most cases, two major strategies were proposed to address the current gender bias in occupational nouns: (1) gender neutralisation, involving the use of one noun to refer to either sex or both sexes, and (2) gender specification, involving the use of parallel terms for male and female incumbents of occupations and professions.

Whereas the selection of one of these strategies was considered relatively unproblematic for some languages (e.g. English), choosing between these strategies engendered substantial debates with regard to others. This is well documented for languages such as Dutch and German. In The Netherlands,[3] the proponents of gender neutralisation emphasised linguistic arguments, whereas those supporting the introduction of gender-specific occupational terminology gave more weight to the social effectiveness principle. Brouwer (1985a, 1985b, 1991a) and Ruysendaal (1983) have argued in favour of gender neutralisation and Van Alphen (1983, 1985) in favour of gender specification. In their argumentation both parties addressed the principles of social effectiveness and linguistic viability. Brouwer and, especially, Ruysendaal interpret social effectiveness of a proposed change as its ability to detract attention away from the category 'sex'. In other words, the aim is to have a society in which a person's sex has no relevance or significance for his or her occupational status. It should make no difference whether a woman or a man does a particular job. Brouwer and Ruysendaal believe that this is best achieved by means of the strategy which *eliminates* differential treatment (i.e. gender neutralisation). Both authors also mention the fact that the negative and trivialising connotations of some female occupational nouns containing derivational suffixes obstruct the social equality of the sexes in the workforce. Huisman (1984) and Brouwer (1991b) report on small-scale surveys among women in the workforce who express a preference for gender-neutral nouns.

For Van Alphen (1983, 1985), on the other hand, social effectiveness means showing that there are an increasing number of women in all areas of the paid workforce and that women are equally as capable as men of engaging in all types of occupations and professions. Linguistically this is best achieved by making women's participation in the (paid) workforce visible, i.e. by having gender-specific occupational nouns.

Both parties also address the issue of linguistic viability of their proposed options. Brouwer and Ruysendaal argue that gender neutralisation/abstraction is the more viable of the two strategies for the following reasons. Firstly, the gender-neutralisation option is more in tune with current linguistic developments in Dutch. The Dutch language is becoming more analytic, disfavouring the use of gender-marking suffixes: existing female-specific occupational titles and nouns have experienced a substantial drop in use, as testified by their reduced entry into the dictionary. A second related reason for favouring the gender-neutralisation option has to do with speaker insecurity regarding the formation of new female-specific nouns. Dutch has four feminine suffixes which are still partially productive, -*e*, -*es*, -*in* and -*ster*. As a result, language users are sometimes faced with the difficult choice of which suffix to use when forming a new female occupational noun. It has been shown that it is not only 'ordinary' language users but also linguists who experience difficulties selecting the appropriate suffix. Brouwer (1991a: 76–7) also points out that Dutch already has a large number of occupational nouns which are gender neutral and from which it is difficult to derive female-specific nouns. She concludes (p. 77):

> The process of feminizing within the Dutch language does not guarantee perfect visibility of women in the employed population; the inconsistency of feminizing would certainly not favour equal rights.

Both Brouwer and Ruysendaal also argue against feminisation because it runs counter to the principle of 'linguistic economy' (least effort/simplicity) and may cause stylistic problems: in generic contexts two nouns will have to be used constantly to guarantee the equal treatment of the sexes. This practice is regarded as cumbersome and awkward.

Van Alphen (1983, 1985) considers the gender-specification strategy to be linguistically viable because, in contrast to Brouwer's and Ruysendaal's evidence, she believes that there is a definite tendency in Dutch to emphasise gender differentiation, as evidenced in the growing feminisation of occupational nouns recorded by Adriaens (1981). According to Van Alphen, some feminine suffixes – especially -*e*, -*euse* and -*rice* as well as -*a* for Latin words – are still very productive and should therefore be used to form new female occupational nouns. In response to the claim that feminine suffixes carry connotations of triviality or are negative, she retorts that it is better to be named, even if there are negative connotations, and be visible than to be invisible. She quotes a study undertaken by the *Contactgroep Emancipatie binnen het Rijksonderwijs* 1982 (Contact Group Emancipation within State Education) which showed that the absence of gender-specific occupational terminology was an obstacle for students to perceive particular jobs and professions as being open to both sexes. Her own more recent work (Van Alphen 1996) confirms this: she also found that the lack of gender-specific terms, especially female-specific terms, acted as a barrier for young girls' job choices.

These two views give a good insight into the decisions and dilemmas facing language planners. Proponents of either view put forward social and linguistic arguments in favour of their proposals. Those who favour gender neutralisation possibly present the stronger linguistic arguments, whereas those favouring feminisation probably present stronger arguments for the social effectiveness of the proposal.

The gender-neutralisation camp believes, or at least hopes, that the elimination of gender specification, especially through the abandoning of feminine suffixes, will not only obscure gender in occupational and professional nouns but will eventually also lead to a change in perception: these titles will no longer instigate male images, in fact they will not instigate any gendered images. Potential problems in achieving this aim are both linguistic and social. Although many of the Dutch feminine gender-marking suffixes may no longer be productive, they have given rise to a substantial corpus of feminine occupational titles, many of which are frequently used – for example *directrice* (female director), *lerares* (female teacher), *boerin* (female farmer), *werkster/schoonmaakster* (female cleaner), *verpleegster* (female nurse), *secretaresse* (female secretary). It is rather uncertain whether the introduction of the gender-neutralisation stragegy will lead to their rapid decline or whether they will remain remnants of a past period. Words like *secretaresse* and *verpleegster* seem unlikely to disappear in the near future. In other words, if the gender-neutralisation strategy is too strictly adhered too, it may fail because of a substantial number of occupational and professional nouns (both female and male) which are likely to resist change. The gender-neutralisation strategy runs a greater risk of social failure. To what extent will this strategy be able to remove gendered imagery from the nouns? In comparison with English, which has also opted for gender neutralisation as its main strategy, Dutch has many more current uses of feminine-specific occupational nouns. Furthermore, these uses are not yet considered unusual or antiquated, as may be the case with some of the English uses (e.g. *manageress, poetess, aviatrix, executrix*). Thus, Dutch possibly starts its gender-neutralisation strategy with a handicap: the presence of many female-specific job titles aside male ones means that female and male imagery of job titles and occupational nouns is quite entrenched and possibly more difficult to remove. If a *verpleegster* will be referred to as a *verpleger*, the female imagery will give way to what is currently male imagery. This male imagery will then have to disappear before the imagery is one of a person whose gender does not matter. The successful outcome of this strategy could be more a genderless imagery associated with occupational titles than a gender equitable imagery.

The Dutch feminisation camp insists on making women linguistically visible in all contexts so that they could not be so easily ignored or forgotten. The feminisation strategy in its extreme form implies that there should be a feminine form for each occupational noun that exists or is introduced in Dutch. It also means that in generic contexts both forms should be explicitly stated to avoid gender bias. This strategy also has its difficulties from both a social and a linguistic perspective. From a social effectiveness perspective, this proposal needs to deal more firmly with the connotations of triviality which plague quite a number of the female occupational nouns. Its main difficulties are, however, of a linguistic nature. Even if there is some (disputed) evidence that female job titles involving gender suffixation are on the increase, there is nevertheless the difficulty of choosing which of the many suffixes will be used to create the new title. Brouwer (1991a: 76) gives some examples of the difficulties:

> Is the female derivation of *arts/dokter* (medical doctor) arts*e* or arts*in/*dokter*es* or dokter*in*? Is the female form of *hoofd* (head) hoofd*es*, following the example of *voogd–voogdes* (guardian), or hoofd*in*, following the example of *waard*–waard*in* (landlord–landlady), and that of *kostwinnaar* (breadwinner) kostwinnar*es* or kostwin*ster*?

The other difficulty faced by all who support the feminisation strategy is that of repetition or duplication in generic contexts. In order for both sexes to remain visible in generic contexts, it is necessary to mention the female and male (or vice versa) forms of the occupational nouns and any other parts which require gender concord. This, however, leads to a considerable amount of lengthening in some instances, especially in spoken language where there is no access to graphemic innovations reducing the linguistic effort. The principle of the least effort (speech economy) is indeed a strong force in many languages and should not be underestimated.

A similar debate took place for the German language,[4] especially in the then Federal Republic of Germany, although here the choice of one strategy over the other seems to be more for ideological reasons than is the case in Dutch. The language planners and linguists who subscribe to a feminist ideology almost all favour gender specification/feminisation as the dominant strategy. Luise Pusch, who supports feminisation as the main strategy, neverthe-less proposed at some stage (see p. 100 a radical form of gender neutralisation (Pusch 1984a). The other party can be best described as those who oppose the feminisation strategy because their main line of argumentation is one of rejecting the feminisation strategy rather than promoting gender neutralisation.

When it comes to judging the degree of social effectiveness of a strategy, the German proponents favouring the feminisation strategy argue that social equality for women in the workforce is linguistically best served by making women's participation vis-ible, i.e. by consistently referring to them in a feminised form. Their opponents, on the other hand, claim that such a strategy is a form of *linguistic apartheid* (e.g. cited in Lorenz 1991) and could lead to linguistic discrimination against women, making it a socially ineffective strategy.

With regard to the linguistic viability of the strategies, the gender-specification camp argues that the German language is particularly suited to the formation of female occupational nouns by gender suffixation. German has basically one main and still productive gender suffix *-in*. Unlike other languages – including Dutch and some of the Nordic languages that have several suffixes to mark feminine gender – German has very few, and only one that is still really productive. There is, therefore, minimal speaker uncertainty in creating new feminine forms: speakers do not have to select the 'right' gender suffix from a wide range of possible choices. The semantic ambiguity of the *-in* suffix is also miminal. The suffix *-in* attached to an occupational noun is now primarily used to mark a referent as female. Its other function, i.e. that of marking the referent as 'the wife of a male incumbent', is now almost defunct in relation to occupational and professional nouns. The product-ive use of *-in* to form new female occupational nouns, therefore, will not lead to misinterpretation or semantic ambiguities.

Opponents and critics of the feminisation strategy argue that there are two major linguistic obstacles to the successful adoption of the gender-specification strategy (e.g. Pflug 1991, Stickel 1988). The first concerns the principle of linguistic economy: the strategy of gender specification proposes the practice of 'gender splitting', for example, by means of graphemic innovations (e.g. *Lehrer/in* or *LehrerIn*). As this form of 'gender splitting' cannot be applied to spoken language, another method has to be found to convey that information leading to a 'proliferation' of forms. A second concern is that of comprehensibility: Pflug (1991) mentions that the practices of gender splitting and gender specification will pose a substantial threat to linguistic comprehension because each referent will have to be disambiguated for sex/gender. He illustrates this with an example taken from the routine meeting rules in the *Landtag* (state parliament). In order to be gender inclusive, the sentence

> Der Präsident, im Abwesenheitsfall sein Vertreter, leitet die Sitzung. [The president, in case of his absence his replacement/representative, chairs the meeting.]

will have to become

> Der Präsident beziehungsweise die Präsidentin, im Abwesenheitsfall sein Vertreter beziehungsweise seine Vertreterin beziehungsweise ihr Vertreter beziehungsweise ihre Vertreterin leitet die Sitzung. [The male or female president or, in case of absence, his or her representative, chairs the meeting.]

Viet (1991) rejects gender splitting because it is stylistically awkward, if not clumsy, and linguistically redundant.

The arguments in favour of or against either the feminisation or gender-neutralisation strategy in German are similar to those expressed in relation to Dutch. Of course there are some differences, especially in relation to the linguistic arguments: in Dutch, the presence of multiple suffixes for gender marking, none of which seems to be particularly productive, and the tendency towards more analytical patterns and structures in the language do hinder the option of gender specification. These linguistic 'problems' do not affect the German case for gender specification: whereas the Dutch solution to this debate would seem to opt for a 'moderate' form of gender neutralisation (i.e. with some use of gender-specification practices), the German solution has been the reverse. Feminisation is generally favoured as the major or base strategy with some influence of the gender-neutralisation strategy.

Similar debates have taken or are taking place with regard to Spanish (e.g. Nissen 1986, Olivares 1984), Italian (Sabatini 1986), French (Houdebine 1988), Danish (Gomard 1985) and Norwegian (Lunde 1985). Although for English little debate has taken place with regard to the best strategy to promote linguistic equality in occupational nomenclature, some authors criticise or warn of the dangers of the gender-neutralisation strategy. Cameron (1985: 85), for instance, is particularly critical of the value and effectiveness of the gender-neutralisation strategy promoted in many English language guidelines. She does not believe that gender neutralisation will lead to linguistic equality of the sexes because

> ... many language-users, when saying or writing common terms that might in principle refer to either sex, simply do not think of them as referring to women. The words are neutral on the surface, but masculine underneath.

To her, non-sexist language guidelines which mainly promote gender neutrality are ineffective: 'They are a purely cosmetic measure which enables us to see justice being done without really doing us justice' (Cameron 1985: 86).

Case study 2: How to change masculine generic *he*?

Alternatives to the masculine generic pronoun *he*

The masculine generic pronoun debate in English provides another good example of evaluation during the planning stage. Although the proposal for an epicene pronoun in English is not a feminist invention (see Baron 1986), the debate about third person pronouns has definitely been stimulated by feminist interest in eliminating gender bias from English.

Various strategies and alternatives have been proposed to replace masculine generic *he*. There are proposals which favour the strategy of *pronoun avoidance*. This involves the avoidance of the third person pronoun by

- recasting the sentence in the plural;
- using the passive mode;
- repeating the generic noun; or
- deleting the pronoun where it is gratuitous (e.g. in the possessive form).

A second major strategy is that of *pronoun replacement*: here we can distinguish between (a) proposals which involve the replacement of masculine generic '*he*' with the second person singular pronoun *you* or with the first person plural *we* and (b) proposals which seek to replace *he* with another third person singular pronoun. The alternatives under proposal (b) include both existing pronouns *one, it, she*, singular *they* and the dual pronoun *he or she* and its many variations such as *she or he, s/he, she/he, he/she*, as well as a new pronoun (e.g. *E, co, thon, tey*[5]).

The strategy of pronoun avoidance cannot be seriously put forward as the *sole* strategy to circumvent the masculine generic *he* problem as the linguistic viability of this option is very doubtful. A language such as English needs pronouns for a range of functions, e.g. anaphoric reference, marking possession. Dropping only one element of the pronoun system (i.e. third person singular) would destabilise the present system of pronouns. It is also unlikely that pronoun avoidance is the best strategy to attain social effectiveness: in the case where the generic noun is repeated to avoid the generic pronoun, it is doubtful to what extent this strategy promotes gender inclusiveness, especially if the generic noun has overt or covert connotations of maleness. Similar arguments can be raised in relation to the proposal in which generic *he* is replaced by *you* or *we*. To my knowledge feminist language planners have only offered the strategy of pronoun avoidance as *additional* to that of pronoun replacement.

Within the pronoun-replacement strategy a series of alternatives are put forward as substitutes for masculine generic *he*. The two alternatives which have been most widely scrutinised are singular *they* (e.g. Bodine 1975, Mackay 1980, 1983) and the introduction of a new epicene or gender-neutral pronoun (e.g. Baron 1986, Henley 1987). In fact, Mackay (1980) proposed a cost–benefit analysis to examine the viability of alternatives for masculine generic *he* and he tested this programme on the alternative singular *they*. According to Mackay (1980: 352)

> a usage should be prescriptively recommended if and only if the benefits of the usage outweigh the costs, where benefits facilitate communication (i.e. the comprehension, learning, and production of the language) and costs make communication more difficult (relative to all other means of expressing the same concept).

Although Mackay (1980) should be credited with the idea of testing the viability of alternatives in a systematic manner before implementing or prescribing them, his proposed programme focuses solely on criteria or factors of linguistic viability. His criteria include simplicity, lexical and conceptual availability, comprehensibility, learnability, imageability, ambiguity and functional issues. There are no criteria, however, to examine the social effectiveness of an alternative. Furthermore, the criteria used by Mackay (1980) to judge the viability of a proposal programme are new and have not been tested on any other form of language subjected to linguistic prescriptivism. Hellinger (1990) is also critical of Mackay's lack of justification of why he gives more weight to certain criteria. In the case of singular *they*, he pays particular attention to the criterion of contextual ambiguity which the replacement of *he* by singular *they* can create in such sentences as 'If a scholar has no faith in their principles, how can they succeed' and 'When a psychiatrist succeeds in helping their patient, they usually set them free from their inhibitions'. Hellinger (1990: 81) writes

> Die Assoziation von sing. *they* zur Kategorie Plural und die damit verbundenen potentiellen Mehrdeutigkeiten werden von Mackay als Hauptargument gegen den Vorschlag feministischer Linguistinnen vorgebracht ... Dieses Argument ist aus zwei Gründen wenig überzeugend. Zum einen sind die Ambiguitäten eine Eigenschaft vieler Sätze, insbes. komplexe Sätze, die Pronomina enthalten ... Auch die formale Identität von singularischem und pluralischem *they* dürfte kaum die Gefahr von Kommunikationszusammenbrüchen (wie Mackay, 1980: 361 befürchtet) heraufbeschwören; auch die Pronomina der 2. Person (*you*) sind im Englischen im Singular und Plural identisch. [The association of singular *they* with the category of plural and the fact that this association has the potential for ambiguities are considered by Mackay to be the main arguments against the proposal by feminist linguists ... This argument is not very convincing for two reasons. First, ambiguities are a characteristic of many sentences, especially complex sentences which contain pronouns ... Also the formal identity of singular and plural *they* should not cause a major threat to communication (as Mackay, 1980: 361 fears), the pronouns for the second person singular and plural (*you*) are also identical in English.]

The proposal to create a new epicene pronoun has been discussed extensively in the work of Baron (1986) who comments that the search for a sex-indefinite pronoun has had a long history in English and was, until recently, not motivated by a feminist concern but by a concern to rectify a structural irregularity in the English language.

In the following paragraphs I review proposals to replace masculine generic he with other pronouns. These proposals include the generic use of *she*, the use of singular *they*, the dual gender-inclusive pronoun *he or she* (and its variations), the pronouns *one* and *it* and the introduction of a new gender-neutral pronoun. I shall assess their appropriateness with reference to the criteria of linguistic viability and social effectiveness.

Generic *she*

The proposal to grant the pronoun *she* generic status takes various forms. Some language planners recommend a straightforward substitution of generic *he* with generic *she* to be adopted by both female and male language users. Others adopt a sex-exclusive use of generic *she* and therefore also of generic *he*: this entails that women use *she* to refer to all generic nouns whereas men would use *he* generically. Yet other proposals introduce the generic *she* to be used in alternation with generic *he*. In terms of social effectiveness, the generic use of *she* to replace or alternate with generic *he* very much succeeds in making women visible but at the expense of a reduced visibility (in case of alternation) or invisibility (in the case of replacement) of men in language.

If the proposal is to replace generic *he* with generic *she*, the problems are simply reversed from a linguistic equality perspective. Indeed, if the aim of a generic pronoun is to be truly gender inclusive, this proposal may make women very visible but at the expense of making men invisible. The current ambiguity or confusion between the masculine pronoun *he* and the generic pronoun *he* would simply be transferred to the feminine pronoun 'she' and the generic pronoun *she*. Both from a social effectiveness and a linguistic viability perspective, the transposing of generic *he* with generic *she* would not lead to a generic pronoun which is truly generic, gender neutral or gender inclusive.

The sex-exclusive approach to the use of generic *he* or *she* has some potential for a more gender-balanced use of generic pronouns. Women would use *she* generically and men would use *he* thus avoiding the present imbalance. From a linguistic perspective, this proposal would be quite radical for English. Although it would not lead to the introduction of a new pronoun or a restructuring of the current pronoun system, it would introduce the phenomenon of sex-exclusive marking of pronouns. In English there are no other instances of sex-exclusive usages of this kind. Its introduction could therefore have an impact on the structural development of the language (i.e. it could perhaps trigger other forms of sex-exclusive use). It certainly will have an influence on the revelation of authorship in language. It would always be clear that the author of a (spoken/written) text is either male or female. This may be most appropriate in the case of speakers or single authors but the question arises which generic use would suit multiple female and male authors. Similarly there is a large body of texts whose authorship is irrelevant, or wishes to remain anonymous (e.g. signs, legislative texts, contracts, information leaflets). Which generic pronoun would be used in such cases?

Another proposal involving generic 'she' is for the alternate use of *he* or *she* in reference to the same generic nouns. In other words, sometimes generic *he* would be used to refer to generic nouns such as *professor*, *lawyer*, *worker*, *cleaner*, *president*, and sometimes generic *she*. There is some historical evidence for this option. For example, Bodine (1975) and Baron (1986) found some evidence suggesting that *she* had been used generically alongside *he* in some dialects of English. This alternation between generic *he* and generic *she* would contribute substantially towards a gender-inclusive inter-pretation of generic pronouns. However, most problematic in this proposal is the issue of alternation. How should this alternation occur to ensure that no gender bias or gender stereotyping is intro-duced? How should alternation occur to avoid too much linguistic ambiguity? If the type of alternation is left up to the individual it will remain idiosyncratic and will hardly contribute to a more equitable use of generic pronouns or to linguistic clarity in relation to generic pronoun use.

The generic *she* proposal has been promoted primarily as a strat-egy of linguistic disruption to attract attention to the gender bias in generic pronouns. However, in the current climate it seems un-likely that such a proposal would receive support from the wider speech community, in particular, men.

Singular *they*

The proposal to replace generic *he* with singular *they* is wide-spread. There is substantial research evidence available to show that singular *they* would indeed be capable of promoting the idea of sex-indefiniteness as a generic pronoun (e.g. studies quoted earlier in this chapter and in Chapter 2). This is reinforced by many people's tendency to use singular *they* not only in reference to indefinite nouns such as *someone*, *anyone*, *everyone*, *person* but also other generic nouns. From a social effectiveness perspective, this option promotes the idea of gender neutrality through the use of a form which is gender neutral. There have been a few studies (see Chapter 2, Gastil 1990) which found evidence that the use of singular *they* calls up less male images than generic *he*. It is the linguistic viability of this proposal which has attracted most attention. As mentioned before, Mackay (1980) undertook a cost–benefit analysis of singular *they* and found that the costs outweigh the benefits in this case. His major objection is that the use of singular *they* creates more ambiguity as illustrated in the examples quoted before, i.e.

- If a scholar has no faith in their principles, how can they succeed?
- When a psychiatrist succeeds in helping their patient, they usually set them free from their inhibitions.

Hellinger (1990) pointed out that this objection is overrated because the ambiguity is not only mainly contextual but ambiguity is also the characteristic of many complex sentences. Mackay's (1980) other objections include the imperfect match between generic *he* and singular *they* in distributional patterns (i.e. lack of identical distribution) as well as the fact that the pronoun *they* can refer to both animate and inanimate referents and can therefore have a dehumanising and distancing effect.

Other language planners and commentators (e.g. Bodine 1975, Baron 1986, Frank and Treichler 1989) have taken a more positive view of singular *they* as a potential replacement for generic *he*. Their main argument has been that singular *they* has a long history of widespread use as a generic pronoun in speech and has also persisted in writing, despite the persistent actions of prescriptive grammarians to eliminate its use. In addition, some recent surveys of non-sexist pronoun use have shown that singular *they* is often the preferred alternative to generic *he* in speech, and sometimes in writing (e.g. Henley and Dragun 1983; Martyna 1978, Pauwels 1989b). However, the persistent prescriptive view that singular *they*, despite its widespread use in speech, is grammatically incorrect, may continue to hamper its promotion throughout the speech community.

Dual, gender-inclusive pronouns

The naming of both third person singular pronouns (hereafter called dual pronoun) *he or she* and its many variations *she or he*, and in writing *s/he*, *he/she*, *she/he* is clearly satisfactory in terms of social effectiveness. The dual pronoun explicitly names both sexes so that there should be no doubt about its gender inclusiveness. Like singular *they*, it is its linguistic viability which is questioned. Its use is considered particularly problematic from a stylistic point of view and from the perspective of speech economy. The use of a dual pronoun has been described as longwinded, cumbersome, pedantic and ugly both in speech and writing. Some have claimed that the constant repetition of a dual pronoun makes comprehension more difficult. Bolinger (1980) believes that its use complicates the anaphoric function of pronouns. He argues that a pronoun in its anaphoric function is an empty word and is therefore de-accented:

we could as well substitute a mathematical symbol [*for generic* he – *author*]. Such virtually empty words behave as empty words normally do: they are de-accented, to attract as little attention as possible. (Bolinger 1980: 95)

According to Bolinger (1980: 96) the use of a dual pronoun does not allow this de-accentuation: 'it refuses to take the back seat that all languages reserve for pure anaphora'. Furthermore, the alternatives *s/he*, *he/she*, *she/he* involving graphemic innovation are considered unsuitable for speech, thus reducing their overall viability.

Finally, limited surveys of people's use of non-sexist pronouns have revealed mixed findings about the suitability of the dual pronoun to replace generic *he*. Henley and Dragun (1983) found that although 61 per cent of their informants reported avoiding the use of generic *he*, the dual pronoun was not the preferred alternative: recasting the sentence in the plural was the preferred option. Bate (1978), on the other hand, noted a high degree of acceptance for *he or she* in her study of sexist language in transition in comparison with the alternatives *s/he* and singular *they*. Martyna (1978) showed that her informants used singular *they*, the pronoun *he or she* and the repetition of the generic nouns as alternative generics in a sentence completion test. Whereas singular *they* was used most in spoken responses, *he or she* were more frequent in written responses. Pauwels (1989b) also found that students had a preference for the dual pronoun in written language and for singular *they* in speech. Gastil (1990) found that the generic interpretation of *he/she* varied between male and female students. He found some evidence that male students may comprehend *he/she* in a manner similar to *he*, casting doubt on the gender-inclusive interpretation of this pronoun.

The pronoun *one*

The assessment of this alternative has received little attention because its linguistic viability is considered very limited. It has a very restricted usefulness in replacing generic *he*. For example, *one* is not considered a viable alternative as a possessive referring to generic nouns other than *one*, *everyone*, and possibly *every man and woman* or *person*. Also, its rather formal and learned character is seen as an obstacle for its widespread use. However, it is capable of conveying the idea of sex-indefiniteness.

The pronoun *it*

Baron (1986) reports that there has been some support for extend-
ing the use of *it* as a 'generic' pronoun replacing *he*. Indeed there
are already some instances of *it* to indicate referents whose sex is
unknown. The most common examples involve the nouns *baby*
and *child*. However, its primary association in English with inanimate nouns may hinder its extension to human referents. It is also
doubtful if a pronoun associated with inanimacy is capable of conveying the idea of sex-indefiniteness of human referents.

A new, sex-indefinite pronoun

In many respects the creation and introduction of a new, sex-
indefinite pronoun would be the most appropriate solution. A
new pronoun – a neologism – is unlikely to have marked male
or female connotations so that its meaning could be truly sex-
indefinite and generic. Its distributional patterns would be identical
to those of generic *he*, i.e. the new pronoun could replace the
masculine generic in all contexts without causing anaphoric or other
ambiguities. Its use would be simple and would not interfere with
stylistic demands. However, the fact that the pronoun is new, that
is lexically unavailable, is considered a major stumbling-block.
Indeed, there is plenty of historical evidence that the introduction
of a new pronoun is doomed to failure. Baron (1986) documents
several attempts (both serious and jocular) over the past two hun-
dred years to introduce a new epicene pronoun in English. So far
all attempts have failed for the new pronoun(s) to gain widespread
acceptance. Nevertheless, some feminist language planners continue
promoting a new pronoun as the best alternative to replace generic
he. However, they realise that without massive support from an
agency or institution capable of influencing language use (e.g. the
media) the efforts to introduce the new pronoun will fail (e.g.
Henley 1987).
    This assessment of the linguistic viability and social effectiveness
of proposed alternatives to generic *he* has shown that none of the
candidates is ideally a suitable replacement. It is therefore not surprising that most language planners for English have abandoned
the idea of finding a sole replacement for generic *he* and instead
recommend a set of alternatives which can replace generic *he* according to context.

A gender-balanced system for honorific titles

The imbalance in honorific titles for women and men in many languages has been the subject of many attempts at linguistic reform. Throughout the centuries women have been primarily defined in terms of the 'man' or 'men' in their lives, i.e. a husband, a father or a son. Men, on the other hand, have seldom been defined by the 'woman' or 'women' in their lives. The references to men as 'Jill's husband', 'Jane's widower' are far fewer than references to women as 'John's wife, or 'Jack's widow'. Men are more likely to be defined and described in terms of their social or professional status in society. It is not surprising then that the current honorific titles for women reflect this. Spender (1980: 27) criticised this asymmetrical practice relating to courtesy titles for women and men as follows:

> The practice of labelling women as married or single also serves supremely sexist ends. There is tension between the representation of women as sex objects and the male ownership rights over women and this has been resolved by an explicit and most visible device designating the married status of women.

In English general courtesy titles for women reveal information about marital status whereas those for men do not. 'Miss + surname' is generally used to refer or address an unmarried female person, irrespective of age, and the title 'Mrs + surname' is used to address married women, including those who have been married. Although there are two courtesy titles for males, 'Mr' and 'Master' which distinguish males primarily in terms of age, only one, 'Mr', is in common use. Men's courtesy titles do not reveal information about their marital status.

In order to rectify the gender imbalance in courtesy titles a range of options are available. Some of these have been suggested in jest, whereas others have received more serious consideration.

First, there is the option which seeks to introduce a differentiation between men in terms of their marital status. It is argued that if men find the information about a woman's marital status relevant, women may want the same information about men. Proposals include the revival of the term 'master' to mean not only young man, but also unmarried man leading to the following system (Hook 1977):

- *Mr* for married men in line with *Mrs* for married women.
- *Master* for unmarried men in line with *Miss* for unmarried women.

The American satirist Ambrose Bierce (1911) suggested the title 'Mh' or 'Mush' for the unmarried man. Other suggestions (serious and in jest) have included two new titles for men to replace the present 'Mister'. Baker, as cited in Lakoff (1975: 91), suggests the titles 'Murm' for the married man and 'Srs' for the unmarried man. Sorrels (1983: 10) selects the titles 'Mrd' for married men and 'Mngl.' for single men.

A second option propagated by some language commentators is to do away with courtesy titles altogether. Among those favouring abolition of courtesy titles, there are nevertheless some who believe that present-day society is not yet ready for a total abolition of titles. They therefore propose the introduction of a universal courtesy title which can be used by and for both women and men, irrespective of marital, social or class status. Suggestions have included *Pn*, *Per* and *Pr* (Person), *Masir* (a contraction of Madam and Sir) and *M*..

A third strategy involves redressing the gender imbalance between male and female courtesy titles by changing female ones. Here two main suggestions have been made. The best known one is that of replacing the present two titles 'Mrs' and 'Miss' by the new title 'Ms' so as to obtain parallelism between the male and female courtesy titles. The other suggestion has been to turn either the courtesy title 'Miss' or 'Mrs' into a general courtesy title for adult women and to abandon the other title. Thus, if 'Miss' was selected as a general courtesy title for women, then 'Mrs' would be abandoned or vice versa. There are arguments in favour of either title to become the general courtesy title. In the case of 'Miss' there is some evidence that in the past 'Miss' has been used to refer to both married and unmarried women (e.g. Baron 1986). In some dialects of English, 'Miss' can still be used in that sense. In favour of 'Mrs' as the general courtesy title is the fact that an earlier meaning of the title was that of an adult woman irrespective of marital status, and the fact that currently most adult women are being addressed as 'Mrs', rightly or wrongly.

Very little assessment of the viability of these three major options has taken place so far. In fact, most of the suggestions with regard to the restructuring of male courtesy titles have been made in jest. This also applies to some extent to the common-gender title proposals. As to the changes of female courtesy titles, evaluations of their viability have only occurred after their implementation (e.g. Atkinson 1987, Pauwels 1987b, 1996). Linguistically speaking, the preferred option, the 'Ms' alternative, involves more radical changes than either the selection of 'Mrs' or 'Miss' as the common courtesy title for women. For 'Ms' to become the female parallel term of 'Mr', the use of 'Mrs' and 'Miss' needs to be abandoned. The processes of change involved are more complex than those leading to the abandoning of one term. After all, the introduction of the new title is not meant to be merely an addition to the present system of titles, i.e. an additional title to reflect a further semantic distinction – for instance, 'Miss' for an unmarried woman, 'Mrs' for a married woman, and 'Ms' for a previously married woman. On the contrary, the new title is meant to *replace* the existing ones in form and is meant to carry only two of the three semantic features associated with the previous titles. The features 'sex' [+ female] and 'age' [+ adult] are kept, but that of 'marital status' is abandoned. The mixture of old and new information associated with a new coinage within a relatively established and stable system may impede its adoption and spread. Furthermore, the pronunciation of the new title 'Ms' is seen to be problematic by both supporters and opponents of the change. Since the title 'Ms', whose origin remains rather obscure, is not generally regarded to be an abbreviation of 'Mistress' (e.g. Hook 1977, Spender 1980, Kramarae and Treichler 1985), 'Ms' ought to be pronounced /mz/, which constitutes an unacceptable consonant cluster in English. A vowel is therefore inserted to make the cluster acceptable. The fact that there are no guidelines regarding the quality of this vowel, e.g. /ɪ/, /ʌ/ or /ə/, is considered problematic because the existence of numerous phonological variants of 'Ms' may result in confusion and even prove detrimental to the present system of titles. Pauwels (1987b: 136) remarks about the 'Ms' proposal:

> It is perhaps questionable whether the 'Ms' proposal is indeed the simplest and most efficient way of remedying the present imbalance in the personal title system. For instance, introducing another personal title for men may have been simpler: a male equivalent for either 'Mrs' or 'Miss' would have filled the lexical gap without having to remove two existing titles ('Mrs' and 'Miss' and replace them by a third ('Ms'). Another alternative would have been to make 'Mrs' the universal personal title for (adult) women . . . and abandon the use of 'Miss' to refer to adult, unmarried women.

As to the question of social effectiveness of the options, it can perhaps be stated that a neologism 'Ms' is more likely to be free from the unwanted connotation of 'married' or 'unmarried'. However, evidence from other languages in which the equivalent term of 'Mrs' has become the new courtesy title shows that the connotation of 'married' is quickly disappearing from the word (see Pauwels 1996).

The assessment of the proposals to redress the gender imbalance in courtesy titles has again shown that none of the alternatives are clearly superior from either a linguistic or a social perspective. Formal language guidelines for English have not pursued the options of a new male courtesy title or a universal courtesy but have chosen to promote the 'Ms' option, usually as an *alternative* to rather than as a *replacement* of the 'Miss' and 'Mrs' titles.

Notes

1. This is less the case in Spanish where derivational gender marking includes both feminine suffixes (e.g. *-isa* and *-esa*) but also suffix alternations in which case the masculine suffix is alternated with the feminine suffix (*presidente/presidenta*; *campesino/campesina*).
2. The *-eure* suffix is promoted primarily in French-speaking Canada.
3. In the Dutch-speaking part of Belgium there were, until recently, no such major debates about which strategy to use. However, the current debates are similar to the earlier Dutch ones (see De Caluwe 1996, Niedzwiecki 1995, Pauwels 1997a, Van Langendonck and Beeken 1996).
4. For a more detailed discussion, see Hellinger (1993) and Samel (1995).
5. See Baron (1986) for an extensive list of new epicene pronouns in English.

5 Implementing non-sexist language change: guidelines

This chapter discusses the implementation stage of feminist language planning (LP). Implementation is concerned with identifying strategies and making decisions on how best to promote the proposed changes. This stage is crucial for a successful outcome of the LP process which is largely dependent on selecting appropriate mechanisms of implementation to maximise the spread and adoption of the changes in the target community. The implementation stage indeed plays a significant part in achieving the ultimate aim of feminist LP: the elimination of gender inequality in language and the creation of a language capable of portraying the sexes as different but equal.

Implicit in this aim is a desire or a need to replace one linguistic norm with another. In the case of feminist language reform (LR), the desire is to replace sexist language uses and sexist forms of discourse, which currently constitute normative usage, with non-sexist language uses and gender-inclusive forms of discourse. In LP terms (see Kloss 1968), this process entails raising forms or varieties of language from the level of 'discouraged' or 'disapproved' use to a level of 'tolerated' and ultimately of 'promoted' use. Many LP efforts, including feminist LP, indeed aim to achieve the status of sole official usage or joint official status for their reforms. Since this process can involve a 'demotion' of a currently promoted variety, it is not surprising that resistance to change can be quite vehement and that language planners need to take this into consideration.

Making decisions about implementing language changes

In the implementation stage decisions need to be made about appropriate mechanisms and avenues to promote the proposed changes. This includes decisions on how to present the proposed changes, how to make the changes known to the target audience, and whether or not to justify the reforms *vis-à-vis* 'traditional' or current usage. Decisions also need to be made about selecting channels of language spread to promote the changes, and about whether or not to introduce 'sanctions' against the non-adoption or non-observance of the changes.

Not all mechanisms of implementation and avenues of language spread are always accessible to language planners. This is especially so in the case of grassroots language planners. Such planners may, for example, have limited or no access to channels of language spread such as the education system, the media, and possibly legislation and language academies. Government-initiated or officially-sanctioned LR and LP does not usually face such restrictions. This does not imply, however, that the reforms from the latter category are always more successful than those from grassroots planners. Language planning research has shown, for example, that the community's attitudes towards the proposed changes play an important role in the promotion and adoption of the changes. This could mean that some forms of grassroots or non-official LP are viewed positively by the community, thus facilitating the adoption and the spread of language change throughout that community with minimal official means of implementation. Language changes imposed upon a community by a government or official agency, on the other hand, may not be adopted despite far-reaching implementation strategies, because of the negative attitudes of the community towards the changes. An important task for language planners, therefore, is to gather information about the target group's attitudes towards the changes. In other words, language planners must assess people's reactions and views on the matter of change before selecting the implementation mechanisms.

Implementation strategies selected by feminist language planners

So far our discussion of feminist LP has highlighted the fact that the feminist LP process is characterised by a great diversity of opinions on how to achieve the aim of non-sexist language use. It can be expected that this diversity of opinion will also characterise the implementation stage.

Promoting change through role models and solidarity

The role model and solidarity strategy is particularly preferred by language planners who favour the strategies of linguistic disruption and of creating a new woman-centred language. The role-model strategy means that language planners become or promote role-models who *lead by example*. These role models (often the language planners themselves) use the promoted changes in their own language use and appeal in this way to other language users (especially women) to adopt the changes. This strategy appeals primarily to the solidarity among women to promote changes. This appeal to others to change their language use is sometimes made explicit, especially in written sources. Mary Daly, whom I have mentioned in previous chapters, is one role model who explains to her readers why she practises linguistic disruption in her writing (see Daly 1978: both preface and introduction). It is usually the language practices of leading feminist activists, thinkers and writers that have stood and still stand as models for changes in the language practices of other language users. Sometimes the language practices adopted by feminist groups (e.g. women's consciousness-raising groups) and those promoted in feminist publications also act as models for the language use of others.

During visits to The Netherlands and Germany between 1992 and 1994 I decided to explore the impact of the language used in two widely distributed feminist magazines in these countries on its readers. The magazines in question were the Dutch *Opzij* and the German *Emma*. I talked to twenty regular readers of *Opzij* (seventeen women and three men between the ages of 20 and 63) and to seventeen readers of *Emma* (all women between 17 and 55) about their views on the language used in these magazines and whether or not it has influenced their own language use. The *Opzij* readers commented that they had not really noticed much linguistic innovation or other language changes promoting gender equality in *Opzij*. Some readers who were very well informed about language issues felt that *Opzij* was lagging behind other feminist magazines in Europe in promoting linguistic change. They attributed this partly to the magazine's orientation towards liberal rather than radical feminism. Most *Opzij* readers claimed that *Opzij*'s main contribution to linguistic change was to diminish or even eliminate stereotypical descriptions of women and men. They mentioned that articles focusing on professional women seldom discussed the women's familial situation except where appropriate, and there was seldom a focus on women's physical appearance. It was mainly the older female readers (55 years and older) and the three male readers who said that this reduction in stereotyped language about the sexes had had an impact on their own language use.

Emma readers were more outspoken about the role of *Emma* in promoting language change and influencing their own language behaviour. All readers claimed that *Emma*'s language practices of 'gender splitting', of using the indefinite pronoun *frau* as well as an increased use of new compounds with *-frau* (e.g. *Zimmerfrau, Frauschaft*) were clearly innovative and promoted gender equality. As to the influence of *Emma* on their own language practices, most readers (16) said that they were inspired by *Emma*'s language practices and this had given them confidence in changing their own language use. The most frequently adopted change was that of creating new compounds with *-frau*. Four readers had also started to use the indefinite pronoun *frau* in a variety of women's only settings. The practice of gender splitting was also adopted by two readers in their own writing, but most readers felt this practice to be too cumbersome.

Implementing feminist language change through the role-model strategy is largely a non-intrusive way of promoting language change. Language users are not confronted with a set of rules, guidelines or recommendations on how to change their language; rather, they encounter changed language practices which they can choose to adopt or not. The role-model strategy is an individual approach to language change: the language use of certain individuals influences that of other individuals. Since different role models may promote different changes, the changes that will be adopted by the community will be many and diverse. If language users copy language practices from their role models without an understanding of the issues, there is always the danger that this copied behaviour may not promote the underlying goal of linguistic equality for the sexes.

Similarly, with other 'non-regulated' forms of language change, change through role-model imitation will be subject to similar forces of language spread. The proposed wave theory of language spread may also account for the way in which feminist language change promoted through the role-model strategy spreads through the community. The changes are probably adopted first by those who recognise or adopt a particular language user as a role model. The changes then spread from these language users to other language users who associate with them, and then on to other language users.

The role-model strategy is undoubtedly an important implementation strategy for feminist LR. It is, however, questionable whether this strategy used on its own is sufficient to achieve the overall aims of feminist LP.

Reform through legislation and edicts from language academies

Another possible avenue for implementing feminist LR is through legislating the reforms. This implementation strategy is more typical in cases of status planning than of corpus planning. For example, raising the status of an indigenous language to that of the new national language of a country may become enshrined in law, i.e. the national language becomes the national language by law, *de jure*.

Sometimes legislative measures and laws can cover language issues although they seldom deal solely with language matters. For example, laws covering the issue of racial vilification affect forms of language use and language practices that are deemed racist.

Feminist LR has not really had recourse to legislation to implement changes. However, some legislative measures which emanated from governments ratifying the United Nations International Convention on the *Elimination of All Forms of Discrimination against Women* had an impact on language. For example, laws dealing with the elimination of sex discrimination and equal employment opportunity affect the use of job titles and occupational terminology. The linguistic exclusion of women in job titles and job advertisements as well as the sexist practices in job interviewing are judged unlawful under this type of legislation. Such legislation has provided a push towards the creation and adoption of non-discriminatory or gender-inclusive terminology in the area of employment.

Implementing feminist language change with the aid of language academies or other language-regulating bodies was neither a widely available nor a favoured option to most feminist language planners. It was not a favoured option because language edicts or regulations impose changes on the community without much clarification for the need to change. Feminist language planners considered the promotion of feminist LR without ensuring that the community understood the need for reform to be ineffectual, if not counterproductive. It was also not a widely available option to feminist language planners as language academies and other language-regulating bodies were often among the most vehement opponents of the proposed reforms. Such bodies are known to regard themselves as the guardians of language, and tend to adopt conservative attitudes towards proposed LR. The promotion of feminist LR was seen to be an activity clearly at odds with their general philosophy on language and LR.

Promoting change through language guidelines and recommendations

Promoting language change through the formulation and distribution of language guidelines and recommendations has been, and continues to be, possibly the most widespread and popular strategy of implementation for feminist language planners. Because of its widespread adoption across language and speech communities, it deserves elaborate attention in this chapter.

I shall firstly discuss the type of language planners who choose language guidelines as their main vehicle of promoting non-sexist language use. Secondly, I shall undertake an examination of the structure and content of existing guidelines based on a comparative analysis of language guidelines for English, German, French, Italian, Dutch and Spanish.

Type of language planners who opt for language guidelines

Promoting non-sexist language change through the formulation or issuing of guidelines is primarily used by language planners who wish to promote *linguistic equality* **of** *and* **for** *the sexes* by rectifying the present gender imbalance in the linguistic representation of the sexes. This is a different goal from that of language reformers whose aim is to develop a woman-centred language which gives linguistic prominence to women, women's views and experiences. It is therefore not surprising that non-sexist language guidelines have been described as a 'verbal Sex Discrimination Act' (Cameron 1985). The promoters of language guidelines also appeal to the speech community as *rational language users*, willing and capable of change, when they are faced with rational arguments about the need for linguistic change. These language planners are of the opinion that language guidelines are the most effective mechanism for the promotion of linguistic reform *in the public arena*: that is, for example, language use in the public media, in public administration and bureaucracy, in legislation and education. Such language is regularly subjected to rules. Furthermore, the selection of guidelines as main mechanism is also motivated by a desire to minimise linguistic disruption or confusion associated with LR. It is argued that providing clear guidelines about why and how to change language will facilitate the process of linguistic spread and adoption by large sections of the community. This argument of minimal disruption is particularly used by language planners whose work is directed at reforming formal and official uses of language (e.g. administrative and legal texts).

The promotion of LR by means of guidelines has been adopted by both feminist grassroots language planners and (semi-)official LP agencies and committees charged with the 'rectification' of linguistic bias against women. Here I use the term 'feminist grassroots' language planners to refer to LP individuals and groups with a personal, political and/or professional commitment to the issue of non-sexist language. Often these language planners have also been instrumental in bringing the issue of linguistic sexism to the public fore and have rallied publicly for non-sexist LR. The terms '(semi-)official' and 'formal language planning agencies' are used for those groups whose concern with LR is mainly the result of legislative measures banning all forms of sex discrimination: they include, for instance, equal opportunity agencies in the workplace, affirmative action groups, standing committees on language use in the media, language academies, *ad hoc* committees on language in organisations. In practice, it is often not possible to demarcate clearly between these types of language planners in terms of personal and professional commitment to the issue of non-sexist language reform. However, the 'official' LP agencies are more likely to be made up of members who represent different interest groups and hold a variety of opinions on the matter.

In the case of the 'grassroots' planners, the formulation of proposals for change in the form of guidelines was often the direct outcome of in-depth discussions, investigations and analyses of linguistic sexism. Individual women, as well as women's committees in professional associations of education, psychology, business, administration, law, the media and the unions, not only discussed sexism in language but often also formulated non-sexist alternatives and developed guidelines for non-sexist language. Such guidelines then became a crucial aid in the planners' attempt to call attention to the problem of sexism in language, and to encourage, convince or pressure specific sectors of the community (e.g. publishing houses, educational institutions, government bureaucracies) into linguistic reform. Since such language planners had no constitutive power to enforce or dictate change, their demands for change could only be phrased in terms of recommendations (rather than norms or rules). This is often reflected in the style of writing found in many of the guidelines, as is illustrated in the following section. In some instances the sector(s) at which the guidelines were aimed adopted the proposals or formulated their own on the model of the former. *The handbook of non-sexist writing for writers, editors and speakers* by Casey Miller and Kate Swift is an example of this: active as editors for educational materials and many other types of publications in the United States, they were regularly confronted with many sexist expressions and practices found in such materials. Not only did they thoroughly investigate frequent and common sexist linguistic practices, as described in their book *Words and women*, but they also found, created and promoted alternative non-sexist forms, phrases and expressions. They aimed their guidelines at writers, editors and public speakers in general. Many of their suggestions and recommendations for non-sexist alternatives were and still are adopted by other agencies, institutions and groups. Their influence has not been limited to the United States but has spread to other English-speaking and some non-English-speaking societies. For German, the guidelines formulated by four feminist linguists in 1980 (Guentherodt *et al.*, 1980) and published in *Linguistische Berichte*, a linguistics journal, had a similar role: they were the result of debates and discussion among feminists concerned with language and were aimed at making professional groups aware of the problem. Although these guidelines were never formally adopted by any group or agency, they did become the basis or reference point for many guidelines formulated at a later stage – for example, the Austrian guidelines formulated by the Ministry for Employment and Social Services in 1987, the Hannover Guidelines in 1989 and the UNESCO German guidelines in 1993.

Earlier in this chapter I mentioned that LP groups had not always recourse to all or to their preferred mechanisms and avenues for implementing change. In some ways the selection of language guidelines as a major instrument for the promotion of non-sexist language use can be seen partly as a result of restricted access to other avenues and means of implementing change. Language guidelines are seen to be less threatening than other forms of implementation: institutions which adopt guidelines can be seen to be supportive of reform without a need to enforce them. The 'guideline' status of many non-sexist language proposals is conferred upon them by the agencies which formulate and/or implement them. The target audience for the guidelines is encouraged, or at best urged, to consider the recommended changes and to adopt them in their language use relating to the agency or institution.

Generally, no sanctions are imposed for non-compliance; indeed, only in very few specific cases have agencies introduced sanctions for non-observance. This is, for example, the case for the use of sexist or androcentric job titles and expressions in job advertisements in countries which have legislation outlawing discrimination in employment on the basis of sex. However, in practice few complaints by individuals or groups are investigated by the relevant authority and even fewer penalties have been imposed on companies or agencies breaching the guidelines relating to non-discriminatory job titles. Hellinger (1990) reports two cases in which companies were taken to court for alleged breach of the regulations regarding gender-inclusive job titles in job advertisements. An airline company was taken to court in Berlin for using the words 'jobholder . . . he . . .' in its English version of a job advertisement. In its defence the company claimed that they had used the terms 'jobholder' and 'he' in a gender-neutral manner. This argument was rejected by the court on the grounds that 'he' could not be interpreted as gender-neutral in this context. The other case brought before the European court concerns a woman who had applied for a job advertised in the paper as *'leistungsbereiten Hochschulabsolventen der Wirtschaftswissenschaften'* ('performance-eager' tertiary graduate of economics). The female job applicant had interpreted the expression as a generic applying to both women and men. She was told that only men were considered for the job. Consequently she took the company to court.

Although other forms of sanctioning could be imposed for non-compliance, this is rarely done. For example, a publishing company with a non-sexist language policy could impose sanctions on authors or editors who do not observe the guidelines. Such sanctions could include a reluctance to consider a manuscript for publication or a delay in publication due to extensive editing. However, they are rarely imposed. It is much more likely that the company will continue to accept manuscripts and books which do not observe the guidelines without any penalties. In some cases, agencies are trying to promote the adoption of guidelines by a form of reward system. For example, a publishing company could indicate the rewards for adopting non-sexist language guidelines. These could include an increased willingness to consider a manuscript for publication or more rapid processing of the manuscript.

The popularity of language guidelines as a major instrument for promoting language change in the public arena is attested by the literally thousands of guidelines which are in circulation throughout

Western Europe, North America, some parts of South America, Australia, New Zealand and, increasingly, parts of Asia (especially Japan). Most widespread are the guidelines in English-speaking countries such as Australia, Canada, Great Britain, New Zealand and the United States. In these countries many public and government agencies, as well as private corporations, have issued non-sexist language guidelines or have adopted a policy of non-sexist language use. For example, almost all major educational publishing houses, educational institutions, government departments, professional organisations as well as a substantial number of private corporations, workers' unions and some organised religious groups have issued guidelines for non-sexist or non-discriminatory language use. Language guidelines are also widespread in German-speaking countries where they have been adopted by many public sector bodies ranging from government departments to local councils. Increasingly they can also be found in the media sector (publishing), organised religious groups and educational bodies. In Spain the Ministry of Education and Science (Ministeria de Educación y Ciencia 1988) has been the main promoter of non-sexist language guidelines. In France, the formulation of language guidelines is mainly the result of legislative measures ensuring equal employment opportunities for women. In 1984 a terminology commission, *Commission de terminologie relative au vocabulaire concernant les activités des femmes*, was set up to investigate questions of nomenclature for women in the workforce. Two years later (March 1986) an official circular was issued to regulate the use of occupational and professional titles for women in bureaucratic and administrative language (*Circulaire du 11 mars 1986 relative à la féminisation des noms de métier, fonction ou titre*). To date language guidelines in France are still largely limited to official agencies, bodies and institutions linked to the government and the public service and bound by this circular. Other French-speaking countries (e.g. Belgium, Switzerland, Canada) are more advanced in the issuing and adoption of non-sexist language guidelines. This is especially so for French-speaking Canada where the influence of feminist language planning for English has facilitated the spread of French guidelines in many public and private sector agencies (see, e.g., Ager 1990, Evans 1985, 1987, Houdebine 1988, Schafroth 1992, 1993). In The Netherlands and Dutch-speaking Belgium guidelines are in circulation targeting mainly language use in educational materials (Mottier 1983, 1996). In the Scandinavian countries of Norway, Sweden and Denmark there are few official or formal guidelines in circulation; however, public discussions in the media, parliament and educational forums have led to the adoption of a range of non-sexist language use practices and the adoption of 'informal' guidelines. The situation in Italy is less clear-cut: informally there are a number of suggestions for the non-sexist portrayal of the sexes in language put forward and recommended by individuals and women's groups, especially in the area of education, but there are to date no official language guidelines. In 1986 Alma Sabatini prepared a document on linguistic sexism in Italian for the *Presidenza del Consiglio dei Ministri* in which she also made some recommendations regarding alternative non-sexist expressions. These recommendations have not been officially accepted but some groups have taken them as a basis for their own language guidelines and suggestions. For Italian-speaking Switzerland guidelines have been developed by an *Interdepartmental Working Party on Judicial and Linguistic Questions concerning the Elimination of Sex Discrimination* (1988). Proposals are also being developed for Greece (personal communication Roula Tsokalidou). In Japan a few of the big media organisations have included some guidelines on avoiding sexist language in their handbooks known as *Kinkushu*, and some of the prefectures in Japan provided guidelines to eliminate the sexist portrayal of women as a result of EEO actions and legislation (personal communication N. Gottlieb and Takagi Masayuki 1992).

Although the number of guidelines produced, published or adopted throughout the world is certainly not a reliable indicator of their effectiveness, it nevertheless serves as an indicator that guidelines are a popular mechanism for the implementation of non-sexist LR and that feminist language planners have had some success in getting organisations and institutions to address the issue and to adopt a policy on non-sexist language use.

Analysis of the guidelines: structure and content

The following discussion of guidelines for non-sexist language use is based on a comparative analysis of existing guidelines for a range of languages including Dutch, English, French, German, Italian and Spanish. My total sample included 136 sets of guidelines, a majority of which (95) were concerned with English from the Unites States, Canada, Australia, New Zealand and Great Britain. Twenty-five sets had come from the German language countries of Austria,

Germany and Switzerland. I had access to 10 sets of guidelines from French-speaking countries including France, Canada and Switzerland. Further guidelines dealt with Dutch in The Netherlands Belgium (3), Spanish from Spain (2) and Italian (1). The guidelines had been issued or formulated by a great variety of agencies and groups ranging from private individuals concerned with non-sexist language use to government agencies. In most cases the guidelines were targeted at a particular audience (e.g. at authors and editors of educational manuscripts, members of an academic community or a professional organisation, at civil/public servants and at journalists) and were focused on the elimination of sexist forms in texts and discourses characteristic of the target audience. All guidelines were primarily concerned with public forms of language use, especially in writing. Although it was not always easy to establish whether guidelines had been produced by grassroots planners or were the product of a (semi-)official LP committee or agency, both types were represented in this analysis.

The most remarkable result of the comparative examination of these guidelines across languages and across speech communities is their striking similarity in terms of structure and contents as well as in terms of the approach taken to the issue of non-sexist LR. This is remarkable considering the differences in the legal, social and economic status of women in the various countries and regions, interlingual differences in the expression of sexism, as well as the differing experiences of, and attitudes towards, LR. In addition, this similarity in contents is also quite remarkable in a time in which national varieties of pluricentric languages (e.g. German, Spanish, French, English and Dutch) seek greater independence from each other and experience difficulties in finding a common solution to other LP or LR issues. For example, spelling reform plans for such languages as English and German are constantly hampered by regional and national concerns and issues affecting a unified approach to spelling reform.

The similarity in contents is, of course, partly the result of the presence of common features of sexism in the languages concerned: invisibility, asymmetry, trivialisation and stereotyping of women and men in language. Although languages may differ in how they express these features (e.g. at lexical, grammatical or discourse level), the latter are present in all the languages under examination.

The similarity in the format and structure of the guidelines can also partly be explained by reference to the common stages and practices in the LP process: the identification of the problem, the justification for change as well as the description of the necessary changes.

However, the main reasons for the structural and content similarity in my view are the close informal networks which exist between grassroots language planners (mainly women) across languages and communities, and the fact that a small number of guidelines stood as the model for many others within the same language and across languages. There is no doubt that English language guidelines (especially American ones) exerted considerable influence on guidelines for languages like French (especially in Canada), Dutch, Spanish (especially in the Americas) and to some extent the Scandinavian languages and German. In fact, some of the early guidelines in Dutch in the early 1980s were almost direct translations of American guidelines for English.

STRUCTURE OF THE GUIDELINES

Although there is substantial variation among guidelines in terms of length and format, most guidelines are published as small booklets, brochures or folders comprising on average between ten and twenty pages. The shortest 'guidelines' take the shape of an editorial statement in which authors, editors and contributors are informed about the non-sexist language policy of the journal, publication or agency and encouraged to use non-sexist language or to consult with existing guidelines. The editorial statements in some language and linguistic journals illustrate the practice of simply encouraging their contributors to adopt non-sexist or non-discriminatory language practices. For example, the journal of the American Modern Language Association (MLA)[1] and the journal of the Applied Linguistics Association of Australia, *The Australian Review of Applied Linguistics*, provide the following guidance to their contributors:

> The MLA urges its contributors to be sensitive to the social implications of language and to seek wording free of discriminatory overtones.

> We encourage contributors to submit their manuscripts in non-discriminatory language. *ARAL, Australian Review of Applied Linguistics.*

Some journals provide examples of what they mean by non-sexist language in their editorial statement. In its notice to contributors the *Women's Studies International Forum* states

> [...] a deliberate attempt should be made to use non-sexist language. Man for example, is not acceptable as a generic term.

At the other end of the scale, there are the guidelines which have book length and are indeed published as handbooks, style manuals or style guides. This format is mainly applied to the English language, partly because of the tradition of handbooks of style in the United States and partly because of the more advanced state of the non-sexist language debate in English language countries. However, similar handbooks have become available for other languages (e.g. Häberlin *et al.* 1992 and Müller and Fuchs 1993 for German). Well-known examples in this category are Casey Miller and Kate Swift's *The handbook of nonsexist writing* (which has both an American and a British edition), Bobbye Sorrels' *The nonsexist communicator*, and the guidelines written by Paula Treichler and Francine Wattman Frank on behalf of the Commission on the Status of Women in the Profession of the Modern Language Association of America in 1989.

Despite a substantial variation in length, the guidelines nevertheless display a very similar structure. Most start off with *an introduction* in which all or some of the following points and issues are raised:

- the language planner's view of the relationship between language and society, and between language change and social change;
- the language planner's motivations for the formulation of language guidelines;
- the purpose and scope of the guidelines;
- a definition, description or illustration of common forms of linguistic sexism.

Depending on the overall length of the guidelines these introductory remarks can range from a few sentences or paragraphs to article length contributions (e.g. Frank and Treichler 1989).

Preceding the main body of the guidelines are often some general comments about the limitations of the guidelines or how to use the guidelines. The main part of the guidelines usually consists of examples of sexist forms and usages together with a list of suggested or recommended alternatives. Sometimes a concluding section is introduced in which the benefits of using non-sexist language are reiterated and reference is made to further sources of information on non-sexist/non-discriminatory language use.

CONTENTS OF THE GUIDELINES

Introductory remarks: justifications, aims, definitions and restrictions
If introductory comments are made on the nature of the relationship between language and society, between language change and social

change, these tend to reflect the interactionist view. Language is seen as shaping as well as reflecting social reality. Linguistic change is argued for on the basis that (a) language should reflect social changes in the relationship between the sexes (linguistic change should not lag behind social change – linguistic lag theory) and (b) linguistic change contributes to as well as enhances social and attitudinal change relating to gender relations and the position of women in society.

An example of the argument that linguistic change can lead to attitudinal and social change is found in the German *Handbuch zur nichtsexistischen Sprachverwendung in öffentlichen Texten* (Müller and Fuchs 1993: 12)

> Sprechen ist gesellschaftliches Handeln, und Frauen in Institutionen und Verbänden, in Verwaltungen und Behörden wissen, dass ein veränderter Sprachgebrauch auch veränderte Sichtweisen mit sich bringt . . . [Speaking is social action, and women in institutions, organisations, in administrations and bureaucracies know that a change in language leads to a change in perspective/attitude . . .]

In longer guidelines, there is often a section on the functions of language and on the role of language in contributing to, or eliminating discrimination.

The main justifications put forward by language planners for the elimination of sexist language use and practices include reference to the linguistic lag theory, reference to the existence of legislation outlawing sex discrimination including in language, reference to the damaging nature of sexist language on people's (mainly women's) self-image and on straining gender relations. In some cases language planners also point out that the use of sexist language contributes to linguistic confusion and ambiguity, leading to inaccuracies. Conversely, the motivations for the formulation of guidelines include the need for language practices to reflect new social practices, the need for linguistic practices to comply with legislative measures about the elimination of sex discrimination and the benefits for both sexes through improved communication about women and men and the representation of the sexes in language.

The statement of the purpose and aims of the guidelines is also very similar across guidelines and across languages. The primary aims of guidelines are usually

- to sensitise (specific) language users to the issue of language and gender discrimination, and
- to offer them a range of viable alternatives to sexist expressions and language practices.

Quite a few guidelines explicitly emphasise the *advisory* rather than *compulsory* character of the guidelines:

> It should be stressed that the guidelines proposed in this book are not an attempt to curb a person's freedom of speech or expression by prescribing which words should be used or by proscribing the use of certain expressions . . .
>
> The main purpose of these guidelines is to alert people to the harm which the use of discriminatory language can create and to suggest alternative expressions. Readers are not obliged to choose a non-discriminatory alternative from those provided in the guide if they can find another one, more suitable to their context or more to their liking. (Pauwels 1991a: 15–16)

The advisory character or status of the guidelines is also reflected in the tone and style of writing: the majority of verbs and speech acts used throughout proposals to promote usage of non-sexist language stress the firm but voluntary nature of the actions that can be taken by the readers. In a majority of English language guidelines non-sexist alternatives are presented to readers and language users as 'suggestions', 'recommendations', 'more suitable formulations' and phrases such as:

- It is suggested that   OR   We suggest . . .
- It is recommended   OR   We recommend . . .
- A better way of formulating . . .
- X could be rephrased as . . .
- Alternative formulations could be . . .
- It is better to avoid . . .

Similar formulations are found in guidelines for other languages:

- Il faut mieux dire . . . (French) [It is better to say . . .]
- Gute Lösungen sind . . . (German) [Good solutions are . . .]
- Zeg liever . . . (Dutch) [It is better to say . . .]

Generally speaking the scope of the guidelines is largely the same across languages and target groups. Most guidelines primarily target the use of written language in (specific) public contexts and documents. Sometimes attention is also drawn to applying the guidelines to various forms of public speech, for example, language use pertaining to radio and television, to public announcements and speeches, and to spoken language use in educational contexts and in meetings. The guidelines produced by the Australia Council (1983: 2) exemplify this approach:

These guidelines apply to all written and visual material, both external and internal. They apply to forms, publications, exhibits, advertising, press releases and speeches. They apply also to internal correspondence, memoranda and directives.

Some guidelines include suggestions or recommendations to extend their use beyond the targeted contexts to private and informal forms of language use. Although most guidelines deal with the avoidance of derogatory expressions about the sexes, and of women in particular, their recommendations do not usually cover the register of swearing or other forms of deliberate derogatory language use.

Most prominent in all guidelines is the treatment of sexism at the *lexical* level (words, expressions and phrases), although linguistic sexism at the grammatical level (both morphology and syntax) as well as at discourse level (organisation of information) does receive a mention or some attention in the more elaborate sets of guidelines.

Central to the guidelines is a definition and/or a description of sexism in language: after all, if one of the main purposes of guidelines is to make people aware of sexism in language it is important to provide a clear description of what sexist language use is, and what its most common forms are in a particular language. Yet with regard to this issue there are substantial differences among guidelines. Only a minority of guidelines actually provide a definition of what is meant by sexism in language. German language guidelines are most consistent in providing a definition of sexist language, as exemplified by this quotation from Hellinger *et al.* (1985: 1):

> Sprache ist sexistisch, wenn sie Frauen und ihre Leistungen ignoriert; sie ist ebenfalls sexistisch, wenn sie Frauen in Abhängigkeit von oder Unterordnung zu Männern beschreibt, wenn sie Frauen nur in stereotypen Rollen zeigt und/oder anspricht und ihnen so über das Stereotyp hinausgehende Interessen und Fähigkeiten nicht zugestanden werden; sie ist sexistisch, wenn sie Frauen immer wider durch herablassende Ausdrücke demütigt und lächerlich macht. [Sexist language is language which ignores women and their achievements, language is also sexist when it describes women as dependent on or submissive to men, when it portrays women in stereotypical roles and/or addresses them only in stereotyped fashion and does not allow the portrayal of women beyond the stereotypes. Sexist language is also language which derogates and ridicules women by means of denigratory remarks.]

Many of the shorter guidelines produced in predominantly English-speaking countries lack a definition or a clear-cut description of what constitutes sexism in language. These are generally guidelines produced by agencies such as government departments, affirmative action agencies, EEO committees of private and public companies, institutions including universities, schools, as well as media organisations. Their readership is often left to its own devices to construct a view of linguistic sexism: such guidelines merely provide a few examples of sexist terms, expressions and practices accompanied by a list of alternative expressions. In some cases, a few explanatory notes are given at the start of each section. For example, the *Language Guidelines* produced by the EEO office at La Trobe University in Australia (1985) simply state

> On the recommendation of the Working Party on the Status of Women, Council adopted on the 4th March 1985, the following guidelines for language use in the University.

If definitions of sexism and sexist language are provided in guidelines, these tend to emphasise the bias against women rather than men in language use, as illustrated by the example above from Hellinger *et al.* (1985). However, this emphasis on discrimination against women in language has received criticism from various sectors of the community, usually publicised via the media: they claim that the definition of sexist language is itself sexist. The consequence of this allegation of bias led some official language planning agencies to rephrase or amend their definitions. A case in point is the Australian *Style manual for authors, editors and printers* (1988). In its fourth edition, the *Style manual* contained the following definition of sexism in language:

> Sexist language is language that discriminates against women by not adequately reflecting their role, status and – often – very presence in society despite the increased participation of women in the work force and public life. (*Style manual* 1988: 111)

Following considerable criticism mainly publicised in the daily print media, the *Style manual* editors amended the definition in the new edition:

> Sexist language is language that expresses bias in favour of one sex and thus treats the other sex in a discriminatory manner. In most instances the bias is in favour of men and against women.

Reactions against this redefining of sexism in language have also been forthcoming from feminist groups and individuals who see this as a form of neutralising the original meaning of sexism. Frank and Treichler (1989: 17), for example, mention Andrea Dworkin's adoption of the term 'woman-hating' instead of 'sexist' because of the 'growing gender-neutral use of "sexism" to mean discrimination against women *or* men'.

Guidelines which opt for a description of the common forms of sexism in the language under examination also show remarkable similarities across languages and contexts.

They describe sexist language as involving the following *issues* and practices:

1. The invisibility of women in language due to the fact that men are considered the norm for the human species: men's characteristics, thoughts, beliefs and actions are viewed as fully or adequately representing those of all humans, male and female inclusive.
2. The portrayal of women's status in reference to that of men: women's linguistic status is considered dependent on, deriving from or submissive to that of men, which is represented as autonomous. By relegating women to a dependent, subordinate position, sexist language prevents the portrayal of women and men as different but equal human beings. This also results in a lack of symmetry in the linguistic portrayal of women and men.
3. The stereotyped portrayal of both sexes which leads to a very restrictive portrayal, particularly of women.
4. The portrayal of women as inferior to men.

Consequently, the majority of guidelines cover the following *areas* of sexism:

1. Generic reference to people by means of nouns, pronouns, idioms and expressions.
2. Nomenclature for men and women in relation to occupations, professions, and offices and related positions.
3. Stereotyped portrayal of the sexes.
4. Asymmetrical practices in the use of titles, terms of address, human agent nouns for women and men as well as descriptions of women and men.

Guidelines resulting primarily from equal employment opportunity or sex discrimination legislation tend to cover only or primarily *issues* (1) and (2), whereas guidelines formulated in response to more broadly-based concerns about linguistic inequality and gender discrimination in language provide advice about *areas* (1)–(4).

Advice on how to use the guidelines   Common to many guidelines are advisory remarks on their use and on their limitations. Readers are usually informed that not all non-sexist alternatives listed are stylistically appropriate in all contexts of language use, and that the list of non-sexist alternatives is not exhaustive. Sometimes the needs of a specific group of language users are highlighted or the specific problems of certain texts are discussed. A typical example of this is the attention paid to the needs of editors in dealing with issues of sexist language use. Another example is the discussion of the special problems relating to the elimination of sexism in legislative texts.

More recently guidelines have also started to include a section in which common concerns and criticisms against the use of non-sexist language are discussed and counteracted. For example, in 1992 a language committee was set up within the Queensland Department of Education in Australia to draft language guidelines on non-discriminatory language. It was adamant about including in the guidelines a large section covering not only possible objections to the use of non-discriminatory language but also some counter-arguments as the following excerpts illustrate:

[EXCERPT 1]
Will I be able to say or write what I want to?
You will be able to say and write what you want. Except perhaps for making discriminatory statements or comments. Using non-discriminatory language does not inhibit your potential to write or say what you want. Each language is so rich and flexible that each thought or idea can be expressed in a variety of ways. Language constantly changes to accommodate language users' needs to express themselves in different ways.

It's too trivial to worry about!
This argument is like a double-edged sword: it is usually raised by people who strongly oppose change in language, yet they use the triviality argument to express their opposition. The previous sections in this guide have clearly shown that people can be hurt by discriminatory language. Being on the receiving end of discriminatory language can have devastating effects on a person's self-image.

This should be avoided at all costs, especially in the context of education in a multicultural society like that in Australia.

[EXCERPT 2]
It curbs my freedom of expression!
The use of non-discriminatory language in no way impinges on your freedom of expression except when your expressions impinge on someone else's freedom and rights.

It makes me look ridiculous!
A feeling of ridicule is usually the consequence of insecurity about the value of using non-discriminatory language. If you feel unhappy, insecure, uncertain about its purpose, then you might find that using it makes you feel uncomfortable. If a particular non-discriminatory expression triggers the feeling of ridicule, you are free to choose another one with which you feel comfortable. Your use of discriminatory language, on the other hand, might expose you to accusations of racism, sexism and other forms of discrimination.

What do I do with discriminatory language in textbooks and in other texts?
Dealing with discriminatory language in existing texts poses more problems than trying to write or speak in a non-discriminatory way. This is because an author composing a text (either written and spoken) is free to choose any strategy which seems acceptable to him or her and with which the author feels comfortable. Meanings (except for those contained in discriminatory expressions) are not altered by being formulated in non-discriminatory language. Here are some suggestions about how to deal with this issue:
(a) Quotations from published works . . .
(b) Editing new works or new editions of published works . . .

[EXCERPT 3]
What's the problem? Language is natural!
The problem is that many speakers feel they are misrepresented in current language use: they are invisible, mainly described in a stereotypical way or only in relation to another group of people.

This argument often results from the erroneous belief that language changes all by itself without the assistance of or interference from language users. The expressions we have in language result from the uses speakers make of it. Speakers and writers constantly change language to suit their needs: that is how language is natural!

You are interfering with proper language!
Non-discriminatory language does not interfere with proper or correct language use. It does not lead to incorrect language use. As a matter of fact, it amends language use to reflect better and more equitably the great diversity of its users.

What if everyone invents their own language?
Non-discriminatory language is not a new language. In most instances, non-discriminatory language is about using the present resources of language in such a way that they represent and treat different people and their characteristics in an equitable way. There is no ground whatsoever to believe that the use of non-discriminatory language will lead to incomprehensibility. On the contrary, non-discriminatory language is often

more accurate than discriminatory language and therefore aids rather than diminishes people's understanding.

Queensland Department of Education 1992: Draft guidelines on Non-discriminatory Language

Main body: sexist language forms and their non-sexist alternatives   The prevalent structure for the main body of the guidelines is one in which the sexist language forms are listed to the left of the page and their non-sexist alternatives on the right (sometimes vice versa). Sometimes a third column is provided in which an explanation for the changes is given, as demonstrated below:

Avoid	*Use instead*	*Why?*
salesgirl	saleswoman	parallel treatment with salesman

or

No	SI
El hombre	Los hombres y las mujeres La humanidad
Los derechos del hombre	Los derechos humanos Los derechos de las personas
El cuerpo del hombre	El cuerpo humano
La inteligencia del combre	La inteligencia humana
El trabajo del hombre	El trabajo humano El trabajo de mujeres y hombres
El hombre de la calle	La gente de la calle
A la medida del hombre	A la medida humana/de la humanidad/del ser humano

Extract from *Propuestas para evitar el sexismo en el lenguaje*, Instituto de la Mujer, Madrid, 1989.

The listing of alternatives is variable: sometimes the alternatives are listed in order of preference, sometimes in alphabetical order or according to the frequency of their use, or sometimes in random order. For example,

Avoid	*Use instead*
Man	human being, person, people, man or woman
chairman	chair, chairperson, head, president
policeman	police officer, policeman/policewoman

Intra- and interlanguage comparisons of guidelines for English, German, French, Dutch and Spanish revealed a considerable degree of similarity with regard to (1) the areas of sexist language covered, (2) the format for the presentation of non-sexist alternatives, (3) the list of sexist expressions and their non-sexist alternatives as well as (4) the strategies used to promote the elimination of linguistic sexism. Intralanguage comparisons furthermore exposed similarities with regard to material illustrating sexist and non-sexist practices.

The similarity in the coverage of sexist and non-sexist expressions concerns the terms, phrases, expressions and practices that have been singled out for treatment or emphasis. At the interlingual level, for example, the equivalents of 'chairman' in the other languages are almost always mentioned in guidelines. Intralingually speaking, English language guidelines often include in the section dealing with the pseudogeneric status of -*man* nouns, the examples *chairman*, *businessman*, *craftsman*, *tradesman*. In the German guidelines we usually find the following 'generic' examples: *der Lehrer* (teacher), *der Kunde* (customer), *der Angestellte* (clerk). Common examples in French guidelines include *auteur* (author), *ministre* (minister), *docteur* (doctor), *maire* (mayor). Perhaps more remarkable at the intralingual level is the high degree of congruence *among* guidelines of non-sexist alternatives for a specific sexist expression or phrase. To continue with the example of 'chairman', most guidelines list as alternatives for this expression the words 'chairperson', 'chairwoman/chairman', 'president', 'convener', 'chair', 'person in the chair' and 'head'.

The most interesting observation emerging from a comparative analysis of language guidelines, however, is the preference for similar strategies to eliminate sexist language use. The interlingual analysis reveals a preoccupation with changes at the lexico-grammatical level of language. In other words, guidelines for non-sexist language address the issue of sexism and its elimination mainly at *word level* (both form and meaning) with some attention to matters of morphology (e.g. gender suffixes). Other grammatical and syntactic matters, as well as other aspects of language which aid in the construction of sexist discourse, are sometimes mentioned in passing but are generally not examined or discussed. There is, for example, little or no discussion of how syntactic constructions can lead to sexist discourse (e.g. the use of the passive voice to hide agency) along the lines of Penelope's examination of English syntax (Penelope 1990). The two issues that do receive some attention include linguistic stereotyping and linguistic asymmetry in the use of terms and expressions for women and men (e.g. men and ladies, Mr X and his wife).

Another common feature which emerged from a comparative interlingual analysis of guidelines is the strong preference for *form replacement* as the main strategy to address the elimination of sexist language. Within the form replacement strategy two main substrategies can be recognised, that of gender neutralisation or gender abstraction and that of gender specification or feminisation. In Chapter 4 I explained that the strategy of gender neutralisation involves obtaining linguistic equality of the sexes by means of neutralising or minimising gender reference or by abstracting from it. The strategy of gender specification, on the other hand, involves striving for linguistic equality by means of explicit reference to both sexes in an equal and parallel manner (often achieved by means of a deliberate process of feminisation). Although there are interlingual differences in the emphasis placed on either of these two substrategies, both strategies are frequently used concurrently in the guidelines for Dutch, English, French, German, Italian and Spanish. For example, in English the replacements suggested for the masculine generic pronoun *he* include both gender-inclusive and gender-neutral alternatives: the dual pronoun *he or she* is promoted alongside singular *they*. Incidentally, this is also found in Danish and Norwegian proposals which recommend both dual pronouns *han eller hun* (Danish/Norwegian) and gender-neutral expressions such as the adjectival noun *vedkommende* (the one in question) for Danish and the equivalent of singular *they*, *dei*, in Norwegian.

A combination of both strategies is also the preferred approach for dealing with non-sexist alternatives for occupational nouns, although most languages do favour one strategy over the other. Guidelines for German, French, Italian and Spanish tend to favour some form of gender specification (feminisation) as their dominant strategy whereas in Dutch and English guidelines usually promote gender neutralisation as their main strategy.

Comparing guidelines for the same language also reveals a preference for a common strategy to address sexism. This applies in particular to the pluricentric languages, English and German. The dominant strategy promoted in language guidelines for English in Australia, Canada, Great Britain, New Zealand and the United States is that of gender neutralisation: gender reference is minimised or neutralised in generic contexts as well as in occupational nouns referring to women or men. Owing to the relative low incidence of nouns which are morphologically marked for gender (e.g. *-man* words or words containing the feminine suffixes *-ess, -trix, -ette*), the adoption of the gender-neutralisation strategy has meant relatively little need for new expressions except perhaps in relation to some *-man* words. These words are being replaced mainly by existing expressions and nouns which are not (or are no longer) morphologically marked for gender rather than by the creation of new compounds with *-person*. For English, variations between guidelines occur mainly in regard to non-sexist alternatives for generic pronouns. Whereas strategies such as the avoidance of a third person pronoun (e.g. pluralisation, repetition of the noun) as well as the use of the dual pronoun *he or she* (and its variations[2]) are universally promoted in guidelines, the other options such as a new pronoun, the generic use of *she* and singular *they* are seldom found in guidelines produced by official or semi-official language planning committees.

In the case of the Dutch language (as reflected in guidelines from The Netherlands) the strategy of gender abstraction or gender neutralisation seems to be the more favoured strategy. Wherever possible, gender-neutral nouns are used to replace gender-specific (mainly male-specific) ones in generic contexts. The use of existing feminine forms of occupational nouns and professional titles seems to be discouraged. However, in relation to the replacement of the masculine generic pronoun *hij* the preferred strategy is that of gender-specification strategy : *hij/zij* or *hij of zij*. It is important, however, to mention that official language planning agencies in Dutch-speaking Belgium and The Netherlands are still debating which strategy to adopt in their official guidelines concerning non-sexist occupational terminology. The *Nederlandse Taalunie* (Dutch Language Union) is currently considering a proposal from the Dutch-speaking part of Belgium. This proposal, prepared by Patricia Niedzwiecki (1994, 1995) is strongly in favour of feminisation. In The Netherlands a similar debate is going on with some planners being strong advocates of gender neutralisation and others of feminisation (see, e.g., OC en W 1996, Pauwels 1997a).

The situation for the German language is the reverse: most non-sexist language guidelines which have been produced in Germany, Austria and Switzerland have opted for promoting linguistic equality for the sexes first and foremost by making explicit reference to both sexes – that is, they promote the strategy of gender specification or feminisation in generic contexts as well as in reference to occupational nouns and professional titles. This is achieved mainly by means of *Paarbildung* (the use of paired expressions), also referred to as 'gender splitting'. In spoken language, gender splitting is achieved by joining the feminine and masculine forms of a noun (or vice versa) by means of the conjunctions *und* (and), *oder* (or), and *beziehungsweise* (respectively). For example,

> *Lehrerin oder Lehrer* (female or male teacher)
> *der Lehrer beziehungsweise die Lehrerin* (the male respectively female teacher)
> *Lehrerinnen und Lehrer* (female and male teachers)

For the written language, there are a number of options which involve contractions using brackets, slashes or the graphemic creation called *Binnen-I* (internal capital I) or *Gross-I* (big capital I). For example,

> *Lehrerin/Lehrer, Lehrer/in, Lehrer(in), LehrerIn* (female and male teacher)

German guidelines differ somewhat in their recommendations regarding the contracted forms. Some[3] point out that contracted forms involving brackets or slashes for feminine endings may reinforce the linguistic subservient status of the feminine form and should therefore be avoided. The use of the option involving *Binnen-I* is seen as limited: nouns whose stem obtain an umlaut in the feminine form are excluded (e.g. *Arzt/Ärztin*) as well as in morphologically marked cases (e.g. the genitive, *des Lehrers–der Lehrerin*). The prevalence of gender specification in German language guidelines has meant a prolific creation of feminine forms for occupational and other human agent nouns mainly by means of the feminine suffix *-in*: for example, new formations include *Kommissärin* (commissioner), *Pilotin* (pilot), *Direktorin* (director). Most guidelines also endorse the use of *-frau* (-woman) to form feminine occupational nouns and professional titles in analogy with *-mann* nouns. For example, 'the term *Dipl.-Kauf***frau** is created in analogy with *Dipl.-Kauf***mann** (qualified merchant), the term *Stadtamt***frau** in analogy with *Stadtamt***mann** (town councillor).

Although gender specification is the main strategy promoted for the German language, all guidelines do offer non-sexist alternatives which follow the gender-neutralisation strategy. The main forms of gender neutralisation include the use of non-gender-specific agent nouns such as those ending in *-person, -kraft, -hilfe* (assistant/aide) as in *Vertrauensperson* (confidante), *Friseurshilfkraft* (hairdresser's help), *Haushaltshilfe* (household help), and the use of adjectival and participial nouns, for example *die Grünen* (the Greens), *der/die Angestellte* (employee), *der/die Studierende* (the student) as well as the use of abstract nouns: for example, the use of the word

Professur (the professoriate) instead of *der Professor/die Professorin* or *die Gruppenleitung* (group leadership) instead of *der/die GruppenleiterIn* (female/male group leader). Some variation also exists with regard to replacing the indefinite pronoun *man* (one), which is seen to be derived from *Mann* (man). Guidelines targeting bureaucracies and other official organisations are less likely to recommend changes regarding *man*, whereas those targeting a more general audience may recommend the use of *frau* in women-only contexts. A similar observation can be made for compound nouns containing a masculine human agent noun, e.g. **Arbeiter***bewegung* (workers' movement), **Wähler***gemeinschaft* (voters' community/electorate), **Leser***briefe* (readers' letters). Recommendations regarding these terms range from no change (because the term is not a human agent noun in itself) to replacing the masculine form by a contracted gender-inclusive form: for example, *Leser***Innen***briefe* or **Leserinnen***briefe* for **Leser***briefe*.

Guidelines for Spanish parallel the German ones in that they tend to recommend the visibility of women through explicit naming (paired forms). For occupational nouns which only exist in a masculine form, a feminine form is created mainly by means of existing derivational suffixes. The gender-neutralisation as well as gender-abstraction strategies are also used: terms like *el profesorado* (professoriate or teaching staff) are being recommended to replace *el professor* in specific generic contexts. Similarly, gender-neutral terms like *asistente dental* (dental assistant) are also being proposed.

The guidelines which have been produced for the French language are primarily concerned with achieving linguistic equality in relation to occupational nouns and professional titles as well as forms of address. In comparison with English and German guidelines, French guidelines are less comprehensive and far-reaching. The use of feminine forms for female incumbents is promoted, as is the use of paired female and male forms in job descriptions and advertisements which are subject to antidiscrimination and equal employment opportunity legislation. However, in many other generic contexts the masculine generic form is still used as the main generic form. Sometimes some compromise is made through the use of the article as in *Monsieur*, **le** *Ministre* and *Madame*, **la** *Ministre*. Feminisation of occupational terms and professional titles is nevertheless the main strategy used to obtain linguistic equality in French-speaking Canada, Switzerland and Belgium as well as in France. The most conservative or minimal changes are found in France: feminisation is achieved by (1) using existing feminine titles, (2) using the feminine definite/indefinite article in front of a masculine-generic term and (3) adding the existing feminine suffixes *-euse* or *-trice* to a masculine noun. In addition to these strategies Canada, Belgium and Switzerland also promote the use of a new feminine derivational suffix *-eure* – for example, *auteure*.

The recommendations made for Italian by Sabatini (1986) clearly favour the strategy of feminisation, or more generally gender specification. Similar to the authors of German guidelines, Sabatini proposes the explicit mention of both sexes in generic expressions, especially occupational nouns and professional titles. In Italian this strategy has a considerable impact on gender agreement relating to adjectives and participles. Sabatini proposes that in the case of multiple nouns, agreement should be with the gender of those nouns which are in the majority. If it is difficult to establish a clear majority, agreement should be with the last noun (see example on p. 100 in Chapter 4). The types of feminisation strategies recommended for Italian are in many respects similar to the French ones: i.e. (1) using existing feminine titles with the exception of those involving the *-essa* suffix because of its belittling connotation, and (2) using the feminine definite/indefinite article in front of a common gender noun (usually ending in *-e*). The Italian guidelines, however, also strongly recommend the creation of new feminine titles by using the *-a* suffix (e.g. *avvocata, capitana* and *professora*).

Concluding remarks: benefits and further resources   The main body of the text is usually followed by some concluding remarks and references to further resources. Often the benefits of using non-sexist language are spelled out again: (1) the elimination of the linguistic inequality of the sexes, (2) a more accurate and realistic portrayal of women, and (3) greater linguistic accuracy by means of eliminating gender ambiguity. Sometimes it is reiterated that the benefits of using non-sexist language outweigh the difficulties. In listing further and alternative resources on non-sexist language use, guidelines produced for languages other than English not only include reference to the same language materials but also to resources in other languages, especially English. This reflects both the model role of English language guidelines as well as their dominant position in the area of feminist language planning.

Some concluding comments on guidelines

There is no doubt that language guidelines have become a major vehicle for implementing non-sexist language reform across many languages and speech communities. They are considered the preferred vehicle for non-sexist language reform in the context of public, official and written forms of communication, i.e. their primary target is to bring about change in language in the public arena. Although there are some exceptions, the tenor of the guidelines is that of strong encouragement and firm recommendations for change. The major roles of the guidelines are to raise awareness and to provide alternatives. In most instances writers of language guidelines assume that their readership may not be (very) familiar with the problematic issue and need to be convinced of making changes. They therefore provide a discussion of the problem at stake. They are also careful to downplay the issue of intent in the use of sexist language: the use of sexist language is usually portrayed as the result of lack of awareness or knowledge or subconscious habit rather than as a deliberate language practice. Changes are seldom presented in a compulsory manner: usually a range of alternatives to a sexist expression are listed and the selection of the preferred alternative is left to the reader.

Guidelines primarily address the issue of reform at the lexico-grammatical level and almost universally adopt the strategy of form-replacement to achieve non-sexist language reform.

Furthermore, the intra- and interlingual analyses of guidelines have revealed a remarkable degree of similarity with regard to the structure, format and strategies adopted in guidelines across languages and speech communities. This seems to confirm in part the common nature of linguistic sexism across languages and in part the informal networking and collaborative practices of non-sexist language planners across speech communities.

Notes

1. Meanwhile the Commission of the Status of Women in the Profession of the Modern Language Association of America has produced extensive guidelines for their members as well as for others interested in non-sexist language guidelines (see Frank and Treichler 1989).
2. In some cases the *s/he* version of the dual pronoun is also avoided because its applicability is limited to written language only.
3. These are usually written by linguists or involve the assistance of a linguist.

6 Evaluating feminist language planning

Evaluation is always a crucial task in every form of language planning (LP). It needs to occur throughout the LP process. In the ideal case, evaluation will indeed occur prior to or during the appropriate stages of LP. However, in reality, this is not always the case, partly because of time or financial constraints. Furthermore, the type of evaluation that is undertaken varies considerably across LP agencies and language planners in accordance with the aims of the reform. Throughout this book I have emphasised that although feminist language reformers share the concern of eliminating gender-biased discrimination from language use and work towards achieving a more gender-fair linguistic treatment and representation, their specific aims and, consequently, their strategies and proposals may vary considerably. In Chapter 4 I discussed the specific aims and strategies which feminist language planners wish to achieve or use. They included causing linguistic disruption to attract attention to the gender bias in language, creating a woman-centred language and achieving linguistic equality of the sexes. The first two aims are more likely to be found among radical feminist language reform (LR) groups using various strategies (see Chapter 4). The latter aim, that of achieving linguistic equality, is more likely to be espoused by liberal feminist reformers whose main strategy has been the promotion of change through language guidelines. My decision to focus on feminist LR as promoted through guidelines in Chapter 5 was primarily influenced by its potential for interlanguage comparisons rather than for ideological reasons. In this chapter I focus again on feminist LR as promoted through language guidelines, mainly because it is easier to assess the changes resulting from the adoption of language guidelines than to pinpoint changes resulting from other forms of feminist LP (for example, feminist LP efforts aiming to disrupt patriarchal discourse or efforts to change the discourses affecting women and women's lives). Assessing the impact of feminist LP efforts to change the discourses of sexuality, of power, of ownership, for example, is a task well beyond the confines of linguistic experts and is a truly multidisciplinary as well as inter-disciplinary undertaking. My focus on the changes linked to guide-lines should therefore not be interpreted as a reflection of their greater importance, but rather as a reflection of my limitations in expertise and the limitations of this book.

The procedures to evaluate changes range from an informal prob-ing of attitudes, small-scale surveys of the target group's attitudes towards planned changes, to careful analyses of people's reactions to proposed reforms. In the following sections I shall discuss the types of evaluations that have occurred or need to occur in relation to feminist LP. Some of these evaluations have already received attention in previous chapters. In that case I shall not elaborate on them further but refer to the relevant chapter.

Assessing the desirability for change

With regard to feminist LP, a first level of evaluation takes place in relation to the question: Should sexist language be changed? Language planners gather views and opinions about the necessity or desirability of LR. The more academic views on this matter were discussed in Chapter 3. In addition, there have been a range of small-scale surveys exploring people's views on the desirability of changing sexist language. In general, such surveys have not only revealed that many respondents acknowledge the existence of a range of sexist practices in language but have also shown that a smaller, but not insignificant, number of respondents favour change. Those supporting change do so for similar reasons to those put forward by feminist language planners. They include:

- Change will make women and men more equal in language.
- Change will help make women more visible in language.
- Change will be instrumental in removing damaging gender stereo-types from language.

There is nevertheless also considerable evidence that feminist LR is still (strongly) opposed by various sectors of the community. A major channel for airing views against feminist LR is the print media, especially newspapers and current affairs magazines. The re-lease of language guidelines on non-sexist (or non-discriminatory) language has usually provided the trigger for such comments. I shall elaborate on these in the section 'Public reactions to language guidelines'. The main arguments put forward by opponents of feminist LR include:

- A denial that language is sexist. Consequently, reform is not needed.
- The claim that non-sexist LR will destroy literary traditions and the historical link with other linguistic traditions.
- The claim or accusation that feminist LR is a kind of censorship which curbs an individual's freedom of expression.
- The claim that the issue is too trivial to warrant attention.

It can be said that there has not been much formal evaluation of the issue 'Should sexist language be changed?', especially not before the introduction of LR plans.

Evaluating reform strategies and alternatives

A second form of evaluation occurs at the level of selecting the strategies for reform, including alternatives to sexist language forms and structures. In Chapter 4 I discussed some examples of this type of evaluation process, which involve assessing the linguistic viability and the social effectiveness of a proposed strategy or alternatives. For example, there has been the assessment of the alternatives to generic *he*, and of the introduction of *Ms* as a universal title for women in English. There has also been some debate among language planners about the preferred strategies to achieve linguistic equality of the sexes. Although there have been few attempts to assess the wider speech community's view of the appropriate strategies to bring about language change, there have nevertheless been some surveys which have assessed people's preferences for certain non-sexist alternatives *within the form replacement* strategy. For example, Brouwer undertook a small-scale survey among Dutch speakers which revealed that most participants were in favour of the gender-neutralisation strategy with regard to occupational nouns. Jaehrling's (1988) comparative study of attitudes towards non-sexist language reform in English and German found that her English-speaking informants on the whole favoured the use of gender-neutral alternatives for occupational nouns, whereas her German informants' responses were less clear-cut, i.e. they favoured either neutralisation or feminisation. Schafroth's (1993) study among French university students showed that they preferred a minimalist feminisation strategy with regard to occupational nouns, i.e. the provision of a feminine and masculine article (determiner) in front of the (masculine) noun. In addition, the public reactions following the release of language guidelines also give some insight into people's views on preferred but mostly, disliked alternatives (see next section).

Public reactions to language guidelines

The numerous reactions following the release of language guidelines and non-sexist language proposals provide an insight into the views of some sections of the community regarding feminist language reform. An examination of these reactions provides valuable information not only on public opinion concerning the issue but it also constitutes feedback on the implementation process and will assist in further processes of planning. Since many of the public reactions, especially those which have been aired in the print media, convey a considerable degree of reluctance and negativity towards accepting reform, their analysis gives a good insight into the reasons why people oppose change.

The most common observation when surveying public reactions to non-sexist language guidelines across languages and countries is their striking similarity: similar arguments and strategies are used to react favourably and, especially, unfavourably to proposed changes.

Negative reactions as well as arguments against proposed changes have been the subject of thorough analysis by, for example, Blaubergs (1980), Stanley (1982), Hellinger and Schräpel (1983), Hellinger (1990) and Ellerington (1989). To my knowledge, public reactions in favour of the planning initiatives have not yet been the subject of such scrutiny (see, however, Ellerington 1989 and Jaehrling 1988 for some discussion of positive reactions in Australia).

The focus on examining negative reactions and arguments is understandable because of language planners' eagerness to discover which (unforeseen) issues and features hamper or obstruct the acceptance of the proposed changes. This information can then be used by language planners to amend proposals, to seek alternative or additional ways of promoting change or to formulate counter-arguments (e.g. Stanley 1982, Hellinger and Schräpel 1983, Frank and Treichler 1989).

Blaubergs' (1980) pioneering analysis of classic arguments against changing sexist language recognises eight different categories of reactions and arguments:

1. Change in language is futile because there is no proven link between the degree of sexism in language and sexism in society. Changing language will therefore not affect changing attitudes to women.
2. The issue of changing language is trivial in the pursuit of gender equality.
3. Non-sexist language guidelines are an infringement against one's freedom of speech.
4. There is no sexism in language.
5. Linguistic evidence, especially word etymology, proves accounts of sexism in language to be wrong.
6. Other forms of authority also disprove the allegation that language is sexist.
7. Change is too difficult and impractical.
8. Historical linguistic and literary traditions will be destroyed because of changes to language.

Stanley (1982) distinguishes between six basic classes which overlap to a large extent with those used by Blaubergs (1980), i.e.

1. a denial that sexist language exists;
2. the accusation that non-sexist language reform curbs or destroys one's linguistic creativity;
3. trivialising the importance of the issue;
4. objecting to the proposed reforms on the grounds that they lack aesthetic appeal;
5. an overall reaction of negativity (i.e. similar to denial);
6. opposition to non-sexist language reform because it implies censorship.

Hellinger and Schräpel (1983) and later Hellinger (1990), who investigated reactions against German guidelines and proposals, note similar arguments to those observed by Blaubergs and Stanley in relation to German. They categorised reactions and arguments against non-sexist language in terms of six strategies,[1] i.e. (1) ignoring, (2) denying, (3) downplaying, (4) warning, (5) downgrading and (6) ridiculing of the non-sexist language reforms.

These examinations reveal two basic trends in the negative reactions to feminist language reform. Firstly, there are those reactions and arguments which *deny* or *refute the claim* that language is sexist, and consequently there is no need for reform. A second major trend is the one which implicitly or explicitly accepts the premise that there is sexism in language but argues, for a variety of different reasons, *that change is not appropriate.*

Not all the arguments pleading against the proposed reforms are exclusive to the issue of feminist LP. Some of the arguments (e.g. denial of the problem, objections for stylistic, and historical reasons) have also been used in other forms of language reform and planning – for example, in debates about spelling reform in English and German.

In the following subsections I shall discuss the various negative reactions against non-sexist language reform drawing upon Hellinger's (1990) model. I shall provide examples for five of the six strategies discussed by her: (1) denial, (2) downplaying, (3) warning, (4) downgrading and (5) ridiculing. The strategy of ignoring will not be discussed here but will be dealt with later in the chapter (sections on evidence of change). I shall provide some examples drawn from a variety of sources to illustrate the various strategies: they include discussions in academic journals, public debates or forums on changing sexist language as well as personal information communicated to me by colleagues mainly in Europe, Australia, New Zealand and the USA. That many examples concern English reflects the advanced stage of the feminist language reform debate in English-speaking countries where reform proposals for non-sexist language use have been discussed since the 1970s.

For each of the strategies I also document the counter-arguments put forward by feminist language planners and those supporting language reform.

In addition I include a case study on media coverage regarding the non-sexist language debate from Australia. I have done this case because it gives a detailed insight into public and some not-so-public reactions to the non-sexist language issue in the late 1980s.

(1) Denial

Various arguments are used to deny the existence of sexism in language and/or the need for change as promoted in guidelines. The main ones include

(a) language is neutral;
(b) authoritative linguistic resources disprove the claim of sexism in language;
(c) historical evidence, especially etymology, disproves this claim;
(d) language does not discriminate against women because 'as a woman I do not feel discriminated in language' (as expressed by women) or because 'my wife/daughter/female friend, etc., does not feel discriminated against in current uses of language' (as expressed by men).

The 'language is neutral' argument is often linked to a belief that there is no relationship between language and culture or between language change and social change. This argument is not only used by linguists and other language experts (as documented in Chapters 3 and 4), but also by self-appointed language commentators as well as by ordinary language users. For example, in Chapter 2 I quoted an extract from a letter written by the staff of the Linguistics Faculty of Harvard (USA) in response to a demand by some students of the Theological Faculty for the elimination of sexist language (especially the masculine generic pronoun *he*): the response (see Chapter 2, p. 69) emphasised that the masculine generic pronoun is simply a feature of grammar in English and can therefore not be seen to obstruct the (linguistic) equality of women. Cross-cultural and cross-linguistic evidence is also provided to sustain this argument. The case of a language such as Turkish is frequently used to deny the relationship between language and culture: Turkish has a gender-neutral third person pronoun, yet Turkish society cannot be seen to be less discriminatory against women. The following extract from a letter to the editor of *The Australian* is an example along those lines:

> Under the pretext of abolishing the word 'man', as in manual, chairman etc. we are led to believe that this will lead to a more equitable society. What, pray, are the equivalent words in the Soviet Union and Arab countries where the status of women is leagues lower than what it is in the English-speaking world? (*The Australian*, 13/10/1988)

Appealing to the infallibility of linguistic authoritative sources such as dictionaries, prescriptive grammars, handbooks and style manuals is another popular defence against the acceptance of non-sexist language reform, especially by the lay person. Frequently, letters to the editor argue along the lines of 'my dictionary states that chairman refers to men as well as women' or 'I learned in school that "he" can mean both he AND she'. For example,

> I was taught that the suffix 'man' denoted 'woman' where appropriate and that has served my generation without insult or discrimination. (*The Australian*, 13/10/1988)

Historical evidence, including folk etymology, is another popular means of denying the 'language is sexist' claim. For example, the suffix *-man* in *chairman* is vehemently denied to be related to the word indicating a male human being.

In reference to your article on non-sexist language (B, October 25), I believe it is necessary for me to inform the majority of people on the relevance of words. Many of the words which have been changed to conform to the 'non-sexist' *Style Manual* have been derived from the Greek root 'Manus' – the hand, ie manmade-handmade; and chairman – taking a hand in the chairing of a meeting. (*The Bulletin*, 15/11/1988)

Reference to an earlier or traditional non-sexist meaning of a term is also used as an argument. For example, in a survey undertaken by an EEO office at a major English-speaking university to find out preferred alternatives to 'chairman' (as in Chairman of a Department) some 'chairmen' (both male and female) deny the gender-specific nature of 'chairman' or regret the 'gender-specific interpretation' of the word:

> After due consideration of your proposal, however, and noting that the word Chairman is gender-neutral, the department recommends that the existing title be retained.

> As pointed out in your memo, the traditional meaning of 'chairman' is 'a person chosen to preside' and this is still the correct meaning if correct is taken to be what the majority of speakers understand.

> . . . I myself regret the corruption of the original meaning. . . . I believe that the phenomenon of increasing women in the position would, in the foreseeable future, make acceptable the original meaning of the term and re-establish the etymology that carries the acceptable connotation of the guiding *hand* and *not* the guiding *man* . . . I recommend the retention of the original term.

A German example cited by Hellinger and Schräpel (1983: 47) concerns the gender neutrality of all occupational nouns in German, except those ending in *-mann*.

> Ich bin der Meinung, daß Berufsbezeichnungen, die nicht die Endung *-mann* oder ähnliches enthalten, geschlechtsneutral sind. [I am of the opinion that occupational nouns which do not contain *-mann* or such like are gender neutral.]

To counter arguments that language is not sexist, feminist language planners usually stress the results of psycholinguistic and psychological tests which have shown that people do not experience or process language as unbiased as claimed by those opposing change. In Chapters 2 and 4 I referred to various studies which examined the understanding of masculine generic terms.

(2) Downplaying

Followers of this strategy usually acknowledge that there is a relationship between social and linguistic change and also admit to the presence of sexism in language use. However, they allege that the problem of sexist language use is not so great as to warrant action. In other words, they downplay the importance of reform. Another view that leads to this strategy is that societal change *must precede* linguistic change in order for the latter to be effective. Linguistic reforms are not supported if they do not follow societal changes because they are not given much hope of succeeding.

> . . . language is a reflection of society and, since planned language change is ill-advised, any forthcoming change must occur first in societal practices. (Quoted in Blaubergs 1978: 246)

The linguist Robin Lakoff (1975: 47) also argues this point in her pioneering work on women and language *Language and woman's place*:

> People working in the women's liberation movement, and other social reformers, can see that there *is* a discrepancy between English as used by men and by women; and that the social discrepancy in the positions of men and women in our society is reflected in linguistic disparities. The linguist, through linguistic analysis, can help to pinpoint where these disparities lie, and can suggest ways of telling when improvements have been made. But it should be recognized that social change creates language change, not the reverse; or at best, language change influences changes in attitudes slowly and indirectly, and these changes in attitudes will not be reflected in social change unless society is receptive already.

Lakoff is therefore not optimistic about planned language reform in relation to parallel titles for women and men, for example, or with regard to the introduction of a true generic third person pronoun in English. Bolinger (1980: 103) argues along the same lines although he does acknowledge that raising awareness of linguistic sexism (possibly through reform proposals, *my comment*) may assist in removing sexism from language use:

> Sexism in language will grow less as women are accepted more, in the roles that men have traditionally occupied. This is a safe historical prediction – but it will come about by applying pressures, of which awareness of the stereotypes and protest against them is one.

Countering this type of negative reaction has been mainly the domain of feminist scholars with linguistic expertise in the area of language. The argument that social change must precede linguistic change is counteracted by the argument that there is an interactive and dynamic relationship between changes in language and changes in society.

Frank (1989: 109) asserts that

> the proposed changes of sexist phenomena in our language are based on *two* premises. One is that language is as Edward Sapir put it, 'a guide to "social reality"'. The other, a modified version of the Sapir–Whorf hypothesis, holds that language influences our worldview and 'powerfully conditions all our thinking about social problems and processes'. (My *italics*)

Stanley (1982: 846) has identified resistance to *planned* language change as an underlying motivation for the argument that social change must precede linguistic change:

> Like Lakoff, proponents of the negativity argument[2] assume that language change occurs without the conscious intervention of speakers, but the evidence to be found in a study of older grammars contradicts this assumption.

Downplaying the importance of feminist language reform is also done by acknowledging that sexist language use exists but that it has been blown out of all proportions by feminist activists for sociopolitical reasons. For German, Hellinger and Schräpel (1983: 48) quote the German linguist, Hartwig Kalverkämper (1979a) who was a vocal opponent of non-sexist language reform in the early German debates. He saw his contribution to the debate as 'der wissenschaftlichen Auseinandersetzung über "Sprache und Geschlecht" die gesellschaftspolitische Schärfe zu nehmen' (to depoliticise the scientific debate about language and gender). Personal communications from many feminist (linguist) colleagues in The Netherlands, France, Belgium, Sweden, Denmark and Norway as well as Japan, Singapore and Hong Kong confirm the prominence of similar views among their colleagues. Frequently they are told that they are of course right in their assessment about sexist language but their proposals, actions or support for non-sexist language proposals are too fanatical, too politicised and not objective. They are told that their association with such proposals may damage their reputation as linguists, language experts or academics.

The reactions of linguists and other language experts who stress the contextual argument can also be seen as expressions of this strategy. They too acknowledge that sexism in language exists but claim that in most cases this use is unintended as the linguistic and situational context will prove. In an early paper on changing prescriptive *he* (masculine generic pronoun) Mackay (1980) argues that contextual information will be able to disambiguate the vast majority of uses of an ambiguous word such as prescriptive *he* whereas in later work he claims that the ambiguity of singular *they* is a stumbling block for its acceptance as an alternative to generic *he* . . .

The contextual argument raised primarily by linguists and language professionals has prompted responses from feminist scholars along the lines of Hellinger and Schräpel's (1983: 51)

> Wir können keine Rücksicht mehr darauf nehmen, ob jemand eine Äußerung vielleicht gar nicht sexistisch gemeint hat; für uns ist es wichtig, wie wir diese Äußerung verstehen. Wir lehnen es ab, weiter auf kontextuelle oder situative Signale zu warten, um entscheiden zu können ob wir nun mitgemeint sind oder nicht. [We can no longer take into account the fact that someone perhaps did not mean an expression to be sexist; for us it is important how we understand this expression. We reject having to wait for (con)textual or situational signals, in order to decide whether or not we are included in the expression.]

Another variation of this strategy could be called the 'low priority' strategy. It again accepts the fact that language is sexist and that change is not only viable but also desirable. However, the issue of change is not given much, if any attention because there are far more important issues affecting women's lives which need to be dealt with. Across the languages that have implemented guidelines there are those who comment that non-sexist language will not stop women from being battered, raped and will not lead to women obtaining equal wages, as an extract from a personal letter to me illustrates:

> Please Ms PAWEL [*sic*] – you are obviously an educated woMAN [*sic*] – turn your skills or your life to something that will *help* the Status of Women not something that is useless – not worth the effort.

The low priority argument which projects a view that sexist language reform is a trivial issue in comparison to more substantive issues such as equal pay or the elimination of sexual violence has drawn the following counter-arguments and responses:

> Some feminists as well as antifeminists find the issue trivial. They generally describe the concern about sexist language as 'silly' or as diverting attention from the 'real' inequalities in society. But the very prevalence of this argument indicates that the concern is not trivial. (Frank 1989: 125)

The Ad Hoc Committee on Sexist Language of the Association of Women in Psychology (1975: 16) counteracts this objection with the following statement:

> The major objection, often even to *discussing* changing sexist language, is that it is a superficial matter compared with the real physical and economic oppression of women. And indeed, women's total oppression must end; we are not suggesting any diversion of energies from that struggle. We are, however, suggesting that this is an important part of it.

The *apologetic approach* to feminist language reform is also a form of downplaying. For example, some authors indicate that they do not oppose changes but that they do not adopt these changes in their own language use for reasons such as aesthetic appeal, clarity, convenience, tradition. In some instances this statement takes the form of an apology.

> In this book the pronouns used to refer to 'learner' and 'teacher' are 'he', 'his', and 'him'. They have been chosen as a stylistic convenience and are intended as unmarked forms. To those readers for whom this convention is not acceptable, I extend my apologies. (Ellis 1985)[3]

and

> Masculine pronouns are used throughout this book for the sake of grammatical uniformity and simplicity. They are not meant to be preferential or discriminatory. (Schiefelbusch quoted in Blaubergs 1980: 143)

and

> In English and in many (most?) other languages, the masculine forms of nouns and pronouns are used as the general, or generic, term. We would have liked to avoid this but found ourselves constrained by common usage. Had we said 'woman's curiosity about herself...,' this would have been interpreted as referring to women. Using the word 'man'... we are sure that the interpretation will be 'man and woman'. (Fromkin and Rodman 1983: 17, quoted in Frank 1989: 127)

Counteracting the apologetic approach is done along the same lines as counteracting the contextual approach.

(3) Warning

The strategy of warning is used both by those who deny and those who acknowledge the existence of sexism. Many who warn against the adoption of non-sexist language proposals argue that the costs of linguistic reform very much outweigh the benefits of such reform.

The strategy of warning highlights the danger emanating from an acceptance of non-sexist language proposals and alternatives. These dangers include loss of clarity, simplicity and aesthetic appeal as well as increased censorship and loss of freedom of speech. Sometimes opponents warn that the adoption of non-sexist language alternatives will not only lead to a breakdown of the link with the language of past generations but will also destroy the authenticity of old texts. Here are some examples:

> Thank you for your draft paper on language guidelines. To my mind, the language it promotes is generally sensible and reasonable, . . . There are, however, some points with which I would take issue. My own view of what constitutes good English revolves around clarity, simplicity and conciseness – in short, conveying the greatest amount of meaning in the fewest and simplest words. Measured by that standard, and despite protestations to the contrary, I find many of the constructions used to avoid sexist language ugly and clumsy. (Extract from a memo by an editor of a university publication to the EEO officer)

> Im Gegensatz zu vielen anderen Frauen, die sich mit diesem Problem befassen, bin ich aber gegen die Verwendung weiblicher Endungen bei Funktions- oder Berufsbezeichnungen, weil sie in den meisten Fällen
> – umständlich,
> – überflüssig,
> – gegen die Interessen der Frau sind. (Viet 1991: 420)
> [In contrast to many other women who concern themselves with this problem I do not approve of the use of feminine suffixes in professional and occupational titles because they are longwinded, superfluous and against the interests of women.]

Sometimes examples are provided to illustrate the loss of clarity, speech economy, etc., when non-sexist formulations are used. In the following example, Viet (1987: 21) demonstrates that adherence to gender splitting in German leads to loss of speech economy and even absurdity:

> Der Student/die Studentin hat das Recht, einen/e oder mehrere Professor/ in/en/innen als Gutachter/in/innen zu wählen. [The (male/female) student has the right to choose one (male/female) or more (male/female) professors as (male/female) supervisor(s).]

Opponents also warn that clarity and comprehensibility are in danger if proposals are introduced and accepted because they run counter to prescribed usage. This argument is particularly used in relation to grammatical features such as gender agreement between nouns and other parts of speech (e.g. for German, Italian, French,

Spanish), number agreement and the third person singular pronoun (English). The promotion of singular *they* as a non-sexist third person pronoun alternative in English language guidelines has attracted severe criticisms from all parts of the community on the grounds that it is linguistically incorrect.

> As for the recommendations themselves, I do object very strongly to the constructions involving the deliberate disagreement between the number of the pronoun and its referential noun. Licence or no licence I would assume it my editorial responsibility to make the noun and pronoun agree in number. In some cases usage is fair argument for the acceptance of an irregular construction but the examples you cite ('a student should present *their* work' and 'when a student is qualified *they* may apply for admission') confuse communication and are entirely unnecessary given the variety of better alternatives available. There's every chance those sorts of constructions were as ill-conceived in the fifteenth century as they are now. (Extract from a memo by a publications officer to the EEO officer)

For German, the use of the indefinite pronoun *frau* to replace indefinite *man* and the breach in gender agreement between indefinite pronouns (e.g. *wer* (who), *jemand* (someone), *niemand* (no one)) and other pronouns (e.g. possessive, relative) are described as a breach against the German pronoun system:

> Im Deutschen werden Beispiele wie *Wir suchen jemand, die uns helfen kann* oder *Wenn frau mit dem Fahrrad fährt, . . .* eine Verletzung des deutschen Pronominalsystems gesehen. [In German examples such as *We are looking for someone, who (feminine) can help us* or *When one (frau instead of man) rides a bicycle . . .* are seen to be a breach against the German pronominal system.] (Hellinger and Schräpel 1983: 52)

Countering the arguments of those who warn that non-sexist alternatives endanger clarity in language, that they are unaesthetic and that they go against the speech economy principle is usually done in the following ways. Non-sexist language alternatives, if chosen appropriately, neither lead to linguistic confusion nor lack aesthetic appeal. Hellinger (1990: 136), for example, comments on Viet's objection to the sentence 'Der Student/die Studentin hat das Recht, einen/e oder mehrere Professor/in/en/innen als Gutachter/in/innen zu wählen' (see above):

> Dieses Beispiel hat Viet aber offenbar selbst erfunden; in dieser Form wird das Splitting von feministischen Linguistinnen nicht vorgeschlagen. Außerdem ist das Splitting nur *eine* Möglichkeit, sprachliche Sichtbarkeit und Symmetrie zu erreichen. [This example must have been invented

by Viet herself because this is not the way in which feminist linguists propose the use of splitting. Besides, splitting is only *one* possibility to achieve linguistic visibility and symmetry.] (Hellinger 1990: 136)

It is also argued that non-sexist forms do not obscure clarity of expression but, on the contrary, increase clarity as they remove ambivalence about whether or not both sexes are included in generic forms or treated symmetrically.

With regard to the issue of speech economy, feminist language planners concede that in some cases the non-sexist alternatives can lead to more longwinded formulations but point out that they consider linguistic equality to be more important than the principle of speech economy (e.g. Hellinger and Schräpel 1983).

In response to accusations that non-sexist language alternatives promote ungrammatical usage, language planners comment that this only occurs with the use of certain alternatives which can be avoided. For example, if language users have problems with the number agreement involving the use of singular *they*, they can use other alternatives which do not affect the grammar. Furthermore, language planners point out that opposition on the basis of correctness arguments is grounded in the belief that language is static. Such a belief fails to recognise that the linguistic reality is one of dynamic processes leading to variability and change.

Non-sexist language reforms are also opposed on historical grounds: proponents of this view claim, often without substantiation, that non-sexist language reform would destroy the cultural heritage of a society by demanding that historical texts and literature be rewritten to conform to non-sexist language standards. In the *American Spectator* (1980), John Simon, an eager crusader for, and self-appointed guardian of, the (American) English language, concludes his review of *The handbook of nonsexist writing* (Miller and Swift) which incidentally he called *A handbook for maidens*,

... by allowing irresponsible alterations in the language, we are not only losing necessary touch with the glories of our literary past, we are also inviting linguistic turmoil ... (Simon 1980: 31)

Feminist language planners have repeatedly stressed that it was never their intention to rewrite historical documents or literary works so as to destroy their authenticity. The only exceptions have been religious texts and national anthems which are not only seen as historical documents of the past but also as contemporary texts which people use as guides in their daily lives or as expressions of their identity. In the case of reform to religious texts, feminist theologians and women in religious organisations have certainly not been the first, or the only ones, to propose changes to the texts.

However, most arguments put forward by means of the strategy of warning relate to censorship and the imminent danger to the freedom of speech. The 'milder' versions of this argument express objection to the rights of publishers, editors, professional organisations to impose or dictate the use of non-sexist language. This seems to constitute a serious curbing of an individual's right to freedom of expression. More radical versions of this argument liken the reform proposals to Orwellian Newspeak, or Kafkaesque language situations. Opponents also warn unsuspecting language users that the proposals are reminiscent of the linguistic manipulation undertaken by fascist governments in Italy and Germany. Here are some examples of news headlines relating to the introduction of non-sexist language reforms: 'Bring on the Ayatollah', 'A new dark age of illiteracy', 'For 1984, read 1988', 'Newspeak'.

'Unsuspecting' and ordinary language users are also warned against bowing to the pressures of a 'vociferous' minority who sets out to interfere or even destroy traditional language:

> Academia has proved to be the Maginot Line in the defense of good sense against panzer regiments of Women's Liberation. Being a citizen of the occupied territory behind it, I have become familiar – as which of us has not? – with one of the most disturbing manifestations of that movement's influence: the warping of language to suit the ideological line of the new feminism. . . . Like all bullies, the new feminists are attacking their easiest target. And make no mistake, language is under attack. (Levin 1981: 217–18)

Refuting the censorship argument has been done in the following ways: many language planners have stressed that their proposals are guidelines or recommendations which neither prescribe nor proscribe usage. Others (e.g. Blaubergs 1980, Frank 1989) have pointed out that those who oppose the non-sexist language proposals most fervently, on the basis that they impose censorship, are often the ones who are strong advocates of style and other language prescriptions.

A third line of counter-argument establishes an analogy with other forms of discriminatory language (e.g. racist language) and comments that censorship or freedom of expression is not a justified defence in the light of sexism in line with reactions against racism, antisemitism or other forms of discrimination.

(4) Downgrading

This strategy involves not only questioning the linguistic expertise of the language planners but also the scientific character of their scholarship. The language planner's work is condemned for its lack of objectivity, its preoccupation with ideology and its sociopolitical dimension. Often personal attacks on the author(s) of guidelines are introduced to destabilise the latter's position not only as an expert but especially also as a normal person (usually woman). Kalverkämper (1979b: 103 and 105) describes the women who allege that language is sexist and propose non-sexist guidelines as being fanatical about their area of research and accuses them of 'agitatorische Verzerrung'. Furthermore the proposals are downgraded by trivialising them. A typical argument is that the existence of sexism is a very trivial matter in the light of other forms of inequality. The case study of Australia media coverage will contain many such examples.

Reactions from feminist language planners to counteract this strategy have been varied: in some cases no reaction or ignoring the accusations is seen as the preferred strategy, as it is considered very unlikely that any logical argument could have an impact on changing the opponent's stance. In other contexts the best strategy is seen to be the presentation of counter-examples. Another strategy used to counteract the derogation or trivialisation of the issue is to retort with comments along the lines of 'If the issue of non-sexist language reform is so trivial in the eyes of the opponents, why do they get so upset and emotional about it?' Finally, feminist language planners comment that they have never tried to hide either their ideological stance or their belief that language is not neutral.

(5) Ridiculing

The vast majority of negative *public* reactions against proposed non-sexist language reform involves the strategy of ridicule. Hellinger (1990: 137) points out that the users of this strategy lack any form of substantial argumentation against non-sexist language reform and therefore attack purely on emotional grounds. She comments that this is done in a variety of ways, some of which involve (1) attacking the linguistic creations of feminism, (2) rewriting historical texts *ad absurdum*, (3) applying certain guidelines without consideration for any linguistic principles (especially word/morpheme boundaries) and (4) ridiculing the proposed changes in jokes, cartoons and comments. Examples will abound in the Australian case study.

The main strategy for counteracting this type of reaction to language proposals has been, and still is, to ignore them.

Evaluating language reform: an Australian case study

The case study concerns the reactions following the launch of the fourth edition of the Australian *Style manual for authors, editors and printers* (hereafter the *Style manual*) in early October 1988. This manual is used extensively by Australian Public Service staff to guide them in matters of style and manuscript conventions. In previous years the Office of the Status of Women, a government office which forms part of the Department of the Prime Minister and Cabinet, had urged that Australian government publications be written in non-sexist language and that, for this purpose, the *Style manual* should include guidelines on how to eliminate sexist practices in language use. In mid-1987 the Office of the Status of Women employed a consultant (myself) to write a report on issues for non-sexist language reform which would form the basis of a chapter in the fourth edition of the *Style manual* to be published in 1988. The chapter on non-sexist language comprised 16 pages in the 409 page manual.

The *Style manual* was by no means the first to introduce guidelines for non-sexist language use in Australia. A range of other organisations, including tertiary institutions, publishers, statutory bodies, trade unions and professional bodies, had already introduced guidelines. For example, in 1984 the Australian Broadcasting Commission introduced guidelines and the Australian Council of Trade Unions did so in 1986. The latter had also attracted considerable media coverage.

The launch of the *Style manual*, however, caused a furore in the Australian print and electronic media: almost 100 per cent of articles, discussions of, and reactions to the *Style manual* were focused on the chapter about non-sexist language. In fact, more than a thousand articles, editorials and readers' letters were published in Australian national and regional newspapers and magazines in a four-week period following the release of the *Style manual*. Having been identified as the consultant, I was seen as responsible for the section on non-sexist language. I was frequently asked to participate in radio and television interviews concerning the issue and also found myself to be the target of public and private positive and negative comments, including abusive and threatening phone calls and letters. My close involvement in this media 'event' allowed me a very detailed insight into people's public and not-so-public reactions to guidelines on non-sexist language use.

Here I shall focus mainly on the reactions found in the print media, particularly the daily newspapers with a national or a state-wide distribution. I shall discuss the extent to which the Australian arguments for and against the introduction of non-sexist guidelines reflect the arguments and strategies mentioned above.

In the first week following the release of the *Style manual*, all major newspapers carried a number of articles, including front page features, editorials, feature articles and comments on the topic. Later in the coverage a large volume of letters to the editor were also published. The majority of coverage, both in terms of articles and coverage, expressed a negative reaction against the chapter and guidelines. Very few if any of the articles engaged in non-evaluative reporting. The language of both headlines and text was evaluative and often quite emotive. The guidelines were described as an attempt to de-sex language, to take sex out of language, to castrate language, to manipulate language, to can the man, to ban words, to outlaw words, to force manufactured words into usage. Typical headlines included

> 'Govt outlaws "middleman" and "tealady" ' (*Brisbane Sunday Mail* 9/ 10/1988)
> 'Man doomed to extinction' (*The West Australian* 6/10/1988)
> 'Pandering to feminism's newspeak' (*The Age* 12/10/1988)

The arguments put forward and the strategies used to reject the guidelines very much reflect those described earlier in this chapter. Although the majority of negative reactions adopted the strategies of denigration and ridicule, as I shall illustrate later, there were nevertheless also examples of the denial strategy, and of warning against the danger of accepting the guidelines.

Etymological debates were a frequent feature in the denial strategy, as illustrated by the following extract

> 'manual' is a handbook which is derived from 'manus' the hand. Similarly, a 'chairman' is one who manages or handles a meeting by presiding from the chair. (*Brisbane Courier Mail* 18/10/1988)

Another interesting etymological example was the word 'ombuds-man' in English. Borrowed from Swedish *ombudsman* into English, opponents of the non-sexist alternatives 'ombudsperson' or 'ombud' asserted that the word had no sexist connotations in the source language(s).

> ... Melbourne's Swedish academics are still giggling over the attempt by language rapists to de-sex 'ombudsman', a word we leased from the frigid north about 20 years ago. In particular, they chuckle when people suggest it should be reduced to 'ombuds' [*sic*]. Without 'man' on the end, they say it means nothing. 'Ombuds' is simply the genitive form of the word delegate 'delegegate'. In Swedish , they say , 'man' in this case, has no gender. It translates as 'one' or 'person', so there is no need to remove it from the title. 'It's the same as your own English ending of "man",' they say, while apologising for having to mention it. (*The Age* 26/10/1988)

Other examples of the denial strategy included the following letters to the editor:

> ... Nobody thinks that a manhole is male and nobody thinks that by saying the word mankind that women are not included or are in any way inferior. (*Sydney Morning Herald* 11/10/1988)

> ... Words such as mankind have always been understood to be gender inclusive ... (*The Age* 11/10/1988)

The strategy of downplaying or downgrading was not so obvious in the media coverage possibly because the arguments presented under this strategy lacked sensationalism:

> Sir: Women have been subject to discrimination in society, and I understand their push for equal rights. However, I cannot possibly comprehend just what can be achieved by changing our natural language (*Herald*, 6 October) ... (*Sydney Morning Herald* 11/10/1988)

The strategy of warning, on the other hand, was well represented among the negative media reactions. Warnings spelled out the threat that non-sexist language guidelines posed for language and 'mankind' (it is unlikely that they use the word humanity). Here is a taste of the smorgasbord of warnings:

> The final result will realise the worst nightmares of Messrs Orwell and Kafka. (*The Australian* 13/10/1988)

> This campaign is not only destroying our fine language ... but is designed to emasculate the virility characteristic of a young and enterprising country. (*The Australian* 13/10/1988)

> The English language, the richest and most precise in the world, incorporating so much history, so much culture, so many traditions, borrowings, ingenuities and inventions, is to be diminished at some myopic, transient, political whim. ... (*The Age* 11/10/1988)

> Feminist zealots, . . . , have removed sexist words from school textbooks. Have they had the effrontery to rewrite passages from our literature, from Shakespeare, from the Bible of 1606, from Burns, Scott, Stevenson, Trollope? Such meddling would be sacrilege . . . (*The Australian* 14/10/1988)

Ridicule, outrage and derogation were, however, the main reactions to the introduction of non-sexist language use. Ridicule often took the form of applying suggested alternatives, especially man, to the extreme. For example,

> If a workman is a worker and the serviceman is a servicer, then a German must be a germ. (*The Australian* 18/10/1988)

> Chess will become very confusing when kings and queens become monarchs. (*The Australian* 20/10/1988)

Other forms of ridicule included

> I suggest a very simple solution to the raging debate on non-sexist language. On Mondays, Wednesdays and Fridays all police officers should be known as policewomen, all flight attendants should be called air hostesses and so on. On Tuesdays, Thursday and Saturdays we use the present system. Sunday is supposedly a day of rest so everyone can call themselves what they damn well like. Wouldn't that be fun! (*The Australian* 28/10/1988)

Many negative reactions were directed at the alleged 'culprits' of this 'linguistic engineering': these included not only the alleged author of the guidelines but also the government that commissioned them, as well as feminists in general. They were accused of mangling or destroying the English language without proper knowledge or authority to change language. They were seen as a radical minority out to destroy the English language and to bring 'normal' women into disrepute. They were described as abnormal women whose lack of femininity was seen to be responsible for their behaviour. Here is a selection of such descriptions:

> Oh what a hoot! Do I understand that these granite faced frustrated feminists hate men so much they have derived a whole new language to eliminate any reference to them? (*The Australian* 13/10/1988)

> It is amazing the trouble a small group of vociferous fepersons suffering from an inferiority complex can do . . . (*Hobart Mercury* 15/10/1988)

> No wonder the Australian female cannot be taken seriously by males in their quest for equal opportunities when we are represented by dehydrated Mses with their psychotic dribblings of human eating sharks. (*West Australian* 11/10/1988)

What are those hairy legs going to do about changing menopause and menstruation?' (*The Australian* 14/10/1988)

A woman MP yesterday slammed the use of non-gender terms such as spokesperson and chairperson; saying women who demanded such expressions usually 'looked like Dracula's mother'. (*The Herald* 19/10/1988)

Outrage is also characteristic of many negative reactions in the press coverage as illustrated below:

What a steaming heap of personure . . . (*Northern Territory News* 9/10/1988)

As a heterosexual male, I take exception to the proposed castration of the English language. (*The Australian* 18/10/1988)

Sir, The public service's mandating the virtual abolition of 'man' is as sensible as a veterinarian gelding the stallions in a stud farm. Feminist misanthropy is blinkered by a tunnel-vision of reality. (*Northern Territory News* 21/10/1988)

The mind boggles at the thought of paranoid bureaucrats with grubby little minds pouring through text books, manuals and even lowly comics in an attempt to neutralise a strong, virile language which has evolved by the very descriptive nature of its character. (*Hobart Mercury* 24/10/1988)

With the printed reactions from readers being predominantly negative, supporters of the guidelines complain about this alleged bias in news coverage:

Dear Ed, you are a male chauvinist pig. You only seem to publish anti-language change letters. And don't say you don't get any in favour . . . I've written four! (*The Australian* 2/11/1988)

Your so-called 'selection' of Letters to the Editor was blatantly one-sided and is an illustration of how much of a struggle is still ahead for women to be taken seriously. (*The West Australian* 13/10/1988)

Although media comments and reactions in support of the guidelines were in the minority, there were some, especially in the 'Letters to the Editor' section. Both articles and letters in support of the guidelines were mainly reactions to the many negative comments published. They are similar to the counter-arguments formulated by feminist language planners.

In 'Letters to the Editor' proponents of the guidelines stress the need for linguistic change because language lags behind social change or because it inhibits change. Readers also comment that women have been wronged in the language practices of the past. Furthermore, readers reject the extreme ridicule displayed by their opponents and expose the misinterpretations spread by opponents of the guidelines. Here are some examples:

> Well, we've all had a jolly good adolescent giggle at the Federal Government's determination to remove certain sexist words and expressions from our language . . . Our language is not being dehumanised. It is responding, as languages must, to an exciting, changing, developing world. It will only be dehumanised by those who wish to freeze it solid for generations. (*Hobart Mercury* 24/10/1988)

> I'm sick of the shallow, puerile and laboured jokes by both men and women against a genuine and reasonable attempt to suggest options to gender-base words which are no longer applicable to today's reality . . . Language is a living thing . . . Long live humankind! (*The West Australian* 25/10/1988)

It is difficult to gauge the representativeness of the readers' comments found in the 'Letters to the Editor' section of newspapers. Nevertheless the (often vitriolic) reactions against guidelines found in the Australian press mirror those found in other English-speaking countries in reaction to non-sexist language. Although the letters section does not allow for analysing the sociodemographic profile of the writers, it is nevertheless possible (to some extent) to compare female and male views on the matter. With regard to the negative reactions, the male–female ratio is about 6 : 4. Men's and women's negative comments differ somewhat in that men are more likely to make statements about the emasculation of language, and about the female language planners as deviant females. They also go to more extremes in their attempts at ridiculing the changes. Women tend to argue that 'traditional' language has served them well and that changes are therefore not necessary. Quite a few also have the attitude of 'I am a feminist but . . .'.

Excluding the letters written by the Minister for, and others linked to, Women's Affairs in reaction to the media coverage, the gender balance of those supporting the guidelines was more or less equal, even with a leaning towards men. Both men and women brought forward similar arguments, which I have mentioned above.

As a concluding remark to this case study I would like to say that the reaction to the fifth edition of the *Style manual* published in 1994 was very subdued, almost non-existent. In the fifth edition the chapter on non-sexist language had been replaced by a chapter entitled 'Non-discriminatory language'. This chapter incorporated the previous guidelines on non-sexist language use, with minor changes, and also covered discriminatory practices in language based on race, ethnicity and disability. One can only speculate about the non-reaction to this edition: perhaps the issue of discrimination through language and the need for change have become more acceptable, or people have become indifferent about proposed changes to languages as such changes are considered trivial in the light of other economic and social changes facing them. Another possibility could be that the inclusion of other 'minority' groups (Australian Aboriginal people, people from non-English-speaking language backgrounds and people with disabilities) has made it more difficult to react negatively for fear of being branded racist. I sincerely hope it is not for this latter reason!

Notes

1. Hellinger (1990) is a reworking of Hellinger and Schräpel (1983) which only distinguish between four strategies. However, both articles recognise the same arguments and reactions but structure them differently.
2. The negativity argument formulated by Stanley (1982) refers to arguments which claim that sexism in language is the result of sexism in society. Attitudes towards women will not be changed on the basis of changing language. The focus should be on changing social structures from which language change will ensue.
3. However, in his more recent work, Ellis (1990) has departed from his earlier practice and uses generic she throughout the text. He introduces this change in a 'Note on Pronouns'.

    In this book I have used 'she' and 'her' to refer generically to learners, teachers, researchers etc. This is a departure from my previous practice, but I have come to realize that the choice of pronouns is an important issue to many women and that, overall, less offence is likely to be caused by the choice of the female gender. (Ellis 1990: viii)

7 Is change occurring?

In this chapter I address what could be considered the most important form of evaluation in the language planning process – that is, an assessment of its results. The question 'Has language change occurred as a result of the planning?' encapsulates this endeavour. Other relevant questions include 'Which changes are spreading?', 'How are the changes spreading throughout the speech community?' and 'What is the status of the changes in use in the community?'. In other words, documenting the process of change involves the following steps:

- Gathering evidence that proposed alternatives are used in a given speech community or group and that they are spreading throughout (parts of) that community or group; that is, who uses what?
- Assessing the status of the alternatives in use: this allows an insight into the progress of language change. For example, the alternatives could be in use but their status is still one of dispreferred or discouraged use. In other cases, the alternatives may be used alongside 'traditional' forms but constitute the recommended usage. In a few instances, the alternatives may even have replaced (displaced) the traditional forms.
- Gathering evidence about the manner in which they are used. Such data will assist in an evaluation of the *effectiveness* of the alternatives. For example, alternatives may be in use but their use in the community is conflicting with the intended use and functions.

Here I focus on the changes emanating *primarily* from the promotion of non-sexist language use through guidelines. By *primarily* I mean that these changes are likely to be linked to the promotion of language reform via guidelines. I am well aware that such changes could also have been triggered or reinforced by other strategies of language reform.

The study of feminist language change is still in its infancy, especially outside English language countries. This is partly related to the fact that other language communities are often in earlier stages of the planning process. Further, the assessments which have occurred so far have focused almost entirely on the impact of the *form replacement* strategy, which is only one of many strategies. For example, there are a number of studies (admittedly small-scale) which have examined such issues as the use of non-sexist generic nouns and pronouns in the print media, and in the speech and the written work of university students as well as the use of gender-inclusive occupational nouns and pronouns in job descriptions and job advertisements. The use of the new courtesy title 'Ms' by women as well as its use in documents has also been examined. Furthermore, there have been some assessments of the impact of non-sexist language guidelines on gender stereotyping in textbooks and other reference texts (e.g. learners' dictionaries) as well as in religious and legal texts. So far most of these assessments have been undertaken for English, although there are also some for German, Dutch and Norwegian. Besides systematic investigations into feminist linguistic change, there is also a wealth of data available on this subject in the form of long-term casual observations made by interested individuals. Talking to friends, colleagues and others with an interest in the subject of feminist linguistic change, I found that many of them keep notes on changes observed in conversations, meetings, lectures, in a variety of print media as well as while listening to the radio or watching TV. Although the data collected through such practices are often no more than impressions, they are nevertheless very useful in establishing trends or even in providing additional information supporting the findings of a systematic, yet small-scale study into feminist language change. Therefore I shall draw upon both sources of data to discuss some examples of these changes.

What kind of changes are occurring?

For change to occur there must be signs of variability in use. This can be at various levels of language use: for example, phonological variation could be a sign of a sound change, grammatical changes may be the result of the variable use of certain linguistic rules, etc. Although variability is a condition of change, it is not necessarily always a sign of change, nor does it automatically lead to change. Sociolinguistic studies, for example, have provided evidence that there are quite a few forms of variability which could be considered to have 'stabilised' in a community (e.g. Romaine 1982). There is the phenomenon of free variation which is not usually associated with linguistic change. Furthermore, to make a claim that variability is a sign of linguistic change, it must be found in a speech community (rather than in one individual) and it must affect more than a single instance of a particular phenomenon/feature. Although these conditions have been formulated for the investigation of unplanned change (e.g. Labov 1972, Weinreich *et al.* 1968), they can nevertheless be applied to instances of planned language change.

The variability resulting from feminist language planning initiatives is indicative of change in progress. The following sections will provide evidence that certain feminist language planning proposals have caused instability to current practices, resulting in a great deal of variability. Although clear-cut evidence does not yet exist that any particular alternative has completely displaced and replaced existing, 'traditional' forms or practices, there is nevertheless sufficient evidence that most proposed alternatives are being used outside the group of originators and that their use is spreading through the speech community at large.

Naming practices: names and titles

Both systematic and casual observations confirm that an increasing number of women have adopted and are adopting naming practices which assert their linguistic independence from men. For example, women increasingly maintain their premarital name (their so-called 'maiden name' or birth name) after marriage in societies where the tradition is for women to adopt their husband's name. In some cases married women in the paid workforce use their birth name in their work environment and their spouse's name in other contexts. Also, more women revert to their birth name after separation or divorce. Another practice which has increased substantially includes the use of hyphenated names by women who are married, i.e. their surnames are made up of their premarital name and their married name. In societies which allow for name changes other than those related to marital status (of women) more women are taking the opportunity to radically change their name to mark the beginning of a new linguistic feminist-oriented identity.

Despite greater legal flexibility in passing the mother's surname on to children, many women and/or heterosexual couples continue to pass on the father's surname to their offspring. This includes feminist women with an interest in linguistic equality: when questioned about this continued practice they mainly stated that it was force of habit. An interesting development is found in Norway where, since the mid-1970s, the normal procedure is for the mother's name to be passed on to offspring unless the parents decide against it. Personal communication with Norwegian colleagues revealed that an increasing number of parents adopt the 'normal' (i.e. unmarked) procedure and pass on the mother's name.

With regard to courtesy or honorific titles, women in English-speaking countries are increasingly using the new title 'Ms'. In the United States a survey conducted by the *Ladies Home Journal* as early as 1972 showed that approximately 34 per cent of 8,074 polled women preferred the 'Ms' salutation. Steinem (1983: 150), founder of *Ms Magazine*, estimated that by the late 1970s one-third of all American women were in favour of 'Ms' as an alternative courtesy title. Jakobson and Insko (1984) examined the use of 'Ms' among first-year students at an American university in the early 1980s, and found that just under 25 per cent used 'Ms'. Pauwels (1987b) polled 250 women across Australia in 1986 and found that just under 20 per cent made personal use of the title 'Ms'. The results of a similar study in 1996 revealed that personal use of 'Ms' had risen to 44.5 per cent (Pauwels (1997c). As for 'Ms' use among Australian female students, Pauwels (1987b) found that in 1975 3.9 per cent of female students used 'Ms', and this had risen to nearly 12 per cent in 1986. The use of 'Ms' by men to women is not yet very widespread. Many men (at least in Australia) are still insensitive to many women's desire to be addressed as 'Ms'. The use of 'Ms' in written materials is high and has steadily increased in the past 15 years. For example, I surveyed a vast selection of miscellaneous print materials produced and distributed by government agencies, insurance companies, banks and other private and public sector agencies in Australia (Pauwels 1987b, 1996), and found that the title 'Ms' appeared in 90 per cent of the surveyed material, although its use was not always in line with the guidelines. Despite the well-publicised 'anti-Ms' stance of some newspapers (e.g. *The New York Times* until recently), the title 'Ms' is now found in almost every major newspaper published in English-speaking countries. Although the frequency with which 'Ms' is being used in the daily press may have increased dramatically, its use does not always reflect the intended meaning (see 'Are the changes effective?' on p. 218ff).

In speech communities where the gender imbalance in courtesy titles was rectified by a redefining of the equivalent of 'Mrs'[1] (e.g. Dutch, German, French, Italian, French, Norwegian, Danish and Swedish) there is evidence that many adult women have adopted the new meaning of 'Mrs', i.e. as a universal courtesy title for women without reference to marital status. A recently completed study by Pauwels (1996) on the use of female courtesy titles in The Netherlands revealed that 85.3 per cent of Dutch women polled in two major cities used the courtesy title 'Mevrouw' in accordance with feminist planning proposals. The women commented that they expected adult women, irrespective of marital status, to use and to be addressed by the courtesy title 'Mevrouw'. Casual observations on this recommended use of 'Mrs' in French, German, Italian, Norwegian and Spanish seem to confirm the findings of the Dutch study: the 'redefined' title of 'Madame', 'Frau', 'Signora', 'Fru' and 'Señora' is increasingly used by and to adult women, irrespective of marital status, and is also found in most official correspondence.

Fasold *et al.* (1990) compared the use of middle initial references in names for men and women in the *Washington Post* over a six-year period starting at 1975 and ending in 1981. Between 1975 and 1981 they found a significant increase in the use of the middle initial in reference to prominent women (prominent men are the group most likely to be given a middle initial). In an earlier study, Fasold (1987) examined whether the practice of using the surname only in subsequent references to people was symmetrical for women and men in newspaper and magazine articles. He found that the gender imbalance characterising second and subsequent references to women (title + surname) and men (surname only) had dramatically changed in the direction of the male practice: the surname only system was becoming the dominant practice for reference to both sexes.

Occupational nouns and professional titles

An important impact on linguistic terminology relating to professional and occupational titles has been the passing of antidiscrimination laws or equal employment opportunity laws. The use of androcentric occupational nouns and related workplace terminology was considered an obstacle to equal treatment in the employment arena. In principle, the use of sexist or non-gender inclusive terminology was in breach of the antidiscrimination laws and could attract penalties. Consequently, several countries and organisations set up terminology commissions with the task of revising occupational nomenclature in order to eliminate sex-bias. Although such revisions were not always considered satisfactory from a feminist language planning perspective, they nevertheless had an overall positive effect on the language used in job advertisements and descriptions: non-sexist job titles and descriptions increased substantially, especially in English-speaking countries. Cooper's (1984) survey of andro-centric generics (including some occupational titles ending in -*man*) in American newspapers reported a dramatic decline in their use (see also the section on generic pronouns). My own recent work in Australia (Pauwels 1997b) confirmed this trend: a survey of 2,000 job advertisements in ten Australian newspapers revealed that only 5.4 per cent of the sampled occupational terms and titles were used in a gender-exclusive (sexist) manner. They included *chairman, cleaning lady, foreman, groundsman, handyman, manageress* and *waitress*. Despite the alleged 'ugliness' of compound nouns involving -*person*, most occupational titles involving -*man* had been replaced by this option. For example, *chairperson, tradesperson, storeperson, barperson.*

The use of non-sexist occupational nouns has also been the topic of several German investigations. Fleischhauer (1983) undertook a contrastive analysis of 5,000 job advertisements in English and German national daily newspapers covering the period 1967 to 1983. Her findings for the English newspapers were that 15 to 25 per cent of job advertisements placed in 1967 could be considered sexist since they employed male-oriented job titles, generic *he* or contained gender-specific descriptions. About 40 to 45 per cent of job advertisements in that period could be classified as non-sexist. Job advertisements in 1983 were found to have eradicated any blatant examples of linguistic discrimination and 34 to 63 per cent could be described as non-sexist. This compares with the follow-ing findings for German: in 1967 job advertisements in one of the German newspapers were structured according to the required sex of the applicant, i.e. there were separate columns of male and female advertisements. In the other newspaper, the *Frankfurter Allgemeine*, 77 per cent of all advertisements were cast in the generic masculine. The situation had not changed much in the job advertisements for 1983. The earlier practice of separating female and male job advertisements had ceased, but the majority of job advertisements were still cast in masculine generic terms although there were a few instances of gender-neutral terms and of the practice of gender splitting. Hellinger (1990) cites a more recent examination of 6,000 job advertisements in German newspapers undertaken by Brockhoff in 1987. Despite the introduction of antidiscrimination legislation covering employment, there were no major changes in the language used in job advertisements. Brockhoff (1987) found that more than 50 per cent of advertisements were directed at men, 25 per cent were directed at women and about 21 per cent were cast in gender-neutral terms. Both Brockhoff and Hellinger comment that, so far, change has been very slow. In the feminist monthly '*Emma*' the great majority of official/formal job advertisements are cast in non-sexist language with a preference for the strategy of splitting (feminisation), although some also display the strategy of gender abstraction.

During periods of sabbatical leave in The Netherlands in 1991 and 1993 I collected 2,000 job classifieds from the Saturday editions of two national newspapers, *De Volkskrant* and *NRC Handelsblad*. The majority of advertisements in both newspapers for both periods were non-sexist. A minority of gender-specific/gender-exclusive advertisements were found, mainly in the restaurant/hotel and entertainment sector. In 1991 approximately 80 per cent of the classifieds were directed at both women and men and did not contain descriptions that were primarily male- or female-oriented. In 1993 this figure had risen to just under 90 per cent. Although such figures seem indicative of a high degree of success, they should nevertheless be treated with caution. In many cases, the gender bias had been removed from the advertisements by adding the descriptors *m/v*, which is an abbreviation of *mannelijk/vrouwelijk* (male/female), or *man/vrouw* (man/woman) to a masculine occupational noun. For example, *direkteur m/v* (director m/f), *assistent-geoloog m/v* (assistant-geologist m/f), *groepsleider m/v* (group leader m/f). In one instance, even a feminine occupational noun *sekretaresse* (secretary) had been given the descriptor *m/v*. The strategies used in the Dutch job advertisements reflected to some extent the competition between the strategies of gender neutralisation and gender specification (feminisation). Although there was a leaning towards gender-neutral occupational nouns there were nevertheless a fair amount of occupational nouns which employed the technique of gender splitting. Examples of the former include adjectival nouns such as *sektordeskundige* (section expert), *sociaal verpleegkundige* (social 'nurse') or gender-abstract nouns such as *hoofd financiën* (head of finances) and gender-neutral nouns such as *leerkracht* (teacher). Dutch has borrowed heavily from English with regard to occupational nouns relating to business, management and computer expertise. These nouns, which are usually gender neutral in

English, are also treated as gender neutral in Dutch. For example, *case manager, bureau coordinator.* Examples of dual forms or splitting include *docent(e)* (lecturer), *service medewerker/ster* (service assistant), *redakteur/redaktrice* (editor). At present in Dutch job advertisements there is not only variability in terms of sexist and non-sexist alternatives but also, perhaps more so, among the strategies for non-sexist terms. This can even be attested in the feminist monthly *Opzij* which oscillates between the two strategies of gender neutralisation and feminisation. In true generic contexts, *Opzij* tends to opt more for gender-neutral nouns or common-gender nouns whereas in reference to a specific woman, the feminisation strategy seems to dominate, such as *docente* (female lecturer), *classica* (female scholar of classics), *onderzoekster* (female researcher) and *politica* (female politician).

Comments and observations made by colleagues in Sweden, Norway and Denmark also confirm a strong trend to use non-sexist terminology in job advertisements. The dominant strategy used is that of gender neutralisation and gender abstraction. The strategy of adding the 'male/female' descriptors is also frequently used.

In France an investigation of 700 job advertisements in the current affairs weekly *L'Express* in 1992 involved 181 different occupational titles and revealed that only 12.5 per cent of the advertisements could be said to be non-sexist. A breakdown of the findings showed that 3.3 per cent employ the feminisation strategy, *un(e) assistant(e) d'ingénieur,* 7.7 per cent attach the descriptors HF (Homme/Femme = Man/Woman) to a masculine generic occupational noun, *ingénieurs HF technico-commerciaux,* 1.1 per cent provide gender-inclusive visual images and 1.1 per cent use gender-neutral language, for instance *Responsable de zone export* (Schafroth 1993). Schafroth (1993) also examined the use of the feminisation strategy when referring to female authors and writers. The French words are respectively *auteur* and *écrivain.* In 'traditional' French neither of these words has a feminine equivalent. However, the Canadian French and some French French proposals for non-sexist occupational titles have included the formations *auteure* and *écrivaine.* Examining the literature sections of the two French national dailies *Libération* and *Le Monde* in September 1991, Schafroth (1993) found no sign of their adoption.

It seems that the impact of equal employment opportunity and antidiscrimination legislation has so far had varying effects on the use of non-sexist language in job descriptions and advertisements. The number of blatantly discriminatory job descriptions has drastically diminished, especially for positions in the public sector as well as in parts of the private sector. Comparisons between countries have not only revealed different approaches to eliminating sexist bias but also different stages in the process of language change. For example, in English-speaking countries a majority of job advertisements in newspapers are cast in gender-neutral language. In The Netherlands a majority of job advertisements are non-sexist. However, in most cases this is reached by means of the minimalist strategy of adding the descriptor (*m/v*) to mainly masculine generic occupational titles. In Germany and France, on the other hand, gender-inclusive advertisements are not yet a *fait accompli*. A substantial number of those German job classifieds which are gender inclusive tend to employ the feminisation strategy. For French, there is not as yet a clear trend.

Generic nouns and pronouns

Closely related to the issue of linguistic change of occupational nouns is that of generic nouns and pronouns in general. The use of non-sexist alternatives in English for masculine generic nouns and pronouns has been investigated in a variety of contexts. Cooper (1984) examined the impact of feminist language planning on masculine generics in the language of several American newspapers and magazines. Over 500,000 words of text were taken from regional, local and national newspapers and magazines (including women's and general science magazines) covering the period 1971–1979. They were analysed in terms of the presence or absence of androcentric generic nouns and pronouns. Cooper's main findings include a dramatic decline in the use of androcentric generics in the period 1971–1979, especially in women's magazines and the general science magazine *The National Geographic*. The form least resistant to change was generic *man*, which was invariably replaced by many of its alternatives. There was also some decline in the use of the generic pronoun *he*: the preferred alternative to generic *he* seemed to be pluralisation, i.e. recasting the sentence in the plural rather than using the dual pronoun *he or she*, *he/she* or *s/he*).

Fasold's (1987) study of the impact of editorial policy regarding non-sexist language on language use in the newspapers found not only a reluctance but also the proscription to use -*person* compounds to replace -*man* generics. Consequently, the newspapers he surveyed recorded minimal use of -*person* compounds except in direct quotations.

Ehrlich and King (1992: 162) summarise the findings of a class project on language reform in the mainstream media of Canada (generating 168 essays):

> The 168 essays submitted on the topic all found that the newspapers' adherence to their own guidelines was sporadic: e.g. usage of the so-called generic *he* and *man* abound.

The students also found many instances of the misuse of *-person* compounds. Men were referred to in more than 80 per cent of cases by *-man* compounds, whereas women were never referred to by *-man* compounds but by *-person* and *-woman* compounds. The *-person* compound is thus seen in purely female terms.

Meyerhoff (1984) examined the use of *he/man* language in a variety of New Zealand news publications (a student newspaper, a monthly publication of the New Zealand Journalists' union, a weekly Radio and TV magazine, a women's magazine and a regional daily newspaper) between 1964 and 1984. She found that the instances of *he/man* language had decreased between 1964 and 1984. The decrease was most substantial for the student and the journalists' union paper and the least for the daily newspaper and the Radio/TV magazine. However, the only publication to support the use of *-person* compounds was the student newspaper.

The use of non-sexist generic nouns and pronouns has also been investigated in the academic environment. Markovitz (1984) compared a range of university documents dating from 1969 to 1972, with matching documents for the period 1978–1979, and examined them in terms of sexist and non-sexist language use. The overall analysis of the document revealed a significant change in language use.

> Sex-linked language as a whole decreased, $t(88) = 3.79$, $p < .005$, and sex-neutral language increased dramatically, $t = 22.40$, $p < .005$. [. . .]. Sex-linked pronouns and generic nouns decreased significantly as expected, $t = 3.33$ and $t = 3.17$, respectively, although the sex-linked generic noun 'chairman' showed little change over time. (Markovitz 1984: 342)

Ehrlich and King (1992) also examined the impact of language guidelines on university documents at York University in Canada. The university's division of humanities pioneered language reform by removing all references to generic *man* from course titles between 1980 and 1982 and in 1985 a non-sexist language policy was formulated. Under the impact of the policy and its steering committee all course titles containing *man* were gradually removed. Ehrlich and King (1992: 160) state that 'most university documents now use non-sexist alternatives to the so-called generic *he*, and *chair* rather than *chairman* is the norm'.

Pauwels (1989b) is a small-scale longitudinal study investigating the use of non-sexist generic nouns and pronouns by seven university students at an Australian university. The students had been chosen because their language had not shown any signs of non-sexist usage of generic nouns and pronouns at the beginning of the study. Subsequently they had become familiar with the issue of linguistic sexism through participation in a course on language and gender and had been exposed to non-sexist language use by their lecturers. Written work – consisting of essays, class exercises and test papers – was collected from each student between 1986 and 1988. The written corpus amounted to approximately 35,000 words per student. The overall findings of this small-scale study include:

- All informants underwent changes in their use of generic pronouns. With the exception of one student, the changes were consistently in the direction of non-sexist language. In 1988 the writing of five informants showed no signs of masculine generic pronoun use.
- The move away from the masculine generic was generally in favour of a greater use of the gender-inclusive *he/she* (and its variations) or the gender-neutral singular *they*.

Although it has not yet been the subject of much systematic investigation (see, however, Kurzon 1989), the use of non-sexist pronouns in academic textbooks has also increased considerably. This is especially the case in textbooks relating to disciplines in the humanities and the social sciences, where besides a considerable use of the pronoun *he or she* (or one of its variants), singular *they*, generic *she* and the alternate use of *he* and *she* have also increasingly been noted.

Avoidance of gender stereotyping

Feminist language planning initiatives have also had an impact on reducing the blatant forms of gender stereotyping previously found in a multitude of texts and text types. The reduction has been noted especially in children's readers as well as in school and textbooks (e.g. Frank 1989). The amount of gender stereotyping found in dictionary entries has also reduced according to studies by Kaye (1989b), Kramarae (1992) and Hennessy (1993). Kaye (1989b) nevertheless notes that women are still portrayed in a negative light in many dictionary entries (i.e. as 'alcoholics and drug addicts').

In the area of the mass media, gender stereotyping is still the norm rather than the exception, despite many regular complaints from readers and viewers. Fasold *et al.* (1990) found that despite improvements in naming practices, gender stereotyping was still a regular feature of articles in the *Washington Post*. The more recent analyses of newspaper language in Britain undertaken by Talbot (1995) confirm this observation. The following is an extract from a 1994 newspaper article on the entry of a new female MP into the House of Representatives (Australia). The extract illustrates that a woman's physical appearance is still an important point in her description:

> The entrance was, as usual, fashionably late. The smile wore that familiar grim determination. The outfit – stern black suit and ruffled blouse – was parliamentary attendant chic, but the hair remained beyond impersonation. (*The Age* 4/5/1994, p. 9)

Where are these changes occurring?

Judging by the studies, comments and observations on non-sexist language use, changes resulting from feminist language reform initiatives are on the increase in several language communities around the world. The changes are found in many contexts of language use: in spoken and written, formal and informal, private and public uses of language in the domains of education, media, law, religion, public administration, as well as in the private sphere. The previous section already highlighted a number of these domains where such changes have taken or are taking place. Indeed this section overlaps considerably with the previous one. However, here I want to focus on *locating* the changes.

Linguistic changes resulting from formal reform proposals (e.g. guidelines for non-sexist language) seem to occur primarily in *written forms* of public and official discourse which need (to be seen) to abide by the recommendations of non-sexist language policy. Admittedly this impression might be influenced by the fact that it is much easier to monitor written documents than spoken interactions for change.

The language of employment advertising

Official descriptions of professional titles and occupational terminology as well as job advertising either in newspapers or professional publications are an important locus for the use of non-sexist and/or gender-inclusive language in communities which have antidiscrimination legislation. The previous section showed, however, that the linguistic changes occurring in relation to job descriptions can often be minimal.

The language of educational administration and bureaucracy

Linguistic changes have also made considerable inroads in the domain of educational administration, especially in English-speaking societies. Studies by Bate (1978), Markovitz (1984) and Ehrlich and King (1992) found that the adoption of a non-sexist language policy by universities had had a considerable impact on the use of non-sexist language in university documents, ranging from regulations, nomenclature and course descriptions to memos and minutes of meetings.

Observations of other forms of administrative and bureaucratic language use have also recorded diminished use of sexist language in favour of non-sexist formulations. As previously mentioned, Pauwels (1996) found that the title *Ms* was being used in 90 per cent of application forms and other printed forms of information gathering in Australia, although this was not always in line with promoted usage. Hellinger (1990) noted an increased use of the title *Frau* in official correspondence for German. Pauwels (1996) noted a similar increase for the use of the title *Mevrouw* in official correspondence in The Netherlands. Casual observations and remarks made by colleagues give the impression that official forms seeking information have become less androcentric as they no longer automatically assume the recipient or applicant of the form to be male. For example, an increasing number of forms ask information about one's partner by using words like 'spouse', '*de-facto* partner' rather than by referring to 'wife'.

The language of educational publications

It seems that educational publications – for example, academic textbooks, school books, first readers and some reference works – also increasingly adopt non-sexist language use, although there is still a scarcity of studies documenting linguistic change in this domain. Frank (1989) mentions that recent preliminary investigations of school books have found evidence that the most blatant forms of sexism have been eliminated. She nevertheless still found some cases of blatant sexism in college textbooks. In 1993 I informally surveyed a range of new academic textbooks on language and linguistics published in English, German and Dutch. Whereas most English textbooks avoided the use of generic *he* and of masculine generic occupational nouns, there was very little evidence in German and Dutch texts of non-sexist language use. In three German books there were some instances of gender splitting, although these were used very inconsistently. For example, splitting occasionally occurred with the words for teacher (*Lehrer/Lehrerin*), for pupil (*Schüler und Schülerin*) and for student (*StudentIn*), but never occurred for words such as 'professor', 'academic' or 'doctor'. The Dutch texts always used generic *he* (*hij*), in reference to common gender nouns. All professional and occupational nouns were either androcentric or gender neutral. Bull (1993) noted that more recent textbooks for school children in Norway displayed a greater tolerance towards the use of generic *she*. Kurzon (1989), who undertook a small-scale study of the use of sexist and non-sexist language in legal texts in Britain and the USA, found very little evidence of the use of non-sexist language in textbooks, especially in Britiain.

The language of the media

Some change is also occurring in sections of the print media. As mentioned earlier, investigations by Cooper (1984), Ehrlich and King (1992), Fasold (1987), Fasold *et al.* (1990), Meyerhoff (1984) and Swan (1992) among others have found evidence of changes in relation to the linguistic portrayal of the sexes in sections of print media. The changes include more balanced and equitable naming practices, gender-neutral and/or gender-inclusive occupational nouns and, in a very few cases, non-sexist generic pronouns. The degree of change varied considerably according to type of publication (e.g. national daily newspaper vs women's magazine), according to sections (e.g. sports pages, political news, human interest story) and according to individual journalist/editor. Women's magazines and popular science magazines were more likely to adopt changes than general interest magazines (e.g. TV and radio weeklies, computer periodicals, car maintenance magazines) and daily/weekly newspapers. Furthermore, the sports section seems to be the most resistant to change: women in sport and sportswomen are invariably referred to as either *ladies* or *girls*. The naming practices for sportswomen and sportsmen are still mainly asymmetrical: for example, men are referred by surname only, women by either first name only or by courtesy title and surname.

Furthermore, the high degree of variability with regard to the changes and innovations in the print media seems to indicate that linguistic change is still in its very early stages. For example, in some leading Australian newspapers I noticed that the new courtesy title for women 'Ms' is used concurrently with 'Mrs' or 'Miss' to refer to the same woman within the same article or feature. However, in one national newspaper at least, there are signs of a greater overall use of the title 'Ms' and of a lesser amount of 'free' variation with either 'Mrs' or 'Miss'.

The language of dictionaries and language reference works

Examinations of linguistic changes in updated, revised and new versions of language reference works such as dictionaries, grammars, style manuals and style handbooks have yielded mixed results. Most feminist language planning commentators have noted a reluctance among 'linguistic' gatekeepers to incorporate changes or to mention rules resulting from feminist language planning. Hennessy (1993) compared coverage of non-sexist issues in three British learners' dictionaries; The *Collins COBUILD English Language Dictionary* (1987), the *Longman Dictionary of Contemporary English* (1987) and the *Oxford Advanced Learner's Dictionary of Current English* (1989). Her overall findings indicate that there is only sporadic coverage of some feminist language issues: i.e. generic *he*, asymmetrical use of word pairs such as *boy/girl*, and the trivialising effect of the *-ess* suffix. The dictionaries, however, fail their users in two ways: firstly, they do not point out that many practices described in the dictionary are considered sexist by considerable numbers of native speakers and, secondly, they do not provide guidance 'which would encourage learners to develop nonsexist idiolects akin to those of many of their native-speaking peers' (Hennessy 1993: 128). Hennessy (1993) did find, however, that all three dictionaries had reduced the stereotyping of women as 'hysterical', 'domineering', 'gossips' or 'nags' in their illustrative phrases. Cannon and Robertson's (1985) investigation of three American dictionaries concluded with the observation that feminist language awareness, planning and policy has had a positive effect on dictionaries providing appropriate counter-items to sexist items but had not been successful in excising sexist ones from being recorded in the dictionary. Kramarae (1992), commenting on dictionary practices, also noticed an attempt among some current editors of American dictionaries to reduce the blatantly sexist illustrative phrases and to include some coinages by the women's movement. However, she remains unconvinced that 'even many more of these kinds of touch-up changes will [not] alter the misogynist makeup of the dictionary' (Kramarae 1992: 136). Schafroth (1993) found that the 1991 edition of the French dictionary *Le Petit Robert* had recognised the feminisation of a few occupational nouns which had previously only been recorded with their masculine gender: they included (**une**) *biologiste* and *architecte*, and *soldate*. In the area of dictionaries there have been other attempts not only to spread linguistic changes but also to change the 'patriarchal' concept of dictionary making. Kramarae and Treichler's (1985) *Feminist Dictionary* and Daly and Caputi's (1987) *Wickedary* are well-known examples of this enterprise for the English language.

Sunderland's (1986) review of 22 pedagogic grammars of English published between 1975 and 1985 found that there has been an increased treatment of some non-sexist language issues since 1975, although in most cases the innovations or non-sexist practices are still given a negative evaluation. Issues dealt with include non-sexist alternatives to the masculine generic pronoun *he*, the use of the *-ess* suffix, the use of *-person* compounds and the courtesy title *Ms*.

The language of religion

Changes in the direction of non-sexist language use are also increasingly found in the documents and texts used by Judaeo-Christian religions: a number of churches set up committees to examine the androcentrism found in the bible, prayers, and other important religious texts. These committees were also given the task of finding appropriate strategies to increase the gender inclusiveness and/or gender neutrality in such texts. In most instances this resulted in non-sexist revisions of existing texts and in some cases new texts were created to highlight female images of God and/or of women's participation in religious life. In English-speaking countries there are now a number of non-sexist/gender-inclusive versions of the Bible in circulation, especially among Protestant-based churches. This can also be said for the Lutheran and other Protestant churches in Germany, parts of Switzerland, in The Netherlands and in Scandinavia. More recently (May 1994) the Vatican announced that it would take into consideration complaints about sexism in its new version of a catholic Bible translation. More liberal synagogues in the United States have also made attempts to reduce the androcentrism in texts.

Greene and Serovic (1989) analysed changes to the marriage ceremony as conducted in the mainstream Protestant churches in the United States, and found that some (minimal) changes had occurred (e.g. the use of the phrase 'husband and wife' instead of 'man and wife'). Greene and Rubin (1991: 82) report that in the United States 'some seminaries are requiring the use of inclusive language by students . . .'. They also examined the effect that the use of non-sexist language use in religious discourse (mainly sermons) had on the religious community. They found that religious ministers who used gender-inclusive language did not suffer negative reactions from their congregation. In fact, the most significant finding of the study was that 'speakers' use of inclusive language *neither* undermined *nor* enhanced listeners' reactions.' (Greene and Rubin 1991: 93). To my knowledge, there have been no investigations of the extent to which congregations and other religious communities make use of the gender-inclusive texts.

Non-sexist language use in spoken interaction

Little is known about the impact of language guidelines on spoken language use. Systematic investigations of the use of non-sexist language in spoken language are only just emerging (e.g. Wetschanow 1995). There is mainly anecdotal evidence of changes in the speech of individuals, either in private or public settings. For example, Kramarae and Jenkins (1987) documented some efforts to change language and to take control of talk made by women attending a feminist scholarship conference at the University of Illinois in 1978. The main categories of language innovation used and discussed by these women included

> (1) talking about the 'problem' – analyzing women's relationship to language – and naming what we discovered; (2) making negative words, such as 'spinster' and 'bitch', positive by redefining them; (3) making positive words negative, such as turning methodology into methodolotry, to challenge male authority; (4) coining new expressions, such as 'gaslighting', which means to drive someone crazy by denying her reality, as the doctor/husband did to his young wife in the move [*sic*] *Gaslight*;

and (5) using metaphors, stories, jokes, and analogies to depict aspects of women's experience for which there are no words in a patriarchal language. (Kramarae and Jenkins 1987: 138)

My own small-scale study on pronominal changes in students' language use (Pauwels 1989b, see also previous section) also collected some information on linguistic changes in the speech of the students. Although I was unable to record the classroom interactions, I kept notes on the students' pronoun and generic noun use in speech during class. The notes contained information about the type of generic nouns and pronouns used in the course of discussions and oral presentations in class. A gradual but steady decline in the use of the masculine generic pronoun was observed in most students over a three-year period. This decline in masculine generic *he* led to an increase in the use of the dual, gender-inclusive pronoun *he or she* and in the use of *singular they*. In fact, all students were found to try to avoid the masculine generic in *some* contexts and on certain occasions. In four of the seven students there were no further instances of a masculine generic pronoun at the end of the period of observation (i.e. 1988). The preferred strategy in speech for four of the seven students was the use of *singular they* to replace masculine generic *he*.

Studies by Bate (1978), Henley and Dragun (1983), Jaehrling (1988) and Pauwels (1987b), among others, which tried to access non-sexist patterns in speech via interviews and questionnaires, shall be discussed in the following section. Further evidence on non-sexist language changes in speech is of an incidental nature. The casual observations and monitoring of language used by newsreaders, programme announcers and presenters on TV and radio in such countries as Austria, Germany, France, Belgium, The Netherlands, Britain, the USA, Australia, Canada, New Zealand, Italy and Spain all confirm that there is still a low degree of non-sexist language use in speech.

Who adopts the changes?

An important aspect in the evaluation of feminist language planning is to identify how the changes spread throughout the community. Here I provide some insights into the types of language user who are adopting the changes.

There is little doubt that the first users of non-sexist language were the women who initiated the demand for change. They were usually socially conscious women involved in the women's movement. These women certainly acted and continue to act as role models for like-minded women (and some men) who embrace ideas of sexual equality. The studies by Adamsky (1981), Bate (1978), Henley (1987), Henley and Dragun (1983), Jaehrling (1988), Pauwels (1987b) also confirm that it is women with a personal involvement in the women's movement or with a commitment to women's issues who are the main and prime users of non-sexist language.

Feminist-oriented publications including magazines, periodicals and books were also among the first to embrace and promote the changes. These publications became an important vehicle of language spread of non-sexist alternatives within the confines of feminist groups and activities. For German, Hoffmann (1979) and Pusch (1984a, 1990) have documented how the women writing for feminist magazines such as *Emma*, *Courage* and others have been at the forefront of linguistic change: they have introduced as well as promoted a series of lexical and grammatical innovations. For example, many writers consistently use gender splitting in reference to human agent nouns. Some also opt for new gender concord rules (see Chapter 4) and use the indefinite pronoun *frau* instead of *man*. Pusch (1984a: 97) furthermore notices their linguistic creativity in order to make women more visible in language: many writers form new compounds involving the prefix or suffix *frau* as in 'Unifrauen, Guerillafrauen, Medienfrauen, Architekturfrauen, Technikfrauen, SPD-frauen . . .' [University women, Guerilla women, media women, women in architecture, women in technology, SPD women . . .] Examples of the use of *Frau* as a prefix are 'Frauenzentren, Frauenzeitungen, Frauenbuchläden, Frauenferienhäuser.' [Women's centres, women's newspapers, women's bookshops, women's holiday cottages] (Pusch 1984a: 98). Similar observations can be made for other feminist publications in other languages. Feminist publications have also been the promoters and spreaders of linguistic creations by the women's movement. For example, words such as *sexism, sexist, male chauvinism, sexual harassment, consciousness raising* have spread to the speech community at large and are increasingly being recorded in mainstream dictionaries. Other innovations and forms of linguistic creativity include semantic 'ameliorations' (e.g. reclaiming or giving positive connotations to words which underwent a process of semantic derogation, as in *hag* and *bitch*), semantic extensions (e.g. the use of the word *Lesbian* for all women-oriented women), reorganisation of semantic boundaries (e.g. the use of *herstory* to highlight the lack of attention to women in history) and other word plays (e.g. *malestream* for *mainstream*) have often originated in the context of feminist publications.

As to the spread of non-sexist language practices beyond the 'originators', Henley (1987: 19) proposed the following:

> . . . we would expect such change to occur first among those most affected by it – women; particularly young, educated, socially conscious, perhaps employed and mobile women, whose active presence will constitute pressure on speakers to use nonsexist forms.

Although there is still a paucity of studies examining or testing these assumptions, the few studies that have been conducted seem to confirm Henley's (1987) comments (e.g. studies by De Silva 1992, Hellinger and Schräpel 1983, Henley and Dragun 1983, Houdebine 1988, Jaehrling 1988, and Wodak *et al.* 1987). For example, De Silva (1992) examined the attitudes and practices of a small group of editors (18) working in Melbourne, Australia. She found that female editors were more likely to detect sexism in manuscripts and were somewhat more likely to change it than their male counterparts.

Hellinger and Schräpel (1983) were concerned with a small-scale study of women's and men's attitudes towards the use of non-sexist language. They observed that gender and level of education had an impact on recognition of sexist practices in language as well as on attitudes towards the use of non-sexist language in the public sphere and in their own language use. Women certainly displayed a greater sensitivity than men to sexist practices in language and also favoured the introduction of non-sexist language in the public sphere more than men. However, their willingness to adopt the changes in their own language use was not much greater than that of men. With regard to the factor of education, their overall finding was that informants who had a higher level of education were more likely to recognise sexist language practices and were on the whole also more likely to recommend changes in the public sphere and in their own language use.

Jaehrling's (1988) comparative study of attitudes towards changing sexist language in German and English was based on Hellinger and Schräpel's methodology and had similar findings: on the whole, women were more supportive of changes than men. Jaehrling (1988) also found evidence that age can affect attitudes towards, and use of, non-sexist language: younger people (especially those between 21 and 30) were more willing to support change than older people (over 50) and were more inclined to make changes to their own language use.

Wodak *et al.*'s (1987) small-scale study undertaken in Austria examined the impact of gender, age, educational level and occupation on non-sexist language practices relating to occupational nomenclature. Their results showed that women were more positive than men towards non-sexist language practices. Most supportive of the changes were women who were public servants, followed by women with higher education (including university degrees). They did not find an impact of age on the results.

Whereas the German studies found people with higher education to be generally more willing to make changes and adopt non-sexist language practices, Henley and Dragun's (1983) study on American English revealed the opposite:

> ... people with less education or who are not students indicate that they find changing their language easier than do people of higher educational status, or who are students. (Henley and Dragun 1983: 7)

Henley and Dragun (1983) found this surprising but suggested that it may be linked to perceived levels of language ownership; people with higher levels of education may have a greater sense of proprietorship of language, which makes them less willing to change: 'when you own something, you don't want to see it changed' (Henley and Dragun 1983: 7).

For French, Houdebine (1988) examined women's and men's views on adopting the strategy of feminisation in relation to occupational terms. She found women to be more in favour of adoption than men. Younger people were also more in favour than older people. In fact, gender differences increased with age, especially over the age of 40.

Gender also seems to affect the motivation for adopting changes. For women, the main motivation to adopt change is usually the result of a personal commitment, whereas that of men is more likely to be guided by either the presence of credible, high status women as role models or a desire to show solidarity with the women around them. For example, Bate's (1978) examination of non-sexist language use in a university context concluded that

> ... second key factor in actuating change, particularly for men, is the presence of significant females who are sufficiently credible to the speaker to be listened to when they propose changing a language habit. (Bate 1978: 149)

Pauwels (1987b) found that the main reason for women to adopt the title *Ms* in Australia was a personal commitment to gender equality and to fighting linguistic discrimination. The latter reason had disappeared by 1996 (Pauwels 1997c).

Besides presenting a profile of the individual language user who is most likely to react positively to the changes and adopt them, it is also important to look at the spread at institutional level. After all, many feminist language planners made a conscious attempt to influence the language behaviour of the speech community by directing their language planning initiatives at 'corporate bodies' (Cooper 1989) and institutions which could act as intermediaries in promoting language change. For example, the adoption of language guidelines by a TV channel may promote the use of non-sexist language by its newsreaders, programme announcers and presenters and thus act as a powerful vehicle for language spread. At this stage there has not yet been a study investigating which corporate bodies lead the way in using non-sexist language.

Nevertheless, the previous sections have shown that there is some evidence of non-sexist language use in many domains, institutions and corporate bodies. It has been noted that the formal adoption of a policy of non-sexist language use by a corporate body or institution is positively correlated to the use of non-sexist language. Fasold (1987) and Fasold *et al.* (1990), as well as Ehrlich and King (1992), were able to demonstrate for sections of the print media and the university sector in the United States and Canada that there was a positive relationship between the adoption of a non-sexist language policy and the use of non-sexist language. Furthermore, if the adoption of language guidelines was linked to or was part of a wider set of initiatives and actions concerning the elimination of gender discrimination, there was a greater likelihood of actual use of non-sexist language (i.e. the non-sexist language policy guidelines were put into practice, see Ehrlich and King 1992).

Institutions and corporate bodies which have adopted guidelines and consequently use non-sexist language vary greatly from society to society. In Australia, for example, it is the public sector more than the private sector which has adopted non-sexist linguistic changes and innovations. Government departments, especially those with a social or community orientation (e.g. Department of Health, Department of Education, Employment and Training, Department of Community Services, Department of Administrative Services, Department of Immigration and Ethnic Affairs, etc.), have made the greatest effort in eliminating sexist language from their documents, specifically those which are client-oriented. The use of non-sexist language is far less widespread in departments such as Veteran Affairs, Primary Industry or Finance. The private sector's use of non-sexist language is minimal in comparison with that found in the public sector. In most English-speaking countries educational institutions are more likely to employ non-sexist language than the commercial media. In Germany institutional use of non-sexist language varies a great deal according to region/state. In France institutional use is almost completely limited to the use of non-sexist professional titles in official documents. A similar situation is found in Italy (Ciccioni, pers. comm.). Changes have also been observed in Japan, the main one being the replacement of the older and more sexist term for women *fujin* with the 'neutral' term *josei* in relation to (local) government and political parties' services for women. For example, Women's Affairs Sections in local governments used to be called *fujin taisakuka*; after the introduction of the Equal Employment Opportunity Act they were renamed *josei kikakuka*. (Nanette Gottlieb, pers. comm.).

Factors promoting or hindering the spread of non-sexist language through the speech community

So far it has been established that a certain degree of instability and variability is present in many speech communities *vis-à-vis* the use of sexist and non-sexist language and that there is some evidence of changes spreading throughout the speech community. On the basis of studies so far it can be said that

- the use of non-sexist language is more evident in writing than in speech;
- non-sexist language practices are found more in formal and public uses of language than in private;
- women are more likely users than men.

The spread of change in relation to non-sexist language reform seems to be positively influenced by the presence of the following factors at individual level:

- An awareness of what constitutes linguistic discrimination and a personal commitment towards linguistic equality of the sexes in line with achieving other forms of gender equality; for women this commitment is often a result of having experienced discrimination, whereas for men the commitment is more likely a result of showing solidarity.

- The presence of important role models (both female and male) who use non-sexist language. The more prestige these speakers have in the community at large, the more likely can their presence exert an influence on other members of the speech community. Although there is a paucity of such role models (female and male) in the domain of the mass media or the public arena, their numbers are increasing rapidly in areas such as education and public administration.
- The presence of a supportive environment in which the use of non-sexist language is tolerated or even encouraged rather than denigrated or ridiculed. Bate (1978), Pauwels (1987b, 1996) and others found that a disincentive for the use of non-sexist language is the fear of embarrassing oneself.
- The presence of an environment in which non-sexist language is the norm or preferred usage and in which sexist language is not tolerated. Although such environments are still in the minority, they are increasing in the domain of education and in certain types of written language.

These factors also apply to the spread of non-sexist language use at corporate or institutional level. At this level, it is relevant to reiterate the importance of language reform 'within the context of a larger sociopolitical initiative whose primary goal is the eradication of sexist practices (e.g. employment equity programmes)' (Ehrlich and King 1992: 152).

The factors hindering the spread of non-sexist language not only include the opposites of the positive factors listed above, but also include the lack of support among the members of high status groups and those who control the communication networks. This implies a reduced level of access to institutions capable of facilitating language spread. Linguistic and communicative objections to certain promoted forms are also factors affecting acceptance and use of the alternatives negatively. Earlier in this chapter, some of these objections put forward by opponents of non-sexist language use were reviewed. For example, the argument of linguistic economy is sometimes used to argue against the German non-sexist practice of splitting, because it not only involves a greater time expenditure on behalf of the speaker but it also necessitates a higher level of concentration for both speaker and hearer. The argument of increased ambiguity is used to oppose the widespread use of *singular they*. The lack of information concerning the pronunciation of *Ms*, an unknown consonant cluster in English, may hinder its more widespread adoption

It is too early to make a realistic assessment of whether the positive factors outweigh the negative ones in the process of non-sexist language change. Such an assessment is also made more difficult by the fact that the process of language change is seldom linear: processes of change and innovation may spread quite quickly through certain sectors of the community, but the spread beyond those groups may proceed very slowly or not at all. Drawing upon findings from diffusion studies, the spread of language change is likely to exhibit an S-shaped curve (Cooper 1989). Initially the adoption of change or innovations is slow, but gathers momentum and speed, then slackens off again, until it reaches a ceiling. Since the number of longitudinal investigations about non-sexist language change relating to the portrayal of women and men is extremely limited, there is little or no evidence to prove or disprove this model. It is true, however, that most of the available studies have shown a reduction in the use of sexist language and some increases in the use of non-sexist language.

Another factor complicating the assessment of the progress of language change is the fact that change towards the use of non-sexist language involves a multiplicity of rules and alternatives. Non-sexist language change is a collective name for a range of changes, lexical, morphological, discoursal, etc. The progress of each of these needs to be examined as part of the overall assessment. The overview of the type of changes in this chapter reveals that there are considerable degrees of difference in the acceptance and usage rates of certain innovations. For example, for English the use of gender-neutral or gender-inclusive occupational nouns in job advertisements and descriptions has advanced to a stage where it could almost be called preferred usage. However, the use of similar terms (especially *-person* compounds) is not very widespread in the mass media (e.g. newspapers). The use of *Ms* as well as other more balanced forms of address for women and men, has also increased substantially. In many contexts the use of generic *he* still dominates and resists any attempt at change. In German, the acceptance and use of gender-inclusive occupational nouns and titles in job advertisements is probably spearheading the change towards non-sexist language. The use of other phenomena (e.g. those affecting gender concord rules) is limited to some feminist users and does not seem to be spreading to the wider community.

Are the changes effective?

A final, but most important, form of evaluation concerns the *effectiveness* of the observed changes; in other words, are the changes and innovations used in a manner for which they were promoted? Indeed, the success of language planning and reform initiatives is not only measured in terms of the acceptance and spread of alternatives throughout a speech community. Assessing the extent to which the adoption and spread of the changes are in line with the intended aims of the reform is also essential.

The main aim of guidelines, for example, was to formulate the promotion of linguistic equality of the sexes. This was to be done by eliminating a range of discriminatory practices, including those that make women invisible, treat women as secondary, trivialise women and their actions, stereotype the sexes, and denigrate women and men. Recommendations for rectifying the gender imbalance in language use included strategies and alternatives that would make women visible in language, would treat them as equals with men and would reduce stereotyped portrayal of either sex. For these recommendations to be considered successful, they need to be accepted and adopted by the targeted speech community in line with the planners' intentions.

Unfortunately, to date there is still little research which has systematically addressed issues of the effectiveness of reform. This is an area in which more research is urgently needed, and here I shall discuss briefly the results of the limited range of studies available on this issue.

Let us first look at the issue of actual use being in line with recommended or intended use. Evidence gathered on new or changed practices in relation to titles for women has revealed mixed results. The results of Pauwels' (1996) research into the use of *Mevrouw* as a universal title of address for Dutch (adult) women were quite positive. A majority of the polled women (85 per cent) used this title in accordance with its intended usage. Marital status no longer featured in their interpretation of the title. Furthermore, the almost complete absence of the title *Juffrouw* (equivalent to 'Miss') on official forms and many circulars is also proof that the 'marital status' is no longer a prominent feature in honorific titles for adult women. Comments from colleagues working in the Nordic countries and Germany seem to indicate a similar trend. There is a similar but not yet such a strong trend in France, Spain and Italy towards the universal use of the title *Madame, Señora, Signora* for adult women irrespective of their marital status. However, such positive evidence is still outstanding for the honorific title 'Ms' in English-speaking countries. Although the use of 'Ms' is definitely on the increase in most English language countries, there is evidence that many misinterpretations of 'Ms' are in circulation. The main misinterpretation concerns the status of 'Ms' versus the 'traditional' titles of 'Mrs' and 'Miss'. 'Ms' was intended to become a parallel to 'Mr' by replacing the titles of 'Mrs' and 'Miss' since the latter distinguished women on the basis of marital status. However, there is strong evidence that neither women nor men interpret 'Ms' as a *replacement* for 'Mrs' and 'Miss' but either as an alternative to 'Miss' or as an *additional* title for women. For Britain, Graddol and Swann (1989) mention that on many official forms only 'Mrs' and 'Ms' are used leading to a merging of 'Miss' and 'Ms'. Penelope (1990) makes similar claims for the use of 'Ms' in the United States. For Canada Atkinson (1987) and for Australia Pauwels (1987b) found that many women did not regard 'Ms' as a universal title for women replacing 'Mrs' and 'Miss', but as an *additional* one to refer to specific categories of women: in the Canadian context 'Ms' was associated with women who were divorced. The Australian study found not only a similar association between 'Ms' and being divorced/separated but also discovered that new features (other than marital status) were introduced to account for a woman's use of the 'Ms' title. These included ideological orientation ('Ms' is used by feminists), professional status ('Ms' is used by wage earning women in white collar positions), lifestyle ('Ms' is used by modern, trendy women) and sexual orientation ('Ms' is used by lesbians). Pauwels (1987b: 151) comments that the varied interpretations and uses of 'Ms' in Australia have not rectified but actually exacerbated the asymmetry between the honorific titles for men and women. Whereas there is still only one (dominant) title for men, there are now three rather than two titles for women: 'Ms', 'Mrs' and 'Miss'. This means that 'today, even more information can be disclosed through a woman's personal title than in the past . . .' (Pauwels 1987b: 151). Pauwels (1987b) also found that misinterpretations or misuse of the title 'Ms' abound on forms and circulars: the only circular found to use 'Ms' in parallelism with 'Mr' was from a linguistic society!! All others either used 'Mrs', 'Miss' and 'Ms' or 'Mrs', 'Ms'. However, a small number of forms had adopted the practice of simply asking for one's preferred title rather than listing them. On a positive note, Pauwels' (1987b) study did find, however, that women who used the title themselves used it in accordance with its intended meaning. Also the follow-up study conducted in 1996 (see Pauwels 1997c) revealed that the number of polled women who understood the title and interpreted it in line with its meaning had risen from 64 per cent to 85 per cent. Similarly the number of women using 'Ms' as intended more than doubled in this ten-year period, i.e. from just under 20 per cent to 44.5 per cent. As to men's use of the title 'Ms' to address women, there is really no more than anecdotal evidence that seems to indicate (at least in Australia) a continuing reluctance to use 'Ms' when addressing women.

Another problematic area concerns the use of new gender-neutral and gender-inclusive generic nouns. Their use and distribution belie their intended meaning, i.e. that of being gender neutral or gender inclusive. This is especially the case with the new *-person* compounds (e.g. chairperson, spokesperson, salesperson, camera-person) which were created or promoted to avoid the androcentric *-man* compounds (chairman, spokesman, etc.). Severals scholars have commented that the use of many *-person* compounds (especially chairperson) is almost exclusively associated with (assumed) female referents. Dubois and Crouch (1987) cite from the *Chronicle of Higher Education* to demonstrate that women are referred to as *chairpersons* whereas men remain *chairmen*. Ehrlich and King (1994) make a similar observation about the use of *-man* and *-person* compounds (and other non-sexist alternatives) in *The New York Times* and two Canadian (Toronto) newspapers, *The Globe and Mail* and *The Star*. The first findings of my current project investigating language changes in the Australian print media confirm the American and Canadian findings: i.e. that certain *-person* compounds, especially 'chairperson' and 'spokesperson', are primarily used to refer to women rather than men. In Norwegian, however, the opposite is occurring with regard to some new gender-neutral nouns. Some of these new terms – e.g. *stortingsrepresentant* (Parliamentary representative), *tillitsvalgt* (chosen representative) – are used more in relation to men than to women (Tove Bull, pers. comm.).

When it comes to interpretation rather than use of gender-inclusive or gender-neutral pronouns, results are also mixed. McConnell-Ginet (1989) comments that trying to use the pronoun *he* generically has become more difficult because more people have become aware of its controversial nature as a generic. Within the Australian university context I have often observed that speakers feel the need to make metalinguistic comments when they use masculine pronouns and nouns in generic contexts. These comments alert the audience that the speaker uses a masculine noun or pronoun on purpose, e.g. to highlight the fact that there are no female incumbents in a particular positions. During the 1980s a spate of experiments[2] were conducted which showed that the use of masculine generic nouns and pronouns called up male mental image. Some studies also revealed that the use of gender-neutral nouns reduced the maleness of the mental imagery. However, a more recent study by Khosroshahi (1989) showed that the use of gender-inclusive or gender-neutral generics as opposed to the masculine ones did not change the mental imagery associated with them (i.e. no significant effect), except in the case of women who had reformed their language:

> All groups were androcentric except women who had reformed their language; androcentric in the sense that when they read a paragraph that was ambiguous with respect to gender, they were more likely to interpret it as referring to a male than to a female character. Even if the paragraph used he or she or they, feminine referents did not become more salient than masculine ones. (Khosroshahi 1989: 517)

Her findings seem to suggest that 'in a literature dominated by male characters initially sex-indefinite words must quickly develop masculine connotations' (Khosroshahi 1989: 517) and that the effective use of an innovation can only occur when there is a personal awareness of and a commitment to change.

In relation to occupational nomenclature, a more positive note is sounded by Hellinger (1990) who noticed that the introduction of the feminisation strategy has led to a smaller number of women being willing to apply for jobs in which the applicant is described in masculine generic terms rather than when the description is gender inclusive.

The fate of some linguistic creations by feminists is discussed by Ehrlich and King (1994). They notice that 'while feminist linguistic innovations (such as *feminism, sexism, sexual harassment,* and *date rape*) pervade our culture, it is not clear that their use is consistent with their intended, feminist-influenced, meanings' (Ehrlich and King 1994: 65). They identify a range of discourse strategies which are 'used systematically by the print media to redefine and depoliticize feminist linguistic innovations' (*ibid.*). Redefinition can occur through the strategies of omitting or obscuring, of expanding and of obliterating. Other commentators (e.g. Morris 1982) have observed the use of similar strategies in the adoption of feminist coinages in dictionaries.

Although there is still a paucity of research assessing the effectiveness of feminist linguistic reform, so far the results have been not too promising. Usage of non-sexist alternatives has definitely increased but their interpretation does not always reflect the intended meanings. In fact, in some cases feminist reforms have been appropriated by a culture and community still hostile, or at least indifferent, to the ideology associated with the reforms. When non-sexist alternatives are used in a sexist community it is not unlikely that '. . . in the mouths of sexists, language can always be sexist' (Cameron 1985: 90). Does this observation thus give credence to the view that language merely reflects social reality (see Chapter 3) and renders language reform futile? Like many others[3] who pose this question, my reply is premised on the view that linguistic meanings are constructed in social practice and that the dominant culture and cultural groups exert immense influence on (trying) to determine linguistic meaning *per se*. However, linguistic meanings are not fixed and are subject to resistance and change from non-dominant groups. Feminist language reform should be seen in this context of challenging the meanings authorised and promoted by the dominant culture:

> While those in power have the authority and influence to make their meanings stick, nonsexist and feminist linguistic innovations challenge the absolute hegemony of these meanings. (Ehrlich and King 1994: 74)

Note

1. This redefining can be seen in terms of either a semantic extension process (i.e. extend the use of 'Mrs' to mean all adult women) or a reclamation process (i.e. *reclaim* the meaning of 'Mrs' as the courtesy title for all adult women).
2. Some of these studies were discussed in Chapter 2 and Chapter 4.
3. See, e.g., Cameron (1985), Ehrlich and King (1992, 1994), McConnell-Ginet (1989), Penelope (1990) and Silverstein (1985).

Concluding remarks

In this book I have been concerned with documenting and discussing women's efforts to address and eliminate the problems surrounding the portrayal of the sexes in language and the treatment of women and men in language practices. I have referred to these efforts as feminist LR initiatives because I consider them a genuine form of LP or LR. I therefore chose to adopt a LP perspective to document and discuss this phenomenon.

Within a LP framework feminist LR can be considered an instance of corpus planning with a social or sociolinguistic focus. The aims of many feminist LP efforts are to expose the inequalities in the linguistic portrayal of the sexes which reflect and contribute to the unequal positions of women and men in society and to take action to rectify this linguistic imbalance. Language action, it is argued, is social action, and to bring about linguistic change is to effect social change. Feminist LR started very much as a grassroots initiative of women active in the women's movements around the world. Although it has retained a strong grassroots base and character, LR in relation to the sexes has at least, in some societies, also become an activity associated with 'femocrats' – feminist-oriented bureaucrats – charged with the formulation and implementation of policies regarding equal opportunity, antidiscrimination, affirmative action, access and equity, etc. This makes feminist LR an interesting case for language planners as it combines a strong grassroots push for change with some official sanctioning of such change.

Another interesting aspect of feminist LR is its international character: concern with the linguistic representation of women and men is not limited to Western societies but is widespread among speech communities around the world. Exposing linguistic inequities is an activity undertaken by a great diversity of people (mainly women) for languages as diverse as Thai and English, Lithuanian and Arabic, Vietnamese and Yoruba, or even Esperanto. These examinations of sexist practices have revealed a multiplicity of ways in which sexism is encoded in languages: sexist practices abound in the structuring of lexicons, affect writing systems, are found in naming practices and in some grammatical patterns. Although the linguistic encoding of sexism certainly varies across languages, common features across languages have nevertheless been established. In summary, it is **man**, his characteristics and activities, rather than woman and her features which is taken as the norm for linguistic expressions and language practices. Language practices are not immune from the 'male gaze' phenomenon, i.e. they reflect a male perspective on the linguistic construction of reality.

The main focus of *linguistic* analyses of sexism so far has been on sexist practices at or below the sentence level. The study of the construction of sexist discourses has only recently emerged as an activity undertaken by linguists working within a critical linguistic or discourse paradigm. Nevertheless, many new investigations of linguistic sexism in languages not previously documented continue to focus on the word or sentence level. This continues to be a weakness in the study of linguistic sexism as discourse studies on racism and sexism have shown (e.g. Van Dijk 1990).

As the nature of feminist LR remains primarily a grassroots movement, the reform initiatives and efforts are not only very diverse but also often *ad hoc* and less 'planned' than more 'official' language reforms. In many respects feminist LR has been as varied as the people who engage in it: ideologies, beliefs about language, attitudes towards and experience with LR, socioeconomic circumstances, and social and cultural values have all impacted on LR efforts, including whether or not to take language action. Indeed, an acknowledgement of discriminatory practices in language use does not automatically trigger action for reform as I explained in Chapter 3. However, in a majority of cases reform initiatives have been proposed. Important actions across speech communities have included *causing linguistic disruption, creating alternative women-oriented discourses*, and *achieving linguistic equality through form-replacement*. Such actions have given rise to many new words and expressions trying to encapsulate a woman's perspective, to word-plays exposing sexist linguistic assumptions and to experiments with grammatical structures and categories to eliminate gender bias. All these initiatives, proposals and practices have established women as active makers and creators of meaning, no longer satisfied with being consumers of language. This constitutes a radical change for women, who have long been cast in the role of passive recipients of language knowledge or, at best, were seen as the 'transmitters' of good language practices (e.g. as infant and primary school teachers). It is perhaps this new role of women as language activists which has been the most threatening aspect of this type of LR to influential sectors of society. It is not surprising, therefore, to find much resistance to change in such language gatekeeping institutions as language academies and the media.

The reform initiatives that have received most widespread attention are those aimed at achieving *linguistic equality* of the sexes. This is partly the result of the link with equal employment opportunity and antidiscrimination legislation. Through incessant lobbying by women activists, recognition came that gender-biased language practices could have an effect on people's (mainly women's) employment opportunities and that there was therefore a need for revising occupational nomenclature and the language of employment advertising practices. The push for achieving linguistic equality of the sexes was of course not only linked to employment practices but more generally to the secondary status of women in society, e.g. in education, the law and the media. The main strategies promoted to achieve this linguistic equality of the sexes involve either making women more visible in language (feminisation or gender specification) or making gender less relevant (gender abstraction) or less transparent (gender neutralisation). These strategies were primarily applied at word level. Although planners across languages have never adopted one strategy to the exclusion of the others, there are nevertheless clear language-specific trends to opt either for the feminisation or the neutralisation/abstraction strategies. In Chapter 4 I discussed the pros and cons of either strategy from a planning perspective, arguing that selecting strategies for change should be guided by the principles of social effectiveness and linguistic viability. Perhaps a weakness of the strategies associated with achieving linguistic equality is that they are prone to being regarded as simply 'surface' or cosmetic measures: changing or eliminating certain language forms may not always alter the language practices in which they are embedded. A classic example is that of *chairperson*, a form created to achieve linguistic equality which was lacking from the generic *chairman*. An examination of its use nevertheless shows that it has not greatly contributed to linguistic gender balance because *chairperson* is seldom used in a true generic sense but mainly as a substitute for *chairman* or *chairwoman* if the person is a woman.

Because of the relatively recent nature of reform proposals and campaigns, especially in relation to many languages other than English, the question of how successful they have been is perhaps still somewhat premature. Indeed studies examining the reactions to the adoption and spread of reform proposals and changes are only slowly emerging and only in relation to a few speech communities (mainly English). Case studies of public reactions to feminist LR show that there still is considerable resistance to change. These negative public and private reactions not only display great similarities across speech communities but also have a great deal in common with reactions to other cases of LR (see, e.g., Cameron 1995). They are often triggered, among other things, by concerns about linguistic ownership and manipulation as well as by a threat to a common belief that language is an organism that lives a life of its own and should suffer no interference.

Despite the still numerous overt rejections of the reform initiatives, there is no doubt that feminist LR has made and continues to make an impact on language practices. Perhaps its greatest impact to date has been to raise people's awareness of the issue. Feminist language campaigns have made it increasingly difficult for substantial sections of the population to ignore this linguistic expression of gender discrimination. Even if the people don't adopt the changes or embrace the principles of such linguistic change, they can no longer ignore its existence. This is, for instance, clear from increased metalinguistic comments in both speech and writing referring to the issue. Examples include apologies for not adopting dual, gender-inclusive generic pronouns, making statements such as 'I do not want to sound sexist, but . . .'.

The many small-scale projects conducted so far for languages such as English, German, Dutch and French nevertheless also show some signs of actual changes occurring and of a spread throughout the speech community: expectedly, educated women in paid employment are the prime movers of change and often act as role models for other women and some men in matters of linguistic change. Changes occur at different rates in different groups of speakers and language communities. For example, in Australia written language use in public sector agencies reflects many of the changes proposed in non-sexist language guidelines, especially in relation to occupational nomenclature, gender-inclusive pronouns and, to some extent, terms of address for women. Blatant gender stereotyping has diminished substantially in English educational texts used in schools;

however, gender stereotyping remains a prominent feature of language practices adopted by the media.

In the LP paradigm formulated by Kloss (1968), non-sexist language use has increasingly gained the status of *tolerated* usage in the speech community at large and, in some circles, even that of *promoted* usage. However, there are still very significant sectors in which it has the status of *dispreferred* use. Only time will tell whether non-sexist language practices move beyond the stage of tolerated use.

Another comment to be made relates to the effectiveness of the changes. Feminist LR was promoted for a variety of reasons. One reason was that linguistic change was seen to lag behind social change, effectively hindering the linguistic reflection of social change. The introduction and adoption of linguistic changes which promote the idea that women in the workforce are equal with men is indeed an effective way to bring linguistic reality onto a level with social reality. In particular, strategies which aim to make women visible in language contribute to the effectiveness of the reform. Another reason for the reforms has been linked to a Whorfian view of the interaction between language and social reality. According to this view language plays a crucial role in effecting social change. Results from hitherto small-scale studies on the impact of gender-inclusive pronouns and nouns in English have been mixed. While some studies have shown that non-sexist nouns and pronouns have had an impact on the cognitive imagery of their users, others have found no such relationship or have only found such a relationship among specific users (e.g. women). In Chapter 3 I alerted readers to the controversial status of this view in the light of substantial counter evidence that language determines thought or the construction of social reality. These mixed results of the studies are therefore not unexpected.

A final point concerns future directions in the study of feminist LR. The documentation of gender bias in language practices remains an important activity, especially for languages not previously subjected to such an analysis. However, such analyses should not be restricted to the word or sentence level but should rather adopt a discourse analytic approach to more fully explore the construction of sexist discourses. Another important area of study is that of evaluating the changes, their spread throughout the community and their effectiveness. This area of study is very much in its infancy with most investigations to date concerned with a handful of European languages and limited to very few phenomena (i.e.

pronouns, occupational nomenclature and gender stereotyping). Such studies would not only contribute to a better understanding of feminist LR processes but also offer insights into the process of (planned) language change.

I hope that this first attempt at documenting, describing and evaluating feminist language reform inspires others to do the same for other languages and language communities.

Appendix: Drafting non-sexist language guidelines

Putting feminist language planning into practice

This appendix is specifically targeted at equal (employment) opportunity and affirmative action staff as well as gender equity committees and agencies concerned about, or responsible for, taking action to ensure the *linguistic equality of the sexes* in public language. Indeed, there is a growing desire and demand for guidance on the elimination of linguistic discrimination against minority groups, including women, in a very diverse range of speech communities. The descriptions of sexism provided in Chapter 2 were testimony to the fact that an awareness of linguistic sexism is present in many speech communities.

Here I draw upon the information presented in Chapters 2, 3, 4 and 5 to provide some practical advice on how to formulate a policy of non-sexist language and draft guidelines for its implementation.

It has been my experience, especially in the Australian context, that equal opportunity, affirmative action or other staff and agencies addressing the issue of sex discrimination in language feel competent to deal with the implementation of non-sexist language proposals and policies but often need or seek guidance with regard to the linguistic aspects of the LP process, including the description and analysis of the phenomenon of linguistic sexism in language, the selection of alternatives to sexist expressions, as well as the selection of strategies available to counteract sexism in language. It is not uncommon to find that such staff have limited access to information and knowledge about LP and linguistic sexism. Although in some instances they can call upon LP professionals and experts to assist them in this task, the vast majority of EEO or AA staff do not have recourse to this expertise because it is non-existent, is unknown to the staff or is unavailable for financial or other reasons.

In the following sections the stages in the process of LP are discussed in practical terms in order to be of assistance to policy makers and to those charged with developing non-sexist language guidelines. In a manner of speaking the following hints can be considered a checklist which directs the formulation and implementation of language guidelines. The hints provided here are based on research findings relating to LP and discrimination, practical experiences with LP and on a dose of common sense about language and linguistic reform. The guidance particularly applies to the preparation of guidelines aimed at instituting *linguistic equality* of the sexes.

In the first two chapters of this book the stages in the process of feminist language planning were outlined. Recognising the different stages in the planning process will help in the final formulation of non-sexist guidelines. Roughly three major stages can be identified:

1. The fact-finding stage
2. The planning stage
3. The implementation stage

Stage 1: The fact-finding stage

In this stage the problem at stake is identified, described and documented. Although in most instances there will be some descriptions or discussions of linguistic sexism for the language and context in question, it may be useful to draw upon the general features of sexist language identified in Chapter 2 for your own discussion of linguistic sexism. It is also imperative that you have sufficient documentation of the features of sexist language (use) for your language. If no description of sexism exists for your language, you may be guided by the issues identified in Chapters 2 and 5. These include:

1. The invisibility of women in language due to the fact that men are considered the norm for the human species: their characteristics, thoughts, beliefs and actions are viewed as fully and adequately representing those of all humans, male and female.
2. The portrayal of women's status in reference to that of men: women's linguistic status is considered dependent on, deriving from, or submissive to that of men, which is represented as autonomous. By relegating women to a dependent, subordinate position, sexist language prevents the portrayal of women and men as different but equal human beings. This also results in lack of symmetry in the linguistic portrayal of women and men.

3. The stereotyped portrayal of both sexes which leads to a very restrictive portrayal, particularly of women.
4. The portrayal of women as inferior to men.

Consequently, the following areas of language use and structure usually deserve attention and examination of how they contribute to sexism:

(a) Generic reference to human beings affecting, e.g. nouns, pronouns, grammatical number and gender agreement.
(b) Nomenclature for men and women in relation to occupations, professions, offices and related positions (mainly at the level of nouns).
(c) Stereotyped portrayal of the sexes at word, sentence and discourse level.
(d) Titles and other forms of address for women and men; human agent nouns for women and men.

Although the attention of the language planner is usually focused on describing and eliminating linguistic sexism at the word level (e.g. nouns, pronouns, expressions, idioms and phrases), an attempt should be made to examine the issue at sentence and discourse level[1] or at least to draw the language users' attention to the fact that eliminating sexism is not primarily a matter of replacing sexist terms with non-sexist ones.

It is also important that the documentation of the sexist expressions and practices in language be relevant to the type of language use with which you are concerned. For example, if you have to provide guidelines for language use relating to the activities of a workers' union, the documentation of sexism in the use of occupational and professional titles relating to your union will be a central issue. To that purpose, it is useful to undertake your own examination/analysis of language in relevant documents and other forms of language use.

Another relevant aspect of the fact-finding stage is to identify the areas of linguistic sexism that are particularly problematic for your organisation and type of communication. For example, the issue of stereotyped portrayals of women and men may be more salient in the context of education and educational materials than in the context of legal discourse. This can be done by means of analysing the materials/texts and by seeking language users' opinions and views on the issue.

It is also helpful to check if other organisations or bodies similar to yours have undertaken analyses of sexist language, have engaged in language planning of this nature and how they have dealt with the planning and the implementation stages. Checking the existence of other guidelines has two main purposes. Firstly, other examples may help you to decide on a suitable format for your guidelines and the aspects of language that they should cover. Secondly, consulting other guidelines relating to your subject matter also ensures that major discrepancies between the latter and yours are avoided. Although you are under no obligation to adopt the alternatives or strategies recommended in other guidelines as they may not suit your context or you may not think them effective, it is nevertheless advantageous for the implementation of your guidelines if they reflect the major principles and strategies promoted in existing guidelines.

Stage 2: The planning stage

In many instances this stage will be the starting-point for your activities as the various forms and expressions of sexist language will often have been documented and examined by other sources. In the planning stage you will need to make decisions about

(a) whether or not to change sexist language forms and reform sexist language practices; and
(b) how to make linguistic changes, and which ones to make.

The information presented in Chapter 3 will assist you in your decision about whether or not to reform sexist language. In many respects your decision to change or not to change sexist language use will hinge upon your view, and your organisation's view, of the relationship between language and society. You should therefore be aware or inform yourself of the various views currently held on the interaction between language change and societal change. Similarly, the discussion in Chapter 4 on how to change or reform sexist language (use) can provide you with assistance regarding the major strategies and the ways of addressing linguistic reform.

If you have not already done so, it is recommended that you set up an advisory or steering committee at this stage which acts as a forum for discussion on strategies to adopt and changes to implement.

Although there is no need to decide upon one single strategy guiding linguistic reform, it is recommended that your approach to reforming/changing sexist language be consistent by selecting one major strategy (e.g. form-replacement) or by using complementary strategies.

If the outcome of your discussions in the advisory committee and/or consultation with target groups favours a strategy of form-replacement either by means of gender neutralisation or gender specification, you will need to pay particular attention to the formulation/development or creation of non-sexist alternative forms and expressions.

Firstly, you must identify which sexist practices, expressions and forms need to be clearly described and which alternative expressions, practices need to be exemplified. It seems sensible to suggest that those practices, expressions and forms that occur most frequently need to be dealt with and illustrated. Secondly, decisions need to be made about the formulation of alternatives: should preference be given to existing non-sexist expressions or should new forms be created? In Chapter 4 it was suggested that the formulation of non-sexist alternatives be guided by the principles of linguistic viability and social effectiveness. *Social effectiveness* means that the proposed alternatives should be chosen in such a way that they are able to promote or bring about the desired social change. That is, the use of non-sexist expressions should not only reflect but also contribute to the equality of the sexes in social life. *Linguistic viability* means that the suggested alternatives should be viable from a linguistic point of view. For instance, it may be more difficult to introduce a new pronoun to replace the masculine generic pronoun *he* than to use the dual pronoun *he or she*. Linguistic viability is tied to some extent to 'linguistic prescriptivism'; if alternative expressions are promoted which, despite their widespread use (singular *they*, for example) are considered to violate deeply ingrained prescriptive rules of language use, their introduction may be severely hampered. It is important to take into account the stylistic and semantic (meaning) range of the sexist and non-sexist expressions. If you are formulating non-sexist alternatives in a language that has previously been analysed for sexism, it would be advisable to consult existing language guidelines with regard to non-sexist alternatives. Some congruity of alternatives across language guidelines has been shown to facilitate adoption (see above). Thirdly, some assessment of the target group's reactions to proposed alternatives needs to be undertaken in order to avoid total rejection of the reform proposals. Following the discussion about strategies and the formulation of alternative forms and expressions, you should give thought to the implementation stage.

Stage 3: The implementation stage

If your aim is to provide guidance on how to achieve linguistic equality of the sexes, the drafting and issuing of non-sexist language guidelines is your most likely mechanism of implementing reform. The publication of the guidelines in the form of a brochure, leaflet or handbook is perhaps the most widespread format, although other options could include distribution in electronic or machine readable format. Here are some pointers for the structure and content of the guidelines:

Know your audience or readership

In order to be effective and successful, your guidelines should be geared to the specific needs of your readers. It is therefore important to know the audience for whom the guidelines are intended. The tone you adopt in formulating guidelines, the explanations of linguistic discrimination and the alternatives you suggest, will all depend on your audience. For instance, if your guidelines are intended for use within a publishing company, you can expect your readers to have a specialist knowledge of language matters. This will allow you to write more elaborately on the nature of linguistic discrimination, but the tone of your writing should not be too didactic. The nature of your readers' work – dealing with written language of any kind – also means that they need fairly extensive guidelines outlining a multitude of strategies and alternatives.

State aim and rationale for the guidelines

It is advisable to indicate the rationale for your guidelines and to provide some insight into the topic of discriminatory language suitable for your specific audience. It is helpful to have at least a working definition of linguistic sexism and to pinpoint the major forms and expressions of sexism in the language in question.

Provide appropriate examples illustrating linguistic sexism

It is important to select examples which clearly demonstrate a particular type of sexist language (use). Examples should be genuine (that is, taken from actual language use) or should be made up on the basis of actual language use. This avoids the problem of describing discriminatory language on the basis of examples unlikely to reflect actual language use. It is also advisable to choose examples relevant to the type of language/discourse with which your target audience is most often confronted. For example, if you are writing guidelines for language used in medical settings, your examples should be taken from medical textbooks, journals, hospital documents, medical brochures, etc. The use of examples taken from, say, political articles in newspapers would not be suitable in this context.

Presenting alternative, non-discriminatory expressions

The greater part of the guidelines is concerned with the provision of non-discriminatory alternative words, phrases and expressions. As indicated above, two main principles guide the selection of non-discriminatory alternatives: *the principle of social effectiveness* and *the principle of linguistic viability*. It is important to cover at least the words, expressions and practices crucial to the language use in your organisation. In many instances the stylistic and semantic range of the sexist and non-sexist categories of expressions, etc., is characterised by a great deal of overlap, although it is seldom identical. This should be pointed out so that readers are made aware of the potential discrepancies and variations between the sexist and non-sexist expressions. It is therefore also recommended that writers of guidelines suggest multiple alternatives for discriminatory expressions, as this minimises stylistic and semantic difficulties.

Sometimes the selection of non-sexist alternatives is further facilitated by the availability of some extensive lists and word finders dealing with non-sexist language. Care should be taken when consulting such sources: they may not adopt a similar strategy or approach to changing sexist language.

Providing motivation for linguistic reform

In Chapter 5 it became clear that introducing linguistic change or linguistic innovations is often met by considerable opposition caused by a range of factors including linguistic insecurity, fear of being ridiculed, normative thinking about language, etc. It is therefore worthwhile not only to address the benefits of using non-sexist language but also to discuss and counteract some of the major forms of opposition to the non-sexist language proposals. Chapter 5 provides an example of how this can be done. Furthermore, the articles by Blaubergs (1980), Stanley (1982) and Hellinger and Schräpel (1983) can provide guidance for this section.

An important feature of the implementation stage is to ensure that the target audience is made aware of the language reforms and that it is encouraged to adopt the latter. Achieving success in this area will vary greatly across target groups and across organisations. The adoption of the linguistic reforms by key people in an organisation who are perceived as role models will greatly enhance the acceptance and spread of the reforms throughout the target community.

Evaluating the reform proposals

Finally, some evaluation of the implementation stage will need to be undertaken in order to assess if any other measures need to be taken to facilitate the adoption of the reforms. Such evaluation could include an examination of the written materials produced and distributed in the organisation, of the public-speaking practices as well as a survey of attitudes and reactions towards the changes within the target community.

Note

1. Some guidance on analysing sexism at sentence and discourse level can be found in, e.g., Penelope (1990).

Bibliography

Abd-el-Jawad, Hassan R.S. (1989) Language and women's place with special reference to Arabic. *Language Sciences* 11(3): 305–24.

Adams-Smith, Diane E. (1987) Inclusive language in Anglican forms of worship: the revised liturgy in the United Kingdom and New Zealand. Poster presented at the International Congress of Applied Linguistics, Sydney, August 1987.

Adamsky, Cathryn (1981) Changes in pronominal usage in a classroom situation. *Psychology of Women Quarterly* 5: 733–79.

Adriaens, Geert (1981) Vrouwelijke beroepsnamen in het Nederlands. Een synchronisch overzicht en een taalevolutieve benadering. Unpublished thesis. Universiteit Leuven.

Aebischer, Verena (1985) *Les femmes et le langage.* Paris: Presses Universitaires de France.

Aebischer, Verena and Forel, Claire (eds) (1983) *Parlers masculins, parlers féminins?* Neuchâtel: Delacheux et Niestlé.

Ager, Dennis (1990) *Sociolinguistics and contemporary French.* Cambridge: Cambridge University Press.

Akkramas, Pakini (1989) Über die sprachliche Ungleichbehandlung von Frauen und Männern im Thailändischen. Paper presented at the *Tagung der deutschen Gesellschaft für Sprachwissenschaft,* University of Osnabrück, February 1989.

Allan, Keith and Burridge, Kate (1991) *Euphemism and dysphemism: language as a shield and weapon.* New York: Oxford University Press.

Arbeitsgruppe der Bundesverwaltung (1991) *Sprachliche Gleichbehandlung von Frau und Mann in der Gesetzes-und Verwaltungssprache.* Bern: Schweizerische Bundeskanzlei.

Arbeitsgruppe Rechtssprache (1990) *Maskuline und feminine Personenbezeichnungen in der Rechtssprache.* Bonn: Deutscher Bundestag.

Atkinson, Donna L. (1987) Names and titles: maiden name retention and the use of Ms. *Women and Language* 10: 37.

Baron, Dennis (1986) *Grammar and gender.* New Haven and London: Yale University Press.

Bate, Barbara (1978) What does 'she' mean? Nonsexist language use in transition. *Journal of Communication* 28: 139–49.

Beattie, James [1788] (1968) *Theory of language* (reprint). Menston: Scolar.

Bebout, Linda (1984) Asymmetries in male–female word pairs. *American Speech* 59(1): 13–30.

Beier, Heidrun (1982) ¿El sombrero o la sombrerera? Zur Genusneutralisierung femininer Formen bei Berufsbezeichnungen. *Fremdsprachen* 26(2): 102–4.

Beligan, Anamaria (1993) Discriminatory language in post-revolutionary Romanian newspapers. Unpublished paper, Department of Linguistics, Monash University.

Bem, Sandra and Bem, Daryl J. (1973) Does sex-biased job advertising 'aid and abet' sex discrimination. *Journal of Applied Social Psychology* 3: 6–18.

Bierbach, Christine (1989) La lengua compañera del imperio macho. Was ist sexistischer: die spanische Sprache oder ihre Wörterbücher? *Tranvía, Revue der Iberischen Halbinsel* 14: 7–9.

Bierbach, Christine and Ellrich, Beate (1990) Sprache und Geschlechter. In Günter Holtus, Michael Metzeltin and Christian Schmitt (eds) *Lexikon der Romanistischen Linguistik*. Bd V, 1. Französisch. Tübingen: Niemeyer, pp. 248–66.

Bierce, Ambrose (1911) *The devil's dictionary*. New York: Dover.

Blakar, Rolv Mikkel (1971) Kan mannssamfunnet sprengast utan språkrevolusjon. *Syn og Segn* 77: 550–61.

Blakar, Rolv Mikkel (1974) Språk og kvinne undertrykking-eit mangesidig problem. *Ventil* 4: 3–10.

Blakar, Rolv Mikkel (1975) How the sex roles are represented, reflected and conserved in the Norwegian language. *Acta Sociologica* 18: 162–73.

Blakar, Rolv Mikkel (1977) *Språk er makt*. Oslo: Pax.

Blaubergs, Maija (1978) Changing the sexist language: the theory behind the practice. *Psychology of Women Quarterly* 2(3): 244–61.

Blaubergs, Maija (1980) An analysis of classic arguments against changing sexist language. *Women's Studies International Quarterly* 3: 135–47.

Bodine, Ann (1975) Androcentrism in prescriptive grammar: singular 'they', sex-indefinite 'he', and 'he or she'. *Language in Society* 4: 129–46.

Bolinger, Dwight (1980) *The loaded weapon*. London: Longman.

Bornemann, E. (1971) *Sex im Volksmund. Die sexuelle Umgangssprache des deutschen Volkes*. Reinbek: Rowohlt.

Bosmajian, Haig (1977) Sexism in the language of legislatures and courts. In Alleen Pace Nilsen *et al.* (eds), pp. 77–104.

Brantenberg, Gert (1977) *Egalias døtre*. Oslo: Novus.

Braun, Friederike (1991) *Mehr Frauen in die Sprache. Leitfaden zur geschlechtergerechten Formulierung*. Kiel: Frauenministerin des Landes Schleswig-Holstein.

Britto, Francis (1988) Effects of feminism on English. *Sophia Linguistica* 26: 139–49.

Brockhoff, Evamaria (1987) Wie fragt Mann nach Frauen? *Die Zeit*, 2.1.1987.

Brouwer, Dédé (1985a) Hoe vrouwelijk is een hoofd? *De Gids* 148: 105–15.

Brouwer, Dédé (1985b) Anders, aber gleich? Über die Bildung weiblicher Berufsbezeichnungen im Niederländischen. In Marlis Hellinger (ed.), pp. 132–47.

Brouwer, Dédé (1991a) Feminist language policy in Dutch: equality rather than difference. *Working Papers on Language, Gender and Sexism* 1(2): 73–82.

Brouwer, Dédé (1991b) *Vrouwentaal*. Bloemendaal: Aramith.

Brouwer, Dédé, Gerritsen, Marinel, de Haan, Dorian and van der Post, Annette (1978) *Vrouwentaal en mannenpraat*. Amsterdam: Van Gennep.

Brown, Goold [1851] (1880) *Grammar of English grammars* (10th edition). New York.

Brownmiller, Susan (1977) *Against our will. Men, women and rape*. Harmondsworth: Penguin.

Bull, Tove (1988) Words and gender. *Nordlyd* 14: 108–17.

Bull, Tove (1990) Til mann og kvinne skapte han dei. *Altaboka 1990*: 89–95.

Bull, Tove (1993) Language and gender research in Norway: an overview. Paper presented at the AILA Congress in Amsterdam, August 1993.

Calvet, Louis-Jean (1989) Femme sous l'influence lexicale. *Le français dans le monde (April supplement 10)* 29/224: 7–8.

Cameron, Deborah (1985) *Feminism and linguistic theory*. London: Macmillan.

Cameron, Deborah (1995) *Verbal hygiene*. London: Routledge.

Cameron, Deborah and Coates, Jennifer (1985) Some problems in the sociolinguistic explanation of sex differences. *Language and Communication* 5(3): 143–51.

Canciani, E. (1913) Piedmontese proverbs in dispraise of women. *Folklore* 24: 91–6.

Cannon, Garland and Robertson, Susan (1985) Sexism in present-day English: is it diminishing? *Word* 36(1): 23–35.

Carson, Julie (1973) The Rumpelstiltskin syndrome; Sexism in American naming traditions. In Dana V. Hiller and Ann Sheets Robin (eds) *Women and men: The consequences of power*. Cincinnati: University of Cincinnati, Office of Women's Studies, pp. 64–73.

Carstensen, Broder (1983) Words of the Year 1982; Wörter des Jahres 1982. *Deutsche Sprache* 2: 174–87.

Cherry, K. (1987) *Womansword: what Japanese words say about women*. Tokyo: Kodansha International.

Cixous, Hélène (1981) The Laugh of the Medusa. In Elaine Marks and Isabelle de Courtivron (eds), pp. 245–64.

Clausen, Jeanette (1982) Our language, our selves. Verena Stefan's critique of patriarchal language. In Susan Cocalis and Kay Goodman (eds)

Beyond the eternal feminine. Critical essays on women and German literature. Stuttgart: Akademischer Verlag H.D. Heinz, pp. 381–400.

Coates, Jennifer (1986) *Women, men and language.* London: Longman.

Coates, Jennifer and Cameron, Deborah (eds) (1988) *Women in their speech communities.* London: Longman.

Cobarrubias, Juan and Fishman, Joshua A. (eds) (1983) *Progress in language planning.* The Hague: Mouton.

Cochran, Effie Papatzikou (1992) Towards degendered English in the ESL classroom: the Medusa Syndrome. *Working Papers on Language, Gender and Sexism* 2(2): 27–36.

Cohen, Jo, Gallagher, Kathleen and Peery, Alice (1983) *Bibliography of materials on sexism and sex-role stereotyping in children's books.* Chapel Hill, NC: Lollipop Power, Inc.

Collins, Ronald K. (1977) Language, history and the legal process: a profile of the 'reasonable man'. *Rutgers-Camden Law Journal* 8(2).

Connors, Kathleen (1971) Studies in feminine agentives in selected European languages. *Romance Philology* 24: 573–98.

Consdi, Eleonora (1987) Rules of address in secondary schools in Catania: linguistic variation and its social/cultural value. *Language in Society* 16(4): 559–64.

Cooper, Robert L. (1984) The avoidance of androcentric generics. *International Journal of the Sociology of Language* 50: 5–20.

Cooper, Robert L. (1989) *Language planning and social change.* Cambridge: Cambridge University Press.

Corbett, Greville (1991) *Gender.* Cambridge: Cambridge University Press.

Crawford, Mary and English, L. (1984) Generic versus specific inclusion of women in language: Effects on recall. *Journal of Psycholinguistic Research* 13: 373–81.

Daly, Mary (1973) *Beyond God the Father: toward a philosophy of women's liberation.* Boston: Beacon Press.

Daly, Mary (1978) *Gyn/ecology: The metaethics of radical feminism.* Boston: Beacon Press.

Daly, Mary in cahoots with Jane Caputi (1987) *Webster's first new intergalactic Wickedary of the English language.* Boston: Beacon Press.

Danet, Brenda (1980) Language in legal process. *Law and Society Review* 14(3): 447–564.

D'Antoni, Francesca (1992) Il sessismo linguistico nel messagio pubblicitario. *Rassegna Italiana di Linguistica Applicata* 24(1): 129–61.

Davis, Juanita (1985) Sexist bias in eight newspapers. *Journalism Quarterly* 59: 456–60.

De Caluwe, Johan (1996) Systematische vervrouwelijking van functiebenamingen. In OC en W – Ministerie van Onderwijs, Cultuur en Wetenschappen, pp. 39–41.

Degh, Linda, Glassie, Henry and Felix, J. Oinas (eds) (1976) *Folklore today: a festschrift for Richard M. Dorson.* Bloomington: Indian University Research Centre for Language and Semiotic Studies.

Delano, Isaac O. (1979) *Owe l'esin oro: Yoruba proverbs–Their meaning and usage*. Ibadan: University Press Limited.

Demonte, Violeta (1982) Lenguaje y sexo. In María Angeles Duran (ed.) *Liberación y utopia*. Madrid: Akal, pp. 61–79.

Densmore, Dana (1970) *Speech is a form of thought*. Pittsburgh: KNOW, Inc.

De Silva, Connie (1992) Editors' attitudes towards changing sexist language. Unpublished essay, M.A. Applied Linguistics Program, Monash University.

Dorodnykh, A.I. and Martynyuk, A.P. (1990) Some reflections on ideas and results of feminist linguistics. *Papers and Studies in Contrastive Linguistics* 25: 177–82.

Driedger, E.A. (1976) Are statutes written for men only? *McGill Law Journal* 22.

Dubois, Betty Lou and Crouch, Isabel (1987) Linguistic disruption: He/ She, S/He, He or She, He-She. In Joyce Penfield (ed.) *Women and language in transition*. Albany, NY: State University of New York, pp. 28–35.

Dundes, Alan (1976) The crowing hen and the easter bunny: male chauvinism in American folklore. In Linda Degh *et al*. (eds), pp. 123–38.

Eastman, Carol M. (1983) *Language planning: an introduction*. San Francisco: Chandler and Sharp.

Eckert, Penelope and McConnell-Ginet, Sally (1992) Think practically and look locally. Language and gender as community-based practice. *Annual Review of Anthropology* 21: 461–90.

Edwards, John (1985) *Language, society and identity*. Oxford: Basil Blackwell.

Ehrlich, Susan and King, Ruth (1992) Gender-based language reform and the social construction of meaning. *Discourse and Society* 3(2): 151–66.

Ehrlich, Susan and King, Ruth (1994) Feminist meanings and the (de)politicization of the lexicon. *Language in Society* 23: 59–76.

Eisenberg, Daniel (1985) The editor's column. Grammatical sexism in Spanish. *Journal of Hispanic Philology* 9(3): 189–96.

Elgin, Suzette Haden (1984) *Native tongue*. New York: Daw.

Elgin, Suzette Haden (1985) *A first dictionary and grammar of Láadan*. Madison: Society for the Furtherance and Study of Fantasy and Science Fiction.

Elgin, Suzette Haden (1988) *A first dictionary and grammar of Láadan*. Madison: Society for the Furtherance and Study of Fantasy and Science Fiction. (Revised edition.)

Ellerington, Kerrie (1989) Reactions to non-sexist language guidelines published in the *Style manual*. Unpublished essay, M.A. Applied Linguistics Program, Monash University.

Ellis, Rod (1985) *Understanding second language acquisition*. Oxford: Oxford University Press.

Ellis, Rod (1990) *Instructed second language acquisition*. Oxford: Blackwell.

Endo, O. (1987) *Kininaru Kotoba* (Worrying Language). Tokyo: Nan'undo.

Escobar, Alberto (1972) *Lenguaje y discriminación social en la sociedad en América Latina.* Peru: Editorial Carlos Mille batres.

Evans, H. (1985) A feminine issue in contemporary French usage. *Modern Languages* 66(4): 231–6.

Evans, H. (1987) The government and linguistic change in France: the case of feminisation. *ASCMF Review* 31: 20–6.

Fairclough, Norman (ed.) (1992) *Critical language awareness.* London: Longman.

Farley, Lyn (1978) *Sexual shakedown: the sexual harassment of women on the job.* New York: McGraw-Hill.

Farmer, J.S. and Henley, W.E. (1965) *Slang and its analogues.* New York: Kraus Reprint.

Fasold, Ralph (1984) *The sociolinguistics of society.* Oxford: Blackwell.

Fasold, Ralph (1987) Language policy and change: sexist language in the periodical news media. In Lowenberg, Peter (ed.) *Language spread and language policy.* Washington, DC: Georgetown University Press, pp. 187–206.

Fasold, Ralph, Yamada, Haru, Robinson, David and Barish, Steven (1990) The language planning effect of newspaper editorial policy: Gender differences in *The Washington Post. Language in Society* 19: 521–39.

Fischer, Paul (1985) Docteure, docteuse, doctoresse? *Lebende Sprachen* 3: 133–6.

Fishman, Joshua A. (ed.) (1974) *Advances in language planning.* The Hague: Mouton.

Fishman, Joshua (1983) Modeling rationales in corpus planning: modernity and tradition in images of the good corpus. In Juan Cobarrubias and Joshua Fishman (eds) *Progress in language planning: international perspectives.* Berlin: Mouton, pp. 107–18.

Fishman, Joshua A., Ferguson, Charles A. and Das Gupta, Jyotirindra (eds) (1968) *Language problems of developing nations.* New York: John Wiley.

Flanagan, Anna M. and Todd-Mancillas, William R. (1982) Teaching inclusive generic pronoun usage: the effectiveness of an authority innovation approach versus an optional innovation-decision approach. *Communication Education* 31: 275–84.

Fleischhauer, Ursula (1983) Sprachpolitik und Sprachwandel: Eine kontrastive Analyse deutsch- und englischsprachiger Stellenanzeigen. Unpublished Staatsexamenarbeit, Universität Hannover.

Foppa, Alaíde (1978) Lo que dice el diccionario. *fem* 6: 52–5.

Frank, Francine W. (1985a) El género gramatical y los cambios sociales. *Espanol Actual* 43: 27–50.

Frank, Francine W. (1985b) Language planning and sexual equality: guidelines for non-sexist usage. In Marlis Hellinger (ed.), pp. 231–54.

Frank, Francine W. (1989) Language planning, language reform, and language change: a review of guidelines for nonsexist usage. In Francine Frank and Paula Treichler, pp. 105–36.

Frank, Francine W. and Anshen, Frank (1983) *Languages and the sexes.* Albany: State University of New York Press.

Frank, Francine W. and Treichler, Paula A. (1989) *Language, gender and professional writing.* New York: Modern Language Association of America.

Frank, Karsta (1992) *Sprachgewalt: die sprachliche Reproduktion der Geschlechterhierarchie. Elemente einer feministischen Linguistik im Kontext sozialwissenschaftlicher Frauenforschung.* Tübingen: Niemeyer.

Freebody, Peter and Baker, Carolyn (1987) The construction and operation of gender in children's first school books. In Anne Pauwels (ed.), pp. 80–107.

Fretheim, Thorstein (1976) On the abolishment of sex-indefinite 'he'. *Working Papers in Linguistics, Oslo* 7: 134–41.

Froitzheim, Claudia (1980) *Sprache und Geschlecht: Bibliographie.* Trier: Universität Trier.

Fromkin, Victoria and Rodman, Robert (1983) *An introduction to language.* New York: Holt, Rinehart and Winston.

Frost, David. L. (1986) The language of liturgy. *Overland* 104: 61–3.

Gal, Susan (1994) Between speech and silence. The problematics of research on language and gender. In Camille Roman, Suzanne Juhasz and Cristanne Miller (eds) *The women and language debate.* New Brunswick: Rutgers University Press, pp. 407–31.

García, Meseguer Alvaro (1977) *Lenguaje y discriminación sexual.* Madrid: Editorial Cuadernos para el Diálogo, S.A. Edicusa.

Gastil, John (1990) Generic pronouns and sexist language: the oxymoronic character of masculine generics. *Sex Roles* 23 (11–12): 629–43.

Gershuny, H. Lee (1973) Sexist semantics. Unpublished PhD dissertation.

Gershuny, H. Lee (1974) Sexist semantics in the dictionary. *Etc.* 31(2): 159–69.

Gershuny, H. Lee (1975) Public doublespeak: the dictionary. *College English* 36(8): 938–42.

Gershuny, H. Lee (1977) Sexism in dictionaries and texts: omissions and commissions. In Alleen Pace Nilsen *et al.* (eds), pp. 143–59.

Gervais, Marie Marthe (1993) Gender and language in French. In Carol Sanders (ed.) *French Today.* Cambridge: Cambridge University Press, pp. 121–39.

Gilbert, Sandra and Gubar, Susan (1985) Sexual linguistics: gender, language and sexuality. *New Literary History* 16(3): 515–43.

Goh, Yeun Yeun (1994) The use of pronouns and attitudes towards sexism in language among undergraduate students. Unpublished essay, M.A. Applied Linguistics Program, Monash University.

Gomard, Kirsten (1985) Sexistische Sprachmuster im Dänischen und Tendenzen des sprachlichen Wandels. In Marlis Hellinger (ed.), pp. 84–95.

González, Iris G. (1978) Words and women: sexism in the language of the church. Paper presented at the International Sociological Association.

González, Iris G. (1982) Sexism in the church: a sociolinguistic-biblical perspective. *Revista/Review Interamericana* 12(2): 185–99.

González, Iris G. (1985) Some aspects of sexism in Spanish. In Marlis Hellinger (ed.), pp. 48–63.

Gorman, Thomas P. (1973) Language allocation and language planning in a developing nation. In Joan Rubin and Roger Shuy (eds), pp. 72–82.

Grabrucker, Marianne (1993) *Vater Staat hat keine Muttersprache*. Frankfurt: Fischer.

Graddol, David and Swann, Joan (1989) *Gender voices*. Oxford: Blackwell and Open University.

Graham, Alma (1975) The making of a non-sexist dictionary. In Barrie Thorne and Nancy Henley (eds), pp. 57–63.

Graham, Alma (n.d.) *Non-sexist language guidelines*. New York: Alma Graham.

Greene, Kathryn and Serovic, J. (1989) Gender construction in the language of marriage. Paper presented at the Twelfth Annual Conference for the Organization of the Study of Communication, Language and Gender, OH, October.

Greene, Kathryn and Rubin, Donald L. (1991) Effects of gender inclusive/exclusive language in religious discourse. *Journal of Language and Social Psychology* 10(2): 81–98.

Groult, Benoîte (1975) *Ainsi soit-elle*. Paris: Denoel/Gonthier.

Groult, Benoîte (1977) *Le féminisme au masculin*. Paris: Denoel/Gonthier.

Guentherodt, Ingrid (1979) Berufsbezeichnungen für Frauen. Problematik der deutschen Sprache im Vergleich mit Beispielen aus dem Englischen und Französischen. *Osnabrücker Beiträge zur Sprachtheorie*, Beihefte 3: 120–32.

Guentherodt, Ingrid (1980) Behördliche Sprachregelungen gegen und für eine sprachliche Gleichbehandlung von Frauen und Männern. *Linguistische Berichte* 69: 22–36.

Guentherodt, Ingrid (1984) Androcentric language in German legal texts and the principle of equal treatment for women and men. *Journal of Pragmatics* 8: 241–60.

Guentherodt, Ingrid, Hellinger, Marlis, Pusch, Luise and Trömel-Plötz, Senta (1980) Richtlinien zur Vermeidung sexistischen Sprachgebrauchs. *Linguistische Berichte* 69: 15–21.

Guerra, Ada Moca (1972) *Primacias de un documento no publicade: El discrimen contra la mujer en Puerto Rico*. Río Piedras: University of Puerto Rico.

Guiraud, Pierre (1978) *Le langage de la sexualité*. Paris: Payot.

Gupta, Anthea Fraser and Lee, Ameline Su Yin (1990) Gender representation in English language textbooks used in the Singapore primary schools. *Language and Education* 4(1): 29–50.

Häberlin, Susanna, Schmid, Rachel and Wyss, Eva Lia (1992) *Übung macht die Meisterin. Richtlinien für einen nicht-sexistischen Sprachgebrauch*. München: Frauenoffensive.

Hagen, Stephen and Emblem, Doug (eds) (1992) *Languages in international business: a practical guide.* London: Hodder and Stoughton.

Hales, Jim (1988) Eine Analyse des Sexismus in Lehrbüchern für Deutsch als Fremdsprache. Unpublished paper, Department of German, Monash University.

Halfmann, Ulrich (1978) Sexolinguistik und Spanischunterricht. Kommunikative Kompetenz beim Wort genommen. *Osnabrücker Beiträge zur Sprachtheorie* 6: 88–102.

Hamilton, Mykol C. (1988) Using masculine generics: does generic he increase male bias in the user's imagery? *Sex Roles* 19: 785–99.

Hampares, Katherine J. (1976) Sexism in Spanish lexicography. *Hispania* 59: 100–9.

Hanssen, Erik and Rajnik, Eugeniusz (1982) Movierung der Personenbezeichnungen im Deutschen und Dänischen. Dänisch–deutsche kontrastive Grammatik. *Arbeitsbericht 5* (Copenhagen).

Harres, Annette and Truckenbrodt, Andrea (1992) Sexism in German foreign language textbooks. *Language and Gender Newsletter* 1992: 4–5.

Harrigan, J. and Lucic, K. (1988) Attitudes toward gender bias in language: a reevaluation. *Sex Roles* 10: 129–40.

Harris, James [1751] (1765) *Hermes, or a philosophical inquiry concerning universal grammar.* London.

Heilman, M. (1975) Miss, Mrs., Ms.,or none of the above. *American Psychologist* 30: 516–18.

Hellinger, Marlis (1980) Zum Gebrauch weiblicher Berufsbezeichnungen im Deutschen-Variabilität als Ausdruck außersprachlicher Machtstrukturen. *Linguistische Berichte* 69: 37–58.

Hellinger, Marlis (1981) Über den Zusammenhang zwischen Sprache und Geschlecht. *Englisch–Amerikanische Studien* 3: 96–107.

Hellinger, Marlis (ed.) (1985a) *Sprachwandel und feministische Sprachpolitik: Internationale Perspektiven.* Opladen: Westdeutscher Verlag.

Hellinger, Marlis (1985b) Reaktionen auf die 'Richtlinien zur Vermeidung sexistischen Sprachgebrauchs'. In Marlis Hellinger (ed.), (1985a), pp. 255–60.

Hellinger, Marlis (1990) *Kontrastive feministische Linguistik. Mechanismen sprachlicher Diskriminierung im Englischen und Deutschen.* Ismaning: Hueber.

Hellinger, Marlis (1991a) Für sprachliche Chancengleichheit. *Universitas* 5: 413–15.

Hellinger, Marlis (1991b) Feminist linguistics and linguistic relativity. *Working Papers on Language, Gender and Sexism* 1(1): 25–37.

Hellinger, Marlis (1993) Guidelines for the equal treatment of the sexes in German. Paper presented at the 10th World Congress of Applied Linguistics in Amsterdam, August 1993.

Hellinger, Marlis and Schräpel, Beate (1983) Über die sprachliche Gleichbehandlung von Frauen und Männern. *Jahrbuch für Internationale Germanistik* 15: 40–69.

Hellinger, Marlis, Kremer, Marion and Schräpel, Beate (1985) *Empfehlungen zur Vermeidung von sexistischem Sprachgebrauch in öffentlicher Sprache.* Hannover: Universität Hannover.

Hellinger, Marlis and Bierbach, Christine (1993) *Eine Sprache für beide Geschlechter: Richtlinien für einen nicht-sexistischen Sprachgebrauch.* Bonn: Deutsche Unesco-Kommission.

Henley, Nancy (1987) The new species that seeks a new language: on sexism in language and language change. In Joyce Penfield (ed.), pp. 3–27.

Henley, Nancy and Dragun, Darlene (1983) A survey of attitudes towards changing sex biased language. Paper presented at the meeting of the American Psychological Association, Anaheim, 1983.

Henley, Nancy, Gruber, Barbara and Lerner, Linda (1985) Studies on the detrimental effects of 'generic' masculine usage. Paper presented at the Eastern Psychological Association Congress, Boston, March 1985.

Henley, Nancy and Kramarae, Cheris (1991) Gender, power and miscommunication. In Nikolas Coupland, Howard Giles and John M. Wiemann (eds) *'Miscommunication' and problematic talk.* Newbury Park: Sage, pp. 18–43.

Hennessy, Margaret (1993) Propagating half a species: gender in learners' dictionaries. In Pam H. Peters (ed.) *Style on the move: proceedings of Style Council 1992.* North Ryde: Macquarie University, Dictionary Research Centre, pp. 120–32.

Herbert, Robert K. and Nykiel-Herbert, Barbara (1986) Explorations in linguistic sexism: a contrastive sketch. *Papers and Studies in Contrastive Linguistics* 21: 47–85.

Herder, Johann Gottfried [1772] (1966) *On the origin of language* (translated by Alexander Gode). New York: Ungar.

Hexengeflüster (1975) Berlin: Frauenselbstverlag.

Hiraga, Masako (1991) Metaphors Japanese women live by. *Working Papers on Language, Gender and Sexism* 1(1): 38–57.

Hjelmslev, L. (1956) *Animé et inanimé, personnel et non-personnel.* Paris: Travaux de l'Institut de Linguistique.

Hoffmann, Ulrich (1979) *Sprache und Emanzipation. Zur Begrifflichkeit der feministischen Bewegung.* Frankfurt: Campus Verlag.

Hook, Donald D. (1977) Sexism in English pronouns and forms of address. *General Linguistics* 14(2): 86–96.

Houdebine, Anne Marie (1988) La féminisation des noms de métiers en français contemporain. In Georges Kassaï (ed.) *Contrastes. La différence sexuelle dans le langage.* Nice: ADEC, pp. 39–71.

Houdebine-Gravaud, Anne-Marie (1989) Une aventure linguistique: la féminisation des noms de métiers, titres et fonctions en français contemporain. *Terminologie et Traduction* 1989: 91–145.

Houssami, Jamal (1994) People's reactions to proposed non-sexist alternatives to generic pronoun 'he'. Unpublished essay, M.A. Applied Linguistics Program, Monash University.

Hughes, Diana L. and Casey, Patricia L. (1986) Pronoun choice for gender-unspecified agent words: developmental differences. *Language and Speech* 29: 59–68.

Huisman, Joke (1984) *Taal over sekse. Een sociolinguistische benadering.* Universiteit van Amsterdam: Instituut voor Algemene Taalwetenschap.

Ibrahim, Muhammad Hassan (1973) *Grammatical gender, its origin and development.* The Hague: Mouton.

Ide, Sachiko (1979) *Onna no kotoba, otoka no kotoba* (Women's words, men's words). Tokyo: Nihon keizai tsuushin sha.

Irigaray, Luce (1977) *Ce sexe qui n'en est pas un.* Paris: Minuit.

Irigaray, Luce (1985) *The sex which is not one* (translated by Catherine Porter). Ithaca: Cornell University Press.

Irigaray, Luce (ed.) (1987) Le sexe linguistique. *Langages* 85.

Irigaray, Luce (ed.) (1990) *Sexes et genres à travers les languages.* Paris: Bernard Grasset.

Jack, Dörte (1987) *Empfehlungen für die (zumindest) sprachliche Gleich-behandlung von Frauen und Männern. Zur Verwendung von Personen-bezeichnungen in universitären Texten.* Bielefeld: Universität Bielefeld, Interdisziplinäre Forschungsstelle Frauenforschung.

Jacobsen, Lis (1912) *Kvinde og mand. En sprogstudie fra dansk middel-alder.* Kristiania and Kopenhagen: Nordisk Verlag.

Jacobson, M. and Insko, W. (1984) On the relationship between feminism and the use of 'Ms'. *Psychological Reports* 54: 388–90.

Jacobson, M. and Insko, W. (1985) Use of nonsexist pronouns as a func-tion of one's feminist orientation. *Sex Roles* 13: 1–7.

Jaehrling, Stephanie (1988) Attitudes to sexist and non-sexist language: a comparative study of German and Australian informants. Unpublished B.A. (Hons) Thesis, Department of German, Monash University.

Janssen-Jurreit, Marielouise (1976) *Sexismus: Über die Abtreibung der Frauenfrage.* München: Carl Hanser.

Jernudd, Bjørn (1973) Language planning as a type of language treatment. In Joan Rubin and Roger Shuy (eds), pp. 11–23.

Jernudd, Bjørn and Das Gupta, Jyotirindra (1971) Towards a theory of language planning. In Joan Rubin and Bjørn Jernudd (eds), pp. 195–215.

Jernudd, Bjørn and Neustupny, Jírí (1986) Language planning: for whom? Comments presented at the International Colloquium on Language Planning in Ottowa (Canada), May 1986.

Jespersen, Otto (1922) *Language, its nature, development and origin.* London: Allen and Unwin.

Joly, André (1975) Toward a theory of gender in modern English. In André Joly and Thomas Fraser (eds) *Studies in English grammar.* Paris: Editions universitaires, pp. 227–87.

Jordan, Rosan A. and de Caro, F.A. (1986) Women and the study of folklore. *Signs* 11: 500–18.

Jugaku, A. (1979) *Nihongo to Onna* (Japanese and women). Tokyo: Iwanami-shoten.

Kalėdaitė, Violeta (1995) Language and gender in Lithuania; past and present. *Nordlyd* 23: 62–9.

Kallioinen, Vilho, Havu, Eva and Hakulinen Luciane (1987) La neutralisation du genre et l'accord grammatical en français. *Neuphilologische Mitteilungen* 88(4): 378–413.

Kalverkämper, Hartwig (1979a) Die Frauen und die Sprache. *Linguistische Berichte* 62: 55–71.

Kalverkämper, Hartwig (1979b) Quo vadis linguistica? – Oder: Der feministische Mumpsismus in der Linguistik. *Linguistische Berichte* 63: 103–7.

Kaye, Patricia (1989a) Laughter, ladies and linguistics – a light-hearted quiz for language lovers and language-learners. *ELT Journal* 43(3): 185–91.

Kaye, Patricia (1989b) 'Women are alcoholics and drug addicts' says dictionary. *ELT Journal* 43(3): 192–5.

Kennedy, C. (1984) *Language planning and language education*. London: George Allen and Unwin.

Key, Mary Ritchie (1975) *Male/female language*. Metuchen, NJ: Scarecrow Press.

Khayyat, Latif (1974) Judeo-Iraqi proverbs on man and wife. *Proverbium* 24: 934–47.

Khosroshahi, Fatemeh (1989) Penguins don't care, but women do: a social identity analysis of a Whorfian problem. *Language in Society* 18: 505–25.

Kidd, Virginia (1971) A study of the images produced through the use of the male pronoun. *Moments in Contemporary Rhetoric and Communication* 1(2): 25–30.

Klann-Delius, Gisela (1980) Can women's language cause changes? Comments on the trouble with linguistics. *Journal of Pragmatics* 4: 537–42.

Klemensiewicz, Z. (1957) Tytuly i nazwy zawodowe kobiet w swietle teorii i praktyki. *Jezyk polski* 37: 101–19.

Kloss, Heinz (1968) Notes concerning a Language-Nation typology. In Fishman, Joshua, Charles A. Ferguson, J. Das Gupta (eds) *Language problems of developing nations*. New York: Wiley, pp. 69–85.

Kloss, Heinz (1969) *Research possibilities on group bilingualism: a report*. Quebec: International Centre for Research on Bilingualism.

Kochskämper, Birgit (1991) Language history as a history of male language policy: the history of German *Mensch, Frau, Mann, Mädchen, Junge, Dirne*... and their Indo-European cognates. *Working Papers on Language, Gender and Sexism* 1(2): 5–17.

Köhler, Hanne and Wegener, Hildburg (1987) *Gerechte Sprache in Gottesdienst und Kirche*. Frankfurt/Main: Evangelische Frauenarbeit in Deutschland.

Kotthoff, Helga (ed.) (1988) *Das Gelächter der Geschlechter. Humor und Macht in Gesprächen von Frauen und Männern*. Frankfurt/Main: Fischer.

Krätzer, Martina (1981) Berufsbeschreibung, Berufsbild und Rollenklischee: zur Beschreibung konnotativer Bedeutungen im Deutschen und Englischen. Unpublished Staatsexamenarbeit, Universität Hannover.

Kramarae, Cheris (1992) Punctuating the dictionary. *International Journal of the Sociology of Language* 94: 135–54.

Kramarae, Cheris and Treichler, Paula (1985) *A feminist dictionary*. London: Pandora Press.

Kramarae, Cheris and Jenkins, Mercilee M. (1987) Women take back the talk. In Joyce Penfield (ed.), pp. 137–55.

Kramarae, Cheris and Treichler, Paula (1990) Words on a feminist dictionary. In Deborah Cameron (ed.) *The feminist critique of language: a reader.* London: Routledge, pp. 148–59.

Kramer, Cheris (1975) Sex-related differences in address systems. *Anthropological Linguistics* 17: 198–210.

Kremer, Marion (1986) Genus und Pronominalisierung im Englischen und Deutschen unter besonderer Berücksichtigung der Personenbezeichnungen. Unpublished Staatsexamenarbeit, Universität Hannover.

Kuiper, S. (1988) Gender representation in corporate annual reports and perceptions of corporate climate. *Journal of Business Communication* 25(3): 87–94.

Kurzon, Denis (1989) Sexist and nonsexist language in legal texts: the state of the art. *International Journal of the Sociology of Language* 80: 99–113.

Labov, William (1972) *Language in the Inner City: studies in the Black English vernacular.* Philadelphia: University of Pennsylvania Press.

Labov, William (1982) Building on empirical foundations. In Winfred P. Lehmann and Yakov Malkiel (eds) *Perspectives on historical linguistics.* Amsterdam: John Benjamins, pp. 17–92.

Lakoff, Robin (1975) *Language and woman's place.* New York: Harper.

Landfald, Aagot (ed.) (1983) *Råd om språk fra Norsk språkråd.* Oslo: Novus.

Lederer, Richard (1984) A quiz about sexist language. *Verbatim* 11(1): 14–15.

Lee, Alicia (1982) People and women people: are women human? A study in sexist language in the media. (manuscript).

Lee, Motoko Y. (1976) The married women's status and role as reflected in Japanese: an exploratory sociolinguistic study. *Signs* 1(4): 991–9.

Lepschy, Giulio (1987) Sexism and the Italian language. *The Italianist* 7: 158–69.

Lepsius, Karl Richard (1880) *Nübische Grammatik.* Berlin: Hertz.

Levin, Michael (1981) Vs. Ms. In Mary Vetterling-Braggin (ed.), pp. 217–22.

Lewis, Mary Ellen B. (1974) The feminists have done it: applied folklore. *Journal of American Folkore* 87: 85–7.

Lind, Åge (1988) A person in their thirties. Some thought on the use of sexist and non-sexist pronouns in modern English as exemplified by situations vacant advertisements. *Moderna Språk* 82(3): 193–202.

Lorenz, Dagmar (1991) Wider die sprachliche Apartheid der Geschlechter. *Muttersprache* 101: 272–7.

Lorraine, Tamsin E. (1990) *Gender, identity and the production of meaning.* Boulder: Westview Press.

Luebke, Barbara (1985) News about women on the A wire. *Journalism Quarterly* 62: 329–33.

Lunde, Katrin (1985) Geschlechtsabstraktion oder-Spezifikation? Entwicklungstendenzen im Bereich der norwegischen Berufsbezeichnungen. In Marlis Hellinger (ed.), pp. 96–122.

Lyons, John (1969) *Introduction to theoretical linguistics.* Cambridge: Cambridge University Press.

Maas-Cahuveau, Claudia (1989) La féminisation des titres et noms de professions au Canada. *Terminologie et Traduction* 1989: 155–66.

Mackay, Donald (1980) Psychology, prescriptive grammar and the pronoun problem. *American Psychologist* 35: 444–9.

Mackay, Donald G. (1983) Prescriptive grammar and the pronoun problem. In Barrie Thorne, Cheris Kramarae and Nancy Henley (eds), pp. 38–53.

Mackay, Donald and Fulkerson, David C. (1979) On the comprehension and production of pronouns. *Journal of Verbal Learning and Verbal Behaviour* 18: 661–73.

Mackay, Donald and Konishi, Toshi (1980) Personification and the pronoun problem. *Women's Studies International Quarterly* 3: 149–63.

Markowitz, Judith (1984) The impact of the sexist language controversy and regulation on language in university documents. *Psychology of Women Quarterly* 8(4): 337–47.

Marks, Elaine and de Courtivron, Isabelle (eds) (1981) *New French feminisms. an anthology.* New York: Schocken Books.

Martin, André and Dupuis, Henriette (1985) *La féminisation des titres et les* leaders *d'opinion: une étude exploratoire.* Quebec: Office de langue française.

Martyna, Wendy (1978) What does 'he' mean? Use of the generic masculine. *Journal of Communication* 28(1): 130–9.

Martynyuk, Alla (1990a) Social relations and sex-stereotyping in language. *Papers and Studies in Contrastive Linguistics* 26: 93–101.

Martynyuk, Alla (1990b) A contrastive study of male and female occupational terms in English and Russian. *Papers and Studies in Contrastive Linguistics* 26: 103–10.

Masayuki, Takagi (1992) *Sabetsu yogo no kiso chishiki.* Tokyo: Doyo Bijutsusha.

McConnell-Ginet, Sally (1983) Review article: language, sex and gender and sexist language. *Language* 59(2): 373–91.

McConnell-Ginet, Sally (1989) The sexual reproduction of meaning: a discourse-based theory. In Francine Frank and Paula Treichler, pp. 35–50.

McConnell-Ginet, Sally, Borker, Ruth and Furman, Nelly (eds) (1980) *Women and language in literature and society.* New York: Praeger.

McFague, S. (1982) *Metaphorical theology: models of God in religious language*. London: SCM Press.

Meijers, J.A. (1952) *Zin en onzin in het Nederlands taalgebruik*. Amsterdam–Antwerpen: Ditmar.

Meredith, Mamie (1930) Doctresses, authoresses and others. *American Speech* 5: 476–81.

Mey, Jakob (1984) Sex and language revisited: can women's language change the world? *Journal of Pragmatics* 8: 261–83.

Meyerhoff, Miriam (1984) A study of sexist and non-sexist language in written New Zealand English. Project paper at the Victoria University of Wellington, New Zealand.

Mieder, Wolfgang (1982) Sexual content of German wellerisms. *Maledicta* 6: 215–23.

Miller, Casey and Swift, Kate (1980) *The handbook of nonsexist writing: for writers, editors and speakers*. New York: Lippincott and Crowell.

Miller, Casey and Swift, Kate (1991) *Words and women. New language in new times*. (Updated.) New York: Harper Collins.

Miller, George (1950) Language engineering. *Journal of the Acoustical Society of America* 22(6): 720–5.

Ministerio de Asuntos Sociales (1989) *Propuestas para evitar el sexismo en el lenguaje*. Madrid: Ministerio de Asuntos Sociales.

Moi, Toril (1985) *Sexual/Textual politics: feminist literary theory*. New York: Methuen.

Monsen, Nina Karin (1973) Solidaritetens semantikk. Et program. In *Festskrift til Arnfinn Stigen*. Oslo, pp. 81–93.

Morris, Meaghan (1982) A-mazing grace: notes on Mary Daly's poetics. *Intervention* 16: 70–92.

Mottier, Ilja (1983) *Marie in woorden: meisjes en taalonderwijs*. 's-Gravenhage: Adviesgroep Leermiddelen.

Mottier, Ilja (1996) Taal en beeldvorming in leermiddelen. In OC en W – Ministerie van Onderwijs, Cultuur en Wetenschappen, pp. 63–7.

Moulton, Janice, Robinson, George M. and Elias, Cherin (1978) Sex bias in language use: neutral pronouns that aren't. *American Psychologist* 33: 1032–6.

Müller, Sigrid and Fuchs, Claudia (1993) *Handbuch zur nichtsexistischen Sprachverwendung in öffentlichen Texten*. Frankfurt: Fischer.

Mufwene, Salikoko S. (1983) Investigating what the words *father* and *mother* mean. *Language and Communication* 3(3): 245–69.

Myers, C. Kilmer (1972) Should women be ordained? *The Episcopalian*, February: 8.

Nakamura, M. (1990) Woman's sexuality in Japanese female terms. In Sachiko Ide and N.A. McLoin (eds) *Aspects of Japanese women's language*. Tokyo: Kurosio Publishers, pp. 147–63.

Nakayama, Masahiko (1993) Linguistic expressions of sexism in Japanese newspapers. Unpublished research paper, M.A. Applied Linguistics program, Monash University.

Nash, Rose (1982) Jobs, gender and civil rights: Puerto Rico Spanish responds to the law. *Word* 33(1–2): 81–95.

Neustupny, Jírí (1970) Basic types of treatment of language problems. *Linguistic Communications* 1: 77–98.

Neustupny, Jírí (1983) Towards a paradigm for language planning. *Language Planning Newsletter* 9(4): 1–4.

Ng, Bee Chin and Burridge, Kate (1993) The female radical: Portrayal of women in Chinese script. *Australian Review of Applied Linguistics* (Series S) 10: 54–85.

Nicholas, Howard, Moore, Helen, Clyne, Michael and Pauwels, Anne (1993) *Languages at the crossroads.* Melbourne: National Languages and Literacy Institute of Australia.

Nichols, Patricia (1988) Language policy and social power: gender and ethnic issues. In Peter H. Lowenberg (ed.) *Language spread and language policy: issues, implications and case studies.* Washington, D.C.: Georgetown University Press.

Niedzwiecki, Patricia (1994) *Alfabetische lijst vrouwelijke titels, ambt-, beroeps-, graad- en functienamen.* Brussel: OCOEC vzw. (Handleiding voor de taalvervrouwelijking. Deel II.)

Niedzwiecki, Patricia (1995) *Handleiding voor de taalvervrouwelijking. Deel I.* Brussel: Kabinet van Onderwijs en Ambtenarenzaken.

Nilsen, Alleen P., Bosmajian, Haig, Gershuny, H. Lee and Stanley, Julia P. (eds) (1977) *Sexism and language.* Urbana, Ill.: National Council of Teachers of English.

Nissen, Uwe Kjær (1986) Sex and gender specification in Spanish. *Journal of Pragmatics* 10: 725–38.

Nissen, Uwe Kjær (1990) A review of research on language and sex in the Spanish language. *Women and Language* XIII(2): 11–29.

Noss, Richard (1967) *Language policy and higher education.* Vol. 3, Part 2 of *Higher Education and Development in Southeast Asia.* Paris: UNESCO and The International Association of Universities.

Nwachukwu-Agaba, J.O.J. (1989) The old woman in the Igbo proverbial lore. *Proverbium* 6: 75–89.

Nye, Andrea (1987) The inequalities of semantic structure: linguistic and feminist philosophy. *Metaphilosophy* 18(3–4): 22–240.

OC en W – Ministerie van Onderwijs, Cultuur en Wetenschappen (1996) *Taal en beeldvorming over vrouwen en mannen.* Den Haag: Ministerie van Onderwijs, Cultuur en Wetenschappen.

Oduyoye, Amba (1979) The Asanate woman: socialization through proverbs (Part 1). *African Notes* 8: 5–11.

Olivares, Carmen (1984) A comment on J.L. Mey's review Article 'Sex and language revisited'. *Journal of Pragmatics* 8: 753–6.

Ott, Maxa (1989) Überlegungen zu einer feministischen Theorie des Sprachwandels. Unpublished paper.

Patthey-Chavez, Genevieve and Youmans, Madeleine (1992) The social construction of sexual realities in heterosexual women's and men's erotic texts. In Kira Hall, Mary Bucholtz and Birch Moonwomon (eds) *Locating Power. Proceedings of the Second Berkeley Woman and Language Conference*. Vol. 2. Berkeley, CA: Berkeley Women and Language Group, University of California.

Patthey-Chavez, Genevieve, Clare, L. and Youmans, Madeleine (1996) Watery passion: the struggle between hegemony and sexual liberation in erotic fiction for women. *Discourse and Society* 7: 77–106.

Pauwels, Anne (ed.) (1987a) *Women and language in Australian and New Zealand society*. Sydney: Australian Professional Publications.

Pauwels, Anne (1987b) Language in transition: a study of the title 'Ms' in contemporary Australian society. In Anne Pauwels (ed.), pp. 129–54.

Pauwels, A. (1988) Non-sexist language. In: *Style manual for authors, editors and printers*, 4th edition. Canberra: Australian Government Publications, pp. 111–27.

Pauwels, Anne (1989a) Some thoughts on gender, inequality and language reform. *Vox* 3: 78–84.

Pauwels, Anne (1989b) Feminist language change in Australia: changes in generic pronoun use. Paper presented at the *Tagung der deutschen Gesellschaft für Sprachwissenschaft*, University of Osnabrück, February 1989.

Pauwels, A. (1991a) *Non-discriminatory language*. Canberra: Australian Government Publishing Service.

Pauwels, Anne (1991b) Sexism and language planning in English-speaking countries: some issues and problems. *Working Papers on Language, Gender and Sexism* 1(2): 17–30.

Pauwels, Anne (1993a) Gender and language reform in Australia. In Pam H. Peters (ed.) *Style on the move: proceedings of Style Council 1992*. North Ryde: Macquarie University, Dictionary Research Centre, pp. 105–19.

Pauwels, Anne (1993b) Languages and the sexes in Australia: research issues and questions. In Gerhard Schulz (ed.) *The languages of Australia*. Canberra: Australian Academy of Humanities, pp. 104–23.

Pauwels, Anne (1993c) Language planning, language reform and the sexes in Australia. *Australian Review of Applied Linguistics* (Series S) 10: 13–34.

Pauwels, Anne (1996) Feminist language planning and titles for women: some crosslinguistic perspectives. In Ulrich Ammon and Marlis Hellinger (eds) *Contrastive Sociolinguistics*. Berlin: Mouton-De Gruyter, pp. 251–69.

Pauwels, Anne (1997a) Non-sexist language policy debate in the Dutch speech community. In Friederike Braun and Ursula Pasero (eds) *Communication of Gender. Kommunikation von Geschlecht*. Pfaffenweiler: Centaurus Verlag.

Pauwels, Anne (1997b) Of handymen and waitpersons: a linguistic evaluation of job classifieds. *Australian Journal of Communication* 24(1): 58–69.

Pauwels, Anne (1997c) Of 'Mses', 'Chairmen' and 'Retromen': linguistic change in the media and the community. *Australian Language Matters* April/May/June: 3.

Pauwels, Anne and Winter, Joanne (1991) Language and gender research in the 1990s: a new forum for ideas. *Working Papers on Language, Gender and Sexism* 1(1): 5–10.

Pavlidou, Theodossia (1985) Sprache und geschlecht im Neugriechischen. In Marlis Hellinger (ed.), pp. 76–83.

Pearson, Judy C., Turner, Lynn H. and Todd-Mancillas, William (1985) *Gender and communication*. Dubuque: Wm C. Brown Publishers.

Penelope, Julia (see also Stanley, J.P.) (1982) Two essays on language and change. I: Power and the opposition to feminist proposals for language change. *College English* 44(8): 840–55.

Penelope, Julia (1990) *Speaking freely*. New York: Pergamon Press.

Penelope, Julia and McGowan, Cynthia (1979) *Woman* and *Wife*: Social and semantic shifts in English. *Papers in Linguistics* Fall–Winter: 491–502.

Penfield, Joyce (ed.) (1987) *Women and language in transition*. Albany: State University of New York.

Perissinotto, Giorgio (1982) Linguistica y sexismo. *Diálogos* 18(104): 30–4.

Perissinotto, Giorgio (1983) Spanish 'hombre': generic or specific? *Hispania* 66(4): 581–92.

Persing, Bobbye Sorrels (1978) (see also Sorrels) *The nonsexist communicator: an action guide to eradicating sexism in communication*. East Elmhurst, N.Y.: Communication Dynamics Press.

Petersen, Pia Riber (1975) Bedepiger, styrkvinder of formandinder. In Sprogn vn. Dansk (ed.) *At fœrdes sproget. Iagttagelser og synspunkter*. Copenhagen: Gyldendal, pp. 53–64.

Pflug, Günther (1991) Der bzw. die Arbeitnehmer- und Arbeitnehmerinnen-Vertreter bzw. Vertreterinnen. Probleme der geschlechtsneutralen Rechts- und Verwaltungssprache. *Universitas* 5: 415–19.

Picò, Isabel (1979) *Machismo y educación en Puerto Rico*. Santurce, P.R.: Departamento de Instrucción Pública.

Pincus, A.R.H. and Pincus, R.E. (1980) Linguistic sexism and career education. *Language Arts* 57(1): 70–6.

Plank, Frans (1985) Movierung mittels Präfix-warum nicht? *Linguistische Berichte* 97: 252–60.

Porecca, Karen (1984) Sexism in current ESL textbooks. *TESOL Quarterly* 14(4): 705–24.

Poynton, Cate (1985) *Language and gender: making the difference*. Geelong: Deakin University.

Prentice, Deborah A. (1994) Do language reforms change our way of thinking. *Journal of Language and Social Psychology* 13(1): 3–19.

Pugsley, Jenny (1992) Sexist language and stereotyping in ELT materials: language, bureaucracy and the teacher. *Working Papers on Language, Gender and Sexism* 2(2): 5–14.

Pusavat, Yoko (1981) Address terms of married mates in contemporary Japan. Paper presented at the conference of Asian Studies of the Pacific Coast, Honolulu, Hawaii.

Pusch, Luise (1984a) *Das Deutsche als Männersprache*. Frankfurt/Main: Suhrkamp.

Pusch, Luise (1984b) 'Sie sah zu ihm auf wie zu einem Gott.' Das Duden-Bedeutungswörterbuch als Trivialroman. In Luise Pusch (1984a), pp. 135–46.

Pusch, Luise (1990) *Alle Menschen werden Schwestern. Glossen zur feministischen Linguistik*. Frankfurt/Main: Suhrkamp.

Rabofski, Birgit (1988) Motion und Markiertheit. Dissertation, Universität Hannover.

Ramsay, Eleanor and Stefanou-Haag, Efrosini (1991) On lies and silence: cross-cultural perspectives on the construction of women's oppression through linguistic omission. *Working Papers on Language, Gender and Sexism* 1(2): 31–42.

Randall, Phyllis R. Sexist language and speech communication contexts: another case of benign neglect. *Communication Education* 34(2): 128–34.

Rendes, Viktoria (1988) Sexism in textbooks: a discussion of 'Unsere Freunde' and 'Deutsch Konkret'. Unpublished paper, Department of German, Monash University.

Rich, Adrienne (1977) *Of woman born: motherhood as experience and institution*. London: Virago Press.

Richards, Graham (1979) Sea without a shore: 1706 proverbs on women and marriage. Unpublished paper, Northeast London Polytechnic.

Ritchie, Marguerite E. (1975) Alice through the statutes. *McGill Law Journal* 21.

Roberts, Bev (1984) Ockers and malespeak. Why women and men don't speak the same language in Australia. *Australian Society* 3(8): 13–16.

Roca-Pons, J. (1963) Arquitecto y arquitecta. *Hispania* 46: 373–4.

Rohwedder, Eberhard (1971) La juez oder la jueza? *Fremdsprachen* 15(2): 138–40.

Romaine, Suzanne (ed.) (1982) *Sociolinguistic variation in speech communities*. London: Edward Arnold.

Römer, Ruth (1973) Grammatiken, fast lustig zu lesen. *Linguistische Berichte* 28: 71–9.

Rubin, Donald I. and Greene, Kathryn L. (1991) Effects of biological and psychological gender, age cohort and interviewer gender on attitudes towards gender-inclusive/exclusive language. *Sex Roles* 24: 391–412.

Rubin, Donald I., Greene, Kathryn L. and Schneider, Deidra (1994) Adopting gender-inclusive language reforms. Diachronic and synchronic variation. *Journal of Language and Social Psychology* 13(2): 91–114.

Rubin, Joan (1971) Evaluation and language planning. In Joan Rubin and Bjørn Jernudd (eds), pp. 217–52.

Rubin, Joan (1973) Language planning: discussion of some current issues. In Joan Rubin and Roger Shuy (eds), pp. 1–10.

Rubin, Joan and Jernudd, Bjørn (eds) (1971a) *Can language be planned? Sociolinguistic theory and practice for developing nations.* Honolulu: The University of Hawaii.

Rubin, Joan and Jernudd, Bjørn (1971b) Introduction: language planning as an element in modernization. In Joan Rubin and Bjørn Jernudd (eds), pp. xiii–xxiv.

Rubin, Joan and Shuy, Roger (eds) (1973) *Language planning: current issues and research.* Washington, D.C.: Georgetown University Press.

Rundhovde, Gunnvor (1980) Pronomena 'han' og 'ho' når ein viser til personnemningar. Talk held at the Norsk Språkråd in January 1980.

Russell, Letty M. (ed.) (1976) *The liberating word: a guide to nonsexist interpretation of the Bible.* Philadelphia: Westminster Press.

Ryen, Else (1976) Det kvinnelige fravær. In Else Ryen (ed.) *Språk og kjøn.* Oslo: Pax, pp. 71–80.

Ruysendaal, Els (1983) Gevraagd . . . Beroepsnamen in beweging. *Tijdschrift voor vrouwenstudies* 14(4.2): 300–5.

Sabatini, Alma (1985) Occupational titles in Italian: changing the sexist usage. In Marlis Hellinger (ed.), pp. 64–75.

Sabatini, Alma (1986) *Raccomandazioni per un uso non sessista della lingua italiana.* Roma: Presidenza del Consiglio dei Ministri, Direzione Generale della Editoria e della Proprietà Letteraria Artistica e Scientifica.

Samel, Ingrid (1995) *Einführung in die feministische Sprachwissenschaft.* Berlin: Erich Schmidt Verlag.

Sautermeister, Christine (1985) La femme devant la langue. In Arbeitsberichte 4, *Frauenthemen im Fremdsprachenunterricht.* Hamburg: Universität Hamburg, Zentrales Fremdspracheninstitut, pp. 63–97.

Schafroth, Elmar (1992) Feminine Berufsbezeichnungen in Kanada und Frankreich. *Zeitschrift für Kanada-Studien* 12.

Schafroth, Elmar (1993) Berufsbezeichnungen für Frauen in Frankreich-Sprachpolitische Maßnahmen und sprachliche Wirklichkeit. *Lebende Sprachen* 2: 64–6.

Schneider, Joseph W. and Hacker, Sally L. (1973) Sex role imagery and the use of generic 'man' in introductory texts. *American Sociologist* 8: 12–18.

Schräpel, Beate (1985) Nicht-sexistische Sprache und soziolinguistische Aspekte von Sprachwandel und Sprachplanung. In Marlis Hellinger (ed.), pp. 212–30.

Schulz, Muriel (1974) How sexist is *Webster's Third? Vis à vis* 2(3): 7–15.

Schulz, Muriel (1975) The semantic derogation of women. In Barrie Thorne and Nancy Henley (eds), pp. 64–73.

Schweizerische Bundeskanzlei (1991) *Sprachliche Gleichbehandlung von Frau und Mann.* Bern: Schweizerische Bundeskanzlei.

Scully, Diana and Bart, Pauline (1973) A funny thing happened on the way to the orifice: women in gynecology text books. In Joan Huber (ed.) *Changing women in a changing society.* Chicago: University of Chicago Press, pp. 283–8.

Scutt, Jocelynne (1985) Sexism in legal language. *Australian Law Journal* 59, 163–73.

Silveira, Jeanette (1980) Generic masculine words and thinking. *Women Studies International Quarterly* 3: 165–78.

Silverstein, Michael (1985) Language and the culture of gender: at the intersection of structure, usage and ideology. In Elizabeth Mertz and Richard J. Parmentier (eds) *Semiotic mediation*. New York: Academic Press, pp. 219–59.

Simon, John (1980) A handbook for maidens. Review of *The handbook of nonsexist writing*. *American Spectator* 13(11): 33–54.

Sorrels, Bobbye M. (1983) *The nonsexist communicator: solving the problems of gender and awkwardness in modern English*. Englewood Cliffs, N.J.: Prentice Hall.

Soto, Debbie Halon, Forslund, Evelyn Florio and Cole, Claudia (1975) Alternative to using masculine pronouns when referring to the species. Paper presented at the Western Speech Communication Association, San Francisco, CA, 1975.

Spears, Joanna S. (1978) Sexism in religious education. *Friends General Conference Quarterly* 2(5).

Spender, Dale (1980) *Man made language*. London: Routledge and Kegan Paul.

Stanley, Julia Penelope (1977a) Gender-marking in American English: usage and reference. In Alleen P. Nilsen, Haig Bosmajian, H. Lee Gershuny and Julia P. Stanley, (eds) *Sexism and language*. Urbana, Ill.: National Council of Teachers of English, pp. 43–74.

Stanley, Julia Penelope (1977b) Paradigmatic woman: the prostitute. In David L. Shores and Carol P. Hines (eds), *Papers in language variation*. Alabama: University of Alabama Press, pp. 303–21.

Stanley, Julia Penelope (1978) Sexist grammar. *College English* 39: 800–11.

Stanley, Julia Penelope (1982) Two essays on language and change. I: Power and the opposition to feminist proposals for language change; II: John Simon and the 'Dragons of Eden'. *College English* 44: 840–54.

Stanley, Julia Penelope and Robbins, Susan W. (1978) Going through the changes: the pronoun *she* in Middle English. *Papers in Linguistics* 11: 71–88.

Stanley, Julia Penelope and McGowan, Cynthia (1979) Woman and wife: social and semantic shifts in English. *Papers in Linguistics* 12: 491–502.

Stannard, Una (1977) *Mrs Man*. San Francisco: Germainbooks.

Stefan, Verena (1976) *Häutungen*. München: Frauenoffensive.

Steinem, Gloria (1983) *Outrageous acts and everyday rebellions*. New York: Holt, Rinehart and Winston.

Stericker, Anne (1981) Does the 'He or she' really make a difference? The effect of masculine pronouns as generics on job attitudes. *Sex Roles* 7: 637–41.

Stern, Rhoda, H. (1976) Review article: sexism in foreign language text-books. *Foreign Language Annals* 9(4): 294–9.

Stickel, Gerhard (1988) Beantragte staatliche Regelungen zur 'Sprachlichen Gleichbehandlung'. Darstellung und Kritik. *Zeitschrift für germanistische Linguistik* 16: 330–55.

Stirling, Lesley (1987) Language and gender in Australian newspapers. In Anne Pauwels (ed.), pp. 108–28.

Style manual (1988) *Style manual for authors, editors and printers* (4th edition). Canberra: Australian Government Publishing Service.

Suardiaz, Delia E. (1975) (1973) Sexism in the Spanish language. Unpublished M.A. Thesis. Seattle: University of Washington.

Sunderland, Jane (1986) The grammar book and the invisble woman. Unpublished M.A. Thesis, Lancaster University.

Sunderland, Jane (1992) Teaching materials and teaching/learning processes: gender in the language classroom. *Working Papers on Language, Gender and Sexism* 2(2): 15–26.

Sutton, William A. (1978) Linguistic sexism in *Time* magazine. Paper given at the 9th World Congress of Sociology, Uppsala, Sweden.

Swan, Toril (1991) Notat om kvinner i norske aviser. In Alhaug Gulbran, Kristoffer Kruken and Helge Salvesen (eds) *Heidersskrift til Nils Hallan*. Oslo: Novus, pp. 453–72.

Swan, Toril (1992) All about Eve: women in Norwegian newspapers in the 20th century. *Working Papers on Language, Gender and Sexism* 2(2): 37–54.

Switzer, Joy (1989) The impact of generic word choices: an empirical investigation of age- and sex-related differences. Paper presented at the annual conference of the Central States Communication Association, Kansas City, Mo 1989.

Takahashi, Minako (1991) Titles and terms for women in English and Japanese. In P.G Fendos Jr (ed.) *Cross-cultural communication: East and West*. Tainan, Taiwan: National Cheng-Kung University, pp. 287–303.

Talansky, Sandra B. (1986) Sex role stereotyping in TEFL teaching materials. *Perspectives* XI(3): 32–42.

Talbot, Mary (1995) Randy fish boss branded a stinker: coherence and construction of masculinities in a British tabloid. *Nordlyd* 23: 259–70.

Thiselton-Dyer, T.F. (1906) *Folk-lore of women*. Chicago: A.C. McClurg and Co.

Thorne, Barrie and Henley, Nancy (eds) (1975) *Language and sex: dominance and difference*. Rowley, Mass.: Newbury House.

Thorne, Barrie, Kramarae, Cheris and Henley, Nancy (eds) (1983) *Language, gender and society*. Rowley, Mass.: Newbury House.

Tittle, Carol, McCarthy, Karen and Steckler, Jane F. (1974) *Women and educational testing: a selective review of the research literature and testing practices*. Princeton, N.J.: Educational Testing Service.

Todd-Mancillas, William (1981) Masculine generics=sexist language. *Communication Quarterly* 29: 107–15.

Todd-Mancillas, William (1984) Evaluating alternatives to exclusive he. *Communication Research Reports* 1: 38–41.

Tong, Rosemary (1989) *Feminist thought*. London: Routledge.

Triandaphyllidis, Manolis (1963) Die 'Abgeordnete' und die Bildung der weiblichen Berufsbezeichnungen (translated from Greek). In Manolis Triandaphyllidis *Sammelwerke*. Bd II. Thessaloniki.

Trible, Phyllis (1973) Depatriarchalizing in biblical interpretation. *Journal of the American Academy of Religion* 41(1): 35–42.

Trible, Phyllis (1976) God, nature in the Old Testament. In *The interpreter's dictionary of the Bible: supplementary volume*. Nashville: Abingdon Press.

Trömel-Plötz, Senta (1978) Linguistik und Frauensprache. *Linguistische Berichte* 57: 49–68.

Trömel-Plötz, Senta (1982) *Frauensprache: Sprache der Veränderung*. Frankfurt/Main: Fischer.

Trömel-Plötz, Senta (ed.) (1984) *Gewalt durch Sprache: Die Vergewaltigung von Frauen in Gesprächen*. Frankfurt/Main: Fischer.

Trömel-Plötz, Senta *et al.* (1981) Richtlinien zur Vermeidung sexistischen Sprachgebrauchs. *Linguistische Berichte* 71: 1–7.

Trudgill, Peter (1974) *Sociolinguistics. an introduction*. Harmondsworth: Penguin.

Tuchman, Gaye (1978) The symbolic annihilation of women in the mass media. In Gaye Tuchman, Allan Daniels and James J. Bénet (eds) *Hearth and home. Images of women in the mass media*. New York: Oxford University Press, pp. 3–38.

Urrutia, Elena (178) Lenguaje y discriminación. *fem* 6: 5–11.

Van Alphen, Ingrid (1983) Een vrouw een vrouw, een woord een woord. Over gelijke behandeling van vrouwen en mannen en de konsekwenties daarvan voor beroepsnamingen in het Nederlands. *Tijdschrift voor Vrouwenstudies* 14(4.2): 307–15.

Van Alphen, Ingrid (1985) Eine Frau – ein Wort: Über die Gleichbehandlung von Frauen und Männern und die Konsequenzen für Berufsbezeichnungen im Niederländischen. In Marlis Hellinger (ed.), pp. 123–31.

Van Alphen, Ingrid (1996) Beroepsnamen en beroepskeuzen v/m; een sociolinguïstische analyse van de beroepskeuzen van 15-jarige meisjes en jongens in Nederland. In OC en W – Ministerie van Onderwijs, Cultuur en Wetenschappen, pp. 42–55.

Van Den Bergh, Nan (1987) Renaming: vehicle for empowerment. In Joyce Penfield (ed.), pp. 130–5.

Van Dijk, Teun (1990) *Racism and the press*. London: Routledge.

Van Haeringen, C.B. (1949) *Neerlandica. Verspreide Opstellen*. 's-Gravenhage: Daamen.

Van Langendonck, Willy and Beeken, Jeannine (1996) Beroepsnamen: toch maar niet vervrouwelijken. In OC en W – Ministerie van Onderwijs, Cultuur en Wetenschappen, pp. 32–8.

Venås, Kjell (1989) Kvinne og manni Gulatingslova. Etter ein idé av Lis Jacobsen. In Eithun Bjørn et al. (eds) Festskrift til Finn Hødnebø 29 desember 1989. Oslo: Novus, pp. 285–303.

Verbiest, Agnes (1988) Taalseksisme: begripsbepaling, balans en prognose. In Korrie Korrievaart (ed.) Vrouwen in taal en literatuur. Amersfoort: ACCO, pp. 50–9.

Verbiest, Agnes (1990) Het gewicht van de directrice. Taal over, tegen en door vrouwen. Amsterdam: Uitgeverij Contact.

Vetterling-Braggin, Mary (ed.) (1981) Sexist language. A modern philosophical analysis. Littlefield: Adams and Co.

Viet, Ursula (1987) Professor/in/en/innen? Gegen die Verwendung von weiblichen Endungen. Universität Osnabrück 2/1987: 21.

Viet, Ursula (1991) Professor/in/en/innen? Gegen die Verwendung von weiblichen Endungen. Universitas 5: 419–21.

Vinje, Finn-Erik (1972) Godt ord igjen. Oslo: Pax.

Violi, Patrizia (1987) Les origines du genre grammatical. Langages 21(85): 15–34.

Vooys, C. G. N. de (1967) Nederlandse spraakkunst. Groningen: Wolters (7th edition).

Wardhaugh, Ronald (1987) Languages in competition. Oxford: Basil Blackwell.

Webster, Sheila (1982) Women, sex and marriage in Moroccan proverbs. International Journal of Middle East Studies 14: 173–184.

Wegener, Hildburg (1990) 'Siehe, das ist meine Beauftragte.' Frauengerechte Sprache in der Übersetzung der Bibel. In Hildburg Wegener, Hanne Köhler and Cordelia Kopsch (eds), pp. 84–101.

Wegener, Hildburg, Köhler, Hanne and Kopsch, Cordelia (eds) (1990) Frauen fordern eine gerechte Sprache. Gütersloh: Verlagshaus Gerd Mohn.

Weinreich, Uriel, Labov, William and Herzog, Marvin (1968) Empirical foundations for a theory of language change. In Winfred P. Lehmann, and Yakov Malkiel (eds) Directions for historical linguistics. Austin: University of Texas Press, pp. 95–195.

Werner, Fritjof (1983) Gesprächsverhalten von Frauen und Männern. Frankfurt/Main: Lang.

Wetschanow, Karin (1995) Als wenns a Grammatikfehler wär: Splittingverhalten einer Gruppe mit links-alternativ feministischer Unisozialisation. Diplomarbeit. University of Wien.

Wheeless, Virginia, Berryman-Fink Cynthia and Serafini, Denise (1981) The use of gender-specific pronouns in the 1980s. Paper presented at the 4th Annual Communication, Language and Gender Conference, Morgantown, West Virginia.

Whorf, Benjamin Lee (1956) Language, thought and reality. Cambridge, Mass.: MIT Press.

Williams, Fionnula (1984) Bachelors' wives and old maids' children: A look at the men and women in Irish proverbs. Ulster Folklife 30: 78–88.

Wilson, Elizabeth and Ng, Sik H. (1988) Sex bias in visuals evoked by generics: a New Zealand study. *Sex Roles* 18: 159–68.

Wodak, Ruth *et al.* (1987) *Sprachliche Gleichbehandlung von Frau und Mann. Linguistische Empfehlungen zur sprachlichen Gleichbehandlung von Frau und Mann im öffentlichen Bereich.* Wien: Bundesministerium für Arbeit und Soziales.

Wodak, Ruth, Kargl, Maria, Wetschanow, Karin and Perle, Ne'la (1997) *Geschlechtergerechte Kommunikation. Theoretische Überlegungen und Analysen.* Wien: Bundesministerium für Angelegenheiten und Verbraucherschutz.

Wolfson, Nessa and Manes, Joan (1980) Don't dear me! In Sally McConnell-Ginet, Ruth Borker and Nelly Furman (eds), pp. 79–91.

Wong, Yee-Cheng (1991) Sexism in modern standard Chinese. Unpublished paper for the MA in Applied Linguistics Program, Monash University.

Xu, R.X. (1988) Nübú zhì qùtán. (On the female radical.) *Yuwén Xuéxí YuYánjiù* 6: 39–40.

Yaguello, Marina (1978) *Les mots et les femmes.* Paris: Payot.

Yordán Molini, Haydée (1976) *La visión de la niña en cinco libros de lecturas escolares.* San Juan, P.R.: Comisión para el Mejoramiento de los Derechos de la Mujer.

Zammit, Susan (1992) *The challenge: choosing to study a LOTE through high school.* Melbourne and Canberra: ACER and DEET.

Zimmermann, Gerhard (1991) Frauenanreden und Frauenbezeichnungen in literarhistorischer Sicht. *Muttersprache* 101: 243–51.

Zumbühl, Ursula (1981) Unterricht in Englisch und Sexismus. Linguistische Analyse eines Englischlehrbuchs. *Linguistische Berichte* 76: 90–103.

Author Index

Abd-el-Jawad, H.R.S. 52, 57
Adamsky, C. 2, 6
Ager, D. 148
Allan, K. and K. Burridge 55
Atkinson, D.L. 136, 218

Baron, D. 26, 38–40, 45, 48–9, 53, 127–9, 131–2, 134, 136
Bate, B. 73, 133, 204, 210, 212, 215
Beattie, J. 40
Beligan, A. 27
Bem, S. and D.J. Bem 71, 118
Bierce, A. 136
Blaubergs, M. 171–2, 179, 183, 234
Bodine, A. 119, 128, 131–2
Bolinger, D. 119, 132–3, 176
Bornemann, E. 53
Bosmajian, H. 29
Brantenberg, G. 101
Brockhoff, E. 198
Brouwer, D. 25, 47–8, 50, 121–2, 124
Brouwer, D., M. Gerritsen, D. de Haan, A. van der Post xi, 102
Brown, G. 46
Brownmiller, S. 55
Bull, T. 205

Cameron, D. xii, 39–40, 70, 89, 90, 126, 221, 225
Cameron, D. and J. Coates xii
Canciani, E. 65

Cannon, G. and S. Robertson 206
Cherry, K. 53, 63–4
Cixous, H. 91
Coates, J. xi
Coates, J. and D. Cameron xi
Collins, R.K. 29
Cooper, R.L. 2–7, 14, 197, 200, 205, 213, 216
Corbett, G. 35–8
Corstensen, B. 24

Daly, M. 31, 98, 100, 102, 141
Daly, M. and J. Caputi 207
Danet, B. 29
De Silva, C. 73, 75, 211
Dorodnykh, A.I. and A.P. Martynyuk 70
Driedger, E.A. 29
Dubois, B.L. and I. Crouch 219

Eckert, P. and S. McConnell-Ginet xii
Ehrlich, S. and R. King 201, 204, 205, 213, 215, 219–20
Eisenberg, D. 100, 114
Elgin, S.H. 104
Ellerington, K. 171
Ellis, R. 179
Evans, H. 148

Fairclough, N. 20
Farley, L. 107
Farmer, J.S. and W.E. Henley 53

Fasold, R. 2, 6, 7, 196, 200–1, 205, 213
Fasold, R., H. Yamada, D. Robinson and S. Barish 196, 203, 205, 213
Fleischhauer, U. 197
Frank, F.W. xiii, 177–9, 183, 203
Frank, F.W. and F. Anshen 52
Frank, F.W. and P.A. Treichler xiii, 84, 132, 152, 156, 171
Freebody, P. and C. Baker 20–2
Froitzheim, C. 17

Gal, S. xii
García, M.A. 24
Gastil, J. 131, 133
Gershuny, H.L. 25
Goh, Y.Y. 73, 75
Gomard, K. 46, 100, 126
González, I.G. 114
Graddol, D. and J. Swann 84, 218
Greene, K. and D.L. Rubin 30, 208
Greene, K. and J. Serovic 208
Guentherodt, I. 29
Guentherodt, I., M. Hellinger, L. Pusch and S. Trömel-Plötz 146
Guiraud, P. 53

Häberlin, S., R. Schmid and E.L. Wyss 152
Hampares, K.J. 25
Harres, A. and A. Truckenbrodt 23
Harris, J. 30, 40
Hellinger, M. xiii, 19, 35, 70, 118, 128–9, 132, 147, 171–2, 181, 197, 204, 220
Hellinger, M. and B. Schräpel 73, 74, 171–3, 177–8, 181–2, 211, 234
Hellinger, M., M. Kremer and B. Schräpel 155–6, 175
Helmsljev, L. 39

Henley, N. xiii, 128, 134, 210–11
Henley, N. and D. Dragun 73, 132–3, 210–12
Henley, N. and C. Kramarae xii
Hennessy, M. 203, 206
Herbert, R.K. and B. Nykiel-Herbert 39, 41–2, 44, 47–8
Hiraga, M. 47, 51, 54, 64
Hoffmann, U. 103, 210
Hook, D.D. 135, 137
Houdebine, A.M. 46, 73, 110, 126, 147, 211–12
Houssami, J. 73

Ibrahim, M.H. 39
Irigaray, L. 91, 105

Jacobson, M. and W. Insko 195
Jaehrling, S. 73, 74, 170–1, 210–11
Jernudd, B. 2, 4, 7, 10
Jernudd, B. and J. Das Gupta 7
Jernudd, B. and J. Neustupny 2
Joly, A. 40

Kallioinen, V., E. Havu and L. Hakulinen 68
Kalverkämper, H. 68–9, 177, 184
Kaye, P. 203
Key, M.R. xi
Khayyat, L. 65
Khosroshahi, F. 220
Kidd, V. 71
Klemensiewicz, Z. 44
Kloss, H. 4, 10, 139, 226
Kochskämper, B. xii, 19, 52
Kramarae, C. 203, 207
Kramarae, C. and M.M. Jenkins 107, 208
Kramarae, C. and P. Treichler 18, 137, 207
Kramer, C. 53, 63
Kurzon, D. 202, 205

Labov, W. 194
Lakoff, R. 52–3, 85, 136

Lepschy, G. 70, 115
Levin, M. 183
Lorenz, D. 125
Lunde, K. 100, 126
Lyons, J. 39

Mackay, D. 71, 72, 128–9, 131–2
Mackay, D. and D.C. Fulkerson 72
Markowitz, J. 201, 204
Marks, E. and I. de Courtivron 88
Martyna, W. 72, 132–3
Martynyuk, A. 48, 85
Masayuki, T. 149
McConnell-Ginet, S. 219
Meijers, J.A. 48
Meyerhoff, M. 201, 205
Miller, C. and K. Swift 18, 26, 29–30
Miller, G. 2
Moi, T. 88
Morris, M. 24, 220
Mottier, I. 148
Moulton, J. 72, 118
Müller, S. and C. Fuchs 152, 153
Myers, C.K. 31

Nakamura, M. 52–3
Neustupny, J. 4, 6, 14
Ng, B.C. and K. Burridge 52, 66
Nichols, P. 23
Niedzwiecki, P. 163
Nissen, U.K. 114, 126
Noss, R. 2

OC en W. 163
Olivares, C. 110, 126
Ott, M. 52

Pauwels, A. xiii, 84, 117, 132–3, 136–8, 154, 163, 195–7, 201, 204, 210, 213, 215, 217–19
Pavlidou, T. 49

Penelope, J. 103, 104, 107–8, 161
Penelope, J. and C. McGowan 19–20, 218
Pflug, G. 125–6
Poynton, C. 19, 56, 58, 63
Pusch, L. 24, 31, 39, 70, 75, 100, 125, 210

Ramsay, E. and E. Stefanou-Haag 106
Rich, A. 55
Ritchie, M.E. 29
Romaine, S. 194
Rubin, J. 7
Ruysendaal, E. 121–2

Sabatini, A. 43, 44, 100, 115, 126, 166
Sautermeister, C. 52
Schafroth, E. 73, 148, 170, 199, 207
Schneider, J.W. and S.L. Hacker 71, 118
Schräpel, B. xiii
Schulz, M. 52–3
Scutt, J. 29
Simon, J. 182
Sorrels, B.M. 86, 136
Spender, D. 55, 60, 87, 106, 135, 137
Stanley, J.P. xiii, 26, 53, 171–2, 177
Stanley, J.P. and C. McGowan 52
Stannard, U. 18, 49, 107
Stefan, V. 107
Steinem, G. 195
Stericker, A. 118
Stickel, G. 125
Sunderland, J. 207
Swan, T. 27, 205

Takahashi, M. 52–3, 60
Talansky, S.B. 6
Talbot, M. 203
Thiselton-Dyer, T.F. 65

Tong, R. 89
Triandaphyllidis, M. 49
Trible, P. 31
Trömel-Plötz, S. 32, 52–3, 68
Trudgill, P. 63
Tuchman, G. 26

Van Alphen, I. 121–2
Van Dijk, T. 223
Van Haeringen, C.B. 48
Viet, U. 126, 180
Violi, P. 39
Vooys, C.G./N. de 48

Wegener, H., H. Köhler and
    C. Kopsch 31

Weinreich, U., W. Labov and
    M. Herzog 194
Werner, F. 53–4
Wheeless, V., C. Berryman-Fink
    and D. Serafini 72
Whorf, B.L. 83
Williams, F. 65
Wilson, E. and S.H. Ng 72
Wodak, R. et al. 211–12
Wolfson, N. and J. Manes 62
Wong, Y.-C. 66

Xu, R.X. 66

Yaguello, M. 29, 39, 40, 44, 49,
    53–5, 56, 61

Subject Index

Academy (language) 4–5, 23, 143
advertisement 27
androcentric ix, 16, 22, 29
Arabic 57, 60
asymmetry 19, 28, 35, 43, 46
  morphological 43, 46–56, 61–3
  semantic 50–3, 157
attitudes 25, 67, 73–7, 170–1
Australia 26, 148, 185–91, 195, 197, 214

Belgium 4, 12, 148
boy(s) 20–1, 52, 58, 103
Britain 26, 148, 205

Canada 12, 26, 148, 213
chairman 160, 175, 186, 224
chairperson 160
Chinese 66
codification 5
corpus planning 4–5, 9–11, 13
creation, creativity 10, 91–8, 103
critical discourse analysis 20

Danish 45–6, 60, 109–11, 162
data-collection ix–x
denial 67–70, 170, 172–5, 187
dictionary 206–7
diminutive(s) 23–5, 58
disruption (linguistic) 98–103, 131, 140, 223
downgrading 184
downplaying 176–9, 187

Dutch 4, 25, 41, 45–6, 48, 51, 57, 60, 110–12, 121–4, 163

écriture féminine 91, 105
elaboration 5
Emma 141–2
epicene pronoun 129
ESL 22–7
experimentation 98

feminisation 28, 112–16, 212, 224
feminism vii–viii, xi, 24
  French 87–92, 105
France 12, 49, 148, 199–200, 214
French 4, 41, 44–5, 50–2, 54, 60, 111–12, 165–6

gender
  abstraction 120, 162–3, 224
  agreement 41–2, 181
  bias 10, 19, 28, 71
  category of 35–8
  common 4
  definition 36
  feminine 36
  formal 37–8
  grammatical 26, 38–41, 68, 99
  inclusive 100
  masculine 36, 40, 179
  metaphorical 40
  natural 37–40

neutralisation 109–12, 121–3, 162–3, 224
semantic 37–8
specification 112–16, 121, 124–6, 162, 164–5
splitting 114–15, 125, 164
systems 36–8
generic
he 26, 71–2, 75, 127–9, 174, 178, 205, 216
noun(s) 41, 112, 118, 179, 200–2
pronoun(s) 41, 115, 118, 127–34, 179, 200–2
she 98, 129, 205
German 4, 25, 41, 44–7, 51, 54, 60, 100, 107, 111–12, 115, 124–7, 162–5
Germany 12, 26, 141–2, 197
girl 21–2, 32, 52, 57, 103
grammar (sexism in) 23, 26
graphisation 2, 5
grassroots 6, 10
Greece 12, 49, 149
Greek 49
guidelines 139–67, 171–92
contents 149–50, 152–66
drafting 228–35
reactions to 171–91
structure 149–51

he/she [he or she] 115, 132–3, 162–3, 200, 202
headline(s) 186
Hebrew 5, 31
honorific(s)
female 27, 204, 217
titles 28, 33, 59–62, 101, 135–8, 176

ideographs 66
idioms 65
interactionist 84, 92, 153
inversion (strategy) 101–2
invisibility 19, 34, 43–4, 112, 157

Italian 41, 43–4, 47, 50, 60, 112–13, 115, 166
Italy 12, 26, 149, 214

Japan 26, 149, 214
Japanese 28, 51, 53–4, 57, 63–4
job advertisements 32, 120, 143, 197–200
Jordan 57–8, 63

Láadan 104–5
lady 28, 30, 52
language change 85, 192–221
language planners (types of) 3, 12–13, 94, 144–6
language planning
definition 2–3
evaluation stage 7–8, 168–221
fact finding stage 7, 13, 16–81
implementation stage 7, 13, 139–67
planning stage 7, 13, 94–138
types 4, 7
lexical
gap 43–6
innovation 24, 99
linguistic
determinism 83, 86–7
economy 125
lag 85, 95
relativity 83
sexism vii, xi, 19
viability 116–17, 119–20
linguistics
contrastive 19, 85
historical 19
systemic 19, 56
Lithuania 10, 17
Lithuanian 17

madonna 35
makers of meaning vii, 10
man 25, 32, 34, 50, 66, 69, 71, 174–5, 201
-man 45, 69, 71, 74–5, 110, 161, 174, 197, 201–2

marked 9
markedness 69–70
media 14, 141, 205–6, 210
metaphors 30, 54
Miss 22, 59–60, 74–5, 86,
    135–8, 218
modernisation 5
modification 10
Mr 33, 59–60, 86, 135–6
Mrs 28, 59–60, 74–5, 86,
    135–8, 196, 218
Ms 26, 33, 86, 136–8, 193, 195,
    216, 218–19

name(s) 18, 56–9, 101, 194–5
naming practices 56–63, 105–7,
    194–6
neologism 96, 108, 134
Netherlands, The 12, 141, 148,
    196, 198–9
noun(s)
  human agent 18, 43, 51,
      109–12, 161, 164–6
  occupational 28, 43, 48–9,
      109–15, 120–7, 161, 164–6,
      196–200
Norway 26, 195, 205
Norwegian 27, 45, 60, 101,
    109–11, 162

one 133–4
Opzij 141–2

Polish 42, 44, 47, 57
political correctness 8
pronoun(s) 27
prostitute 53–4
proverbs 65

reclaiming 102, 104, 107
renovation 5, 10
replacement 162, 170, 193
ridiculing 184, 188, 215
role model 140–2, 215

Romanian 27
Russian 47, 57

sanctions 147
semantic derogation 19, 51–2
sex 50–1, 53–6, 64
sexism 16–80
  common features 9, 34–5
  definition of 155–6
sexuality 30, 50–1, 53–6, 63, 91,
    105, 107
singular *they* 98, 131–2, 181–2,
    216
social effectiveness 116–19
sociolinguistic 7, 211–12
Spain 12, 148
Spanish 25, 41, 50–2, 60, 100,
    111, 113, 165
speech community 14, 66, 73
standardisation 5
stereotyping (gender) 19–24,
    27–8, 35, 57, 63–5, 102,
    157, 202–3
style manual(s) 23, 26, 152,
    185–6
Swedish 45, 110
Switzerland 29, 148
suffix(es) 43, 46–8, 61, 109–11,
    122, 163
Symbolic Order 88–91, 105

USSR (former) 48
US 26, 195, 197, 205, 213

virgin 25, 30

warning (strategy of) 67, 179–83
woman 25, 29–30, 34, 50, 66,
    100
woman-centred (language) 104–9
women's movement xi, 10, 17, 24
whore 30, 35, 102, 109

Yin and Yang 32